Judging Complicity

JUDGING COMPLICITY

*How to Respond to
Injustice and Violence*

GISLI VOGLER

EDINBURGH
University Press

Edinburgh University Press is one of the leading university presses in the UK. We publish academic books and journals in our selected subject areas across the humanities and social sciences, combining cutting-edge scholarship with high editorial and production values to produce academic works of lasting importance. For more information visit our website: edinburghuniversitypress.com

We are committed to making research available to a wide audience and are pleased to be publishing an Open Access ebook edition of this title.

© Gisli Vogler, 2024, 2025, under a Creative Commons Attribution-NonCommercial licence

Edinburgh University Press Ltd
13 Infirmary Street
Edinburgh EH1 1LT

First published in hardback by Edinburgh University Press 2024

Typeset in 11/13 Adobe Sabon by
by Manila Typesetting Company

A CIP record for this book is available from the British Library

ISBN 978 1 3995 2252 6 (hardback)
ISBN 978 1 3995 2250 2 (paperback)
ISBN 978 1 3995 2248 9 (webready PDF)
ISBN 978 1 3995 2247 2 (epub)

The right of Gisli Vogler to be identified as the author of this work has been asserted in accordance with the Copyright, Designs and Patents Act 1988, and the Copyright and Related Rights Regulations 2003 (SI No. 2498).

Contents

Acknowledgements	vii
Introduction	1
1. Debates on complicity and the problem of responsiveness	16
2. Judgement and the potential in human plurality	34
3. Judgement following Arendt: from pluralism to social conditioning	64
4. Social conditioning and analytical dualism	86
5. Responding to complicity through an improved ethos of reality	114
6. Resisting complicity through an ethos of reality in practice	135
Conclusion: A new approach to judging complicity	162
Bibliography	169
Index	184

Acknowledgements

This book is based on my PhD research project which I completed at the University of Edinburgh in 2019. I am immensely grateful to Ersev Ersoy and Beatriz Lopez at Edinburgh University Press, the anonymous reviewers of the book manuscript, and Mihaela Mihai, who guided me in turning the thesis into a book. I am indebted to the examiners of my doctoral thesis, Hartmut Rosa and Andy Hom, whose research and conversations inspired me to think the core ideas in this book further.

I would like to thank the European Research Consortium for the financial assistance which allowed me to write the PhD thesis, and the principal investigator of the ERC Greyzone Project, Mihaela Mihai, for accepting me on her project. I thank the political theory research groups at Leeds and Edinburgh for providing a friendly environment in which to advance my knowledge of contemporary political theory. I am deeply grateful to my former supervisors Mihaela Mihai and Mathias Thaler for providing support above and beyond what could be expected, both in reading and commenting on previous drafts of the thesis and in providing guidance, expert knowledge and academic exemplars to aspire to. I also thank Stuart McAnulla and Jonathan Dean, who took on this project in its early stages and gave me the confidence to develop my own thoughts. Thank you above all to my parents and my brother and sister, as well as my friends around the world, for their unwavering support and interest in my progress and wellbeing. Their confidence in my abilities gave me the necessary motivation to complete this thesis. To Maša I owe gratitude for her guidance, patience and inexorable love of ambiguity.

Introduction

How should those profiting from injustice and violence respond to their complicity? And how can they remain responsive when faced with the many ways in which they are entangled in an unjust world? We[1] are at a deciding moment in affluent (Western) societies when it comes to addressing these kinds of questions. On the one hand, there is cause for optimism: the last decade has seen a significant shift towards open discussion of patriarchal society, institutional racism, capitalist exploitation and the destruction of the environment, amongst many other contemporary political problems. Social movements such as #MeToo, Black Lives Matter, Fridays for Future and Occupy Wall Street have helped turn assuming responsibility for violence and injustice into a dominant political issue. As a consequence, unjust practices, as diverse as Amazon's working conditions and the Oxfam sexual exploitation scandal, are met with global condemnation. Debates about how those benefiting from exploitation and expropriation can act more responsibly now pervade many aspects of everyday life, from what to eat and wear, to who has what kind of opportunities. On the other hand, societies continue to be characterised by a failure to act upon the omnipresent demands for facing up to one's involvement in injustice. Racism, sexism and ableism, and the exploitation of minorities, poorer countries and people, and nature all remain integral parts of human existence. The re-emergence of reactionary populist forces and parties in the US and large parts of Europe, together with the consolidation of power by authoritarian leaders across the world, has exacerbated the problem.

The enduring failures by complicit actors to address injustice are cause for much despair and frustration. However, they have also served as catalysts for a sustained scholarly reflection on the complexities of complicity and how to address them (Beausoleil, 2019;

Hayward, 2017; Mihai, 2022; Schaap, 2020). It is my intention in this book to contribute to this interrogation and to think further how people can appropriately respond to their complicity in injustice and violence. To this end, I begin with a constructive evaluation of recent scholarship on complicity.

The debates on complicity, political judgement and social conditioning

Researchers have fundamental disagreements about how to define and address complicity. These disagreements are linked, in my reading, to diverging approaches to how people (can) make judgements about complicity, which, in turn, are informed by different views on how judgements and actions are shaped by their social context. Broadly speaking, debates on complicity consist of a dominant moral and legal philosophical framework and its critics.

The dominant position defines complicity in terms of separate contributions to a principal act of wrongdoing (Kadish, 1985; Lepora and Goodin, 2013). Typical examples include a lookout during a heist or a police officer who turns 'a blind eye' to a crime. The position adheres to methodological individualism, that is, the view that society is the aggregate of the motivations and actions of independent actors and that these actions and motivations should be the main focal point of discussions on complicity (Kutz, 2000: 4). It focuses on (relatively) easily identifiable acts of contributing to wrongdoing by an individual person that are morally problematic and that sometimes meet the standard of being culpable under the law. The vision of society connects with a conception of moral judgement as the subsuming of past action by this individual actor under pre-given standards of behaviour. The job of the individual is to use their capacity for reason and the parameters of logic and morality to identify morally problematic behaviour and avoid it (Kutz, 2000: 13; Lepora and Goodin, 2013: 12). Similarly, anyone evaluating the actions taken must judge them against these parameters of reason and morality. A focus on complicity, that is, (in)action that contributes to, but remains distinct from, the principal act of wrongdoing – for instance a consumer who buys cheap clothes made by sweatshop labour – throws up complex cases in which blame is more difficult to pin down. However, this does not change, but merely complicates, the assumption that we can judge what is blameworthy behaviour, and what is not.

Criticisms of the dominant framework are by now well established and will not be central to this book. Instead, I focus on three alternative approaches to complicity: Iris Marion Young's social connection model, a poststructuralist complicity-as-being theory and an ethics-of-responsiveness approach that aims to extend the first two. I take them to provide highly sophisticated ways of thinking about complicity and a suitable foundation for my own response to the problem of complicity in injustice. The critical alternatives highlight that most moral wrongs, such as the destruction of the environment or sweatshop labour, are actually structural forms of injustice and violence (Sanders, 2002; Young, 2011). By 'structural', or 'systemic', the term I prefer to use,[2] they mean that we cannot easily trace the unjust outcome (the prevalence of sweatshop labour, for instance) back to the motivations and actions of individual people. We may rightfully challenge individual acts as unjust or violent, for example a company that tries to make a profit by not looking too closely at their suppliers' working conditions. However, we will fail to identify any one person, or group, which is morally blameworthy or legally culpable for the existence of sweatshop labour. This is because the system itself is unjust, meaning that even if all actors behave in morally and legally appropriate ways according to social standards, the outcome may still be unjust (that is, produce sweatshop labour). While individual companies may rightly be criticised for prioritising profit over working conditions, it is the structures of the global economy that often leave companies with equally morally questionable choices. For instance, global value chains are characterised by an uneven distribution of values in favour of pre- and post-production processes, that is, research and development on the one hand and marketing on the other, leaving little money to distribute for those helping to actually manufacture products, from mobile phones to clothing (Van Buren and Schremp-Stirling, 2022). Within this context, complicity becomes something more fundamental that occurs 'naturally', whether we want it to or not, by virtue of our existence within societies that are unjust and steeped in violence.

The emphasis on how action is situated in complex social processes leads the three critical alternatives to reject a primary concern with making judgements about individual culpability and blameworthiness. In their place, Young highlights that when we judge something to be a socially produced injustice, we invite some responsibility for the unjust status quo because we recognise that it is wrong and must be changed (Young, 2001: 18; 2011: 73, 165). We therefore have a shared responsibility to use the resources available to us to transform injustice. According to the complicity-as-being approach, judgements on the inevitability of complicity should lead us to acknowledge our individual responsibility to challenge injustice and violence (Sanders, 2002). Lastly, the ethics of responsiveness raises serious doubts about the ability and willingness of the privileged to judge their complicity, given the systemic nature of such injustice and violence (Beausoleil, 2014, 2017; Coles, 2016; Hayward, 2017; Loacker and Muhr, 2009; Oliver, 2010; Schiff, 2014). In response, its proponents suggest ways in which the processes of disavowal and denial can be interrupted, temporarily at least, to potentially engender acknowledgement of one's complicity and help tackle injustice.

This book affirms these key developments in complicity literature and extends the important insights by delving more deeply into the process and practice of judging complicity. To this end, I turn to a key thinker within the literature on political judgement, Hannah Arendt.[3] Arendt notes that in judging that a thing is good or bad, right or wrong, and so on, judgement helps us position ourselves in the world and refine our understanding of it (Arendt, 1981a: 193). Judgement for Arendt is therefore not just a process that allows us to subsume cases under relevant standards of moral behaviour. Nor is it simply a tool that helps us make judgements about injustice by analysing (complicity in) structural processes. Judgement for Arendt is an integral part of our individual and collective engagement with reality. Our capacity to make adequate judgements on complicity is therefore connected to the qualities of that engagement and potentially a powerful means by which we can help improve it. This is the key point I want to highlight and explore throughout this book: the link between judgement, complicity and our engagement with reality and the way we can improve our relationship with reality as the foundation for tackling complicity in injustice. First, however, I note that Arendt developed her argument about judgement against the backdrop of immense violence and to fully understand it we first need to situate her thought.

Arendt was born in Germany into a Jewish family and completed her studies and PhD with two leading German philosophers, Martin Heidegger and Karl Jaspers. In the 1930s Arendt actively helped to combat the rise of Nazi Germany, before fleeing from Nazi persecution to France and eventually the United States. Informed by this context, Arendt observed an 'irritating incompatibility between the actual power of modern man [sic] [. . .] and the impotence of modern men to live in, and understand the sense of, a world which their own strength has established' (Arendt, 1973: viii). For Arendt, then, a big problem in modernity is the loss of a capacity to understand and come to terms with a reality that facilitates immense violence and injustice. In response, she sought to find new ways for people to create a flourishing, hospitable world that reconciles the powers of humans to create a world in their own fashion and a human need to come to understand that world (Arendt, 1973). Specifically, Arendt highlighted the potential in politics as a space that allows people to come together and exchange opinions with others on issues of common interest. In doing so, the political refines people's understanding of the shared world, without denying their diverging perspectives on it, and potentially facilitates collective action towards improving that world (Arendt, 1998). Judgement plays an important role for this politically sustained (sense of) reality because it gives meaning to what appears in public and provides the standards by which to evaluate action. The person judging, in turn, benefits from the access to different perspectives and from exchanging their opinion on an issue with fellow judges. This has a bearing on the use of the term 'political': political judgement for Arendt does not describe a distinct type of judgement that distinguishes itself from other judging practices through its political content. Instead, according to Arendt, judgement becomes political wherever a person formulates it through active engagement with a community of judges. I therefore will use 'judgement' and 'political judgement' interchangeably in this book whenever I refer to this politically embedded form of judgement.

Arendt teaches us, in my reading, that a pluralist politics concerned with improving our sense of reality is key to sharpening our judgements on complicity. Arendt's perspective on judgement and pluralism contrasts with twentieth-century political theory about judgement and heightened pluralism. Contemporary societies are characterised by an increased diversity in beliefs and values that produce fundamental disagreements. The development led to a convergence of two dominant positions in political thought between the 1960s and the 1990s: European critical theory, emerging from the Frankfurt School and its key representative Jürgen Habermas, overlapped with the tradition of Anglo-American philosophical and political liberalism, notably John Rawls and his followers. The two positions are broadly supportive of pluralist, liberal democracy, but also interpret the heightened pluralism as a burden on our capacity to make judgement that needs to be managed (Rawls, 1993: 54ff.). They alleviate this problem by turning to models of public deliberation that adhere to standards of reasoning which largely remain outside the debate (cf. Azmanova, 2012: 89; Zerilli, 2016a: 152). The consequence is that the 'concept of judging is eliminated and the just enjoys a pyrrhic victory: freed from the limitations of the politically particular, it becomes politically futile' (Azmanova, 2012: 120). This understanding of judgement links with the account of moral judgement introduced above, and it is problematic for the very same reasons. In contrast, Arendt and her followers see human plurality – the fact that people share a world and can only make it hospitable and meaningful together – primarily as a source of, rather than an obstacle to, good judgement (Arendt, 1982; Azmanova, 2012; Mrovlje, 2018; Zerilli, 2016a). They argue that judgement cannot (nor does it need to) rely on narrow or abstract standards of reason to guide it and do not see public discussion and the fundamental disagreements that come with it as a deterrent from making appropriate judgements. Moving back to the broader concern with judging complicity, we can say that for Arendt a community's public opinion formation process inevitably shapes how we judge complicity. Exchanges of opinions can be a means to strengthen our individual perspectives on complicity; however, for this to be the case, we need to develop a sensitivity for how a society can use this potential in pluralism by giving space to political action and judgement. In making judgements, we also need to challenge efforts to constrain or displace human plurality.

But how can we affirm the potential in human plurality to improve our judgements without treating human plurality as merely another standard that, if applied appropriately, will lead to 'valid' judgements (cf. Azmanova, 2012; Vogler and Tillyris, 2021; Zerilli, 2016a)? As we will see in Chapters 2 and 3, Arendt's solution is that judgement can gain critical purchase on reality – what she calls, drawing loosely on Immanuel Kant, general or intersubjective validity – without, however, gaining the coercive power claimed by *a priori*, decontextual or even universal standards of morality and reason. By this she means that incorporating a plurality of perspectives helps judgement move beyond 'merely' expressing an opinion or addressing a particular issue or context; at the same time, it gains this meaning from the historical context and position from which it was articulated, and it is still an opinion rather than an irrefutable fact or truth. This dependence on context and partial perspective is not a problem for judgement because judgement serves precisely to relate to and improve that context. Judgement is objective not in the sense that others must accept its validity and arrive at the same conclusion based on appropriate reasoning – something I discuss in Chapter 3 and above as a concern for orthodox judgement theorists. It is objective in the literal sense of being orientated towards an object or issue, for example sweatshop labour, that shapes judgement and is shaped by it. Judgements are furthermore objective to the extent that different judges have the object in common, that is, it is the same object that different people engage with, and yet view from distinct perspectives. The 'objectivity' this judgement gains emerges both from the interaction with a range of different perspectives and positions (human plurality), and from the interrelationship between judge (subjective) and context (objective reality). The challenge then is not how judgements can claim validity, but how to embed an (improved) account of human plurality within a refined understanding of this interrelationship. Such an approach to what is known as the phenomenon of social conditioning must not give up on the coming together of objectivity and subjectivity but see it as essential to developing an improved engagement with reality that helps us judge and respond to complicity.

Over the past decade, judgement and complicity literature has turned to social theory to expand its understanding of social conditioning, commonly understood as the question to what extent thought and action are the product of their social context and vice versa. In particular, some invoke Pierre Bourdieu's contribution to the debate on the relationship between structure and human agency. They seek to use his work to counterbalance a tendency in earlier judgement and complicity scholarship to locate the critical potential within the mental capacities of the judge and to reduce complicity to individual, decontextualised action (Azmanova, 2012; Kornprobst, 2014; Mihai, 2016b; Schiff, 2014; Weidenfeld, 2013; Young, 2011). This book is indebted to their insights on the imbrication of judgement with issues of power and injustice, which I will bring to bear throughout my discussion of how to judge complicity. My turn to social theorist Margaret Archer serves a related, but different purpose: to complement Arendt's theorising on human plurality and political judgement by shedding further light on the interplay between structure and agency that frames human plurality. In her own words, Archer continues Arendt's project 'to put forward a model [of society] that is *recognisably human*' (Archer, 2016: 138, original emphasis).[4] She suggests that it is in accounting for the distinct properties and powers of a person and their context that we come to understand (social) reality. Again, a short introduction of this key thinker for this book is helpful.

Archer (1995) responded to tendencies in the social sciences to explain social phenomena by emphasising either structural or agential capacities, or by highlighting their inseparability. According to Archer, these forms of conflation cannot explain the contribution of both structures (networks of relationships between social positions) and agency (distinct capacities of each human being). In response, she proposes a model of social transformation in which structures pre-date agency, which, in turn, transforms structure. The analytical distinction allows a closer look at their interrelated but distinct properties and causal powers, which are often empirically difficult to separate. Following investigations into the role of structure, Archer has spent the last two decades working on a systematic account of human agency that avoids two tendencies: to attribute either the causal contribution of human agency to social processes and practices – for instance, when we say that it is capitalism and not individual politicians, estate agents or landlords that is to blame for the housing crisis – or the contributions of social processes and practices to the thoughts and actions of individual actors. Archer has shed light on the development of a sense of self and personal identity, and more recently, on modes of reflexivity through internal conversations and their transformation in late modernity (Archer, 2000, 2003, 2007, 2012). I take from her thought the insight that the interplay of structures and agency inevitably shapes how we think about responding to complicity. The coming together of the distinct properties and powers of structure and agency is also the strength of our engagement with reality beyond a reliance on supposedly pre-given standards. By attending to dualism, which includes challenging conflating approaches to social conditioning, we can make sure that our responses to complicity benefit from the potential in both the subjective and the objective dimension to human existence.

INTRODUCTION

Towards an improved ethos of reality

As set out earlier, this book focuses on the link between complicity, judgement and our engagement with reality. Specifically, it argues that judgements on complicity must be understood as part of the broader effort that all humans pursue, in myriad different ways, to establish a suitable stance towards themselves and the world in and around them. The stance helps us interpret our situation and what actions to pursue to meet our concerns, needs and desires. It does this by filtering a complex social reality through our immediate needs as well as who we think and feel we are, and who we want to be, for example a conservative, patriot and caring father. I call this stance an 'ethos of reality'.[5] The term 'ethos' serves here to indicate that it is both a highly personalised – and open-ended, imperfect – practice and a normative project. Drawing on Archer and Arendt, this book maps out dimensions to the ethos of reality along which it could be improved. I propose the cultivation of an ethos attentive to the interplay of the three components of human experience: structure, agency and plurality.

Admittedly, what 'attentiveness' and 'structure', 'agency' and 'plurality' mean can vary extensively. I nonetheless challenge reductive positions that put unwarranted weight on only one of these three components in their account of social conditioning and change. I object to overreliance on the cultivation of responsive individuals, for example through anti-racism training (overemphasising receptive agency), or on the role of structural crisis, for instance the waning of the imperialist Western nation state which exposes its underlying racist structures (displaying an overarching focus on structure), or on the dissolution of conflict through consensus amongst a plurality of views, for example public discussions on racism in the wake of reported racial violence (overestimating the potential of collective responses to injustice). I will argue that, because they are insufficiently attentive to the contribution that all three elements – structure, agency, plurality – continuously and simultaneously make to social transformation, such positions fail to address adequately how we should respond to complicity. To find the right balance between attentiveness to the complex interplay of structure, agency and plurality and the need to make concrete judgements on complicity, and taking appropriate action informed by this judgement, is undoubtedly difficult. More often than not, we are likely to end up reducing reality to our preferred vision of the world. The challenge of establishing a suitable engagement with reality can also be at odds with our (immediate) reactions to injustice and violence. Nonetheless, I argue that the benefit of humans actively participating[6] in the transformation of unjust practices ultimately depends to a significant extent on avoiding, and indeed combating, the repeated and systematic reduction of the distinct properties and powers of structure, human agency and plurality in our engagement with reality.

In making this argument, the book brings together three debates – on complicity, on political judgement and on structure–agency. At different stages of my argument, the book provides an overview of the current state of the three debates and my contribution to them. With regards to political judgement literature, I take up the challenge of complementing Arendt's emphasis on human plurality with an appropriate subject- and object-focus, or theory of social conditioning. My approach seeks to displace what Zerilli (2016a) terms radical forms of subjectivism or objectivism, which reduce reality to human perceptions of it or entail a desire for transcendence of the merely 'subjective' or 'partial' understanding of social formations. The two forms are interrelated, with the tendency to attribute causal force to either (social) structures or human agency. In its place, I draw from Archer (2003) a subjectivism that recuperates the ethical value of humans' sense of self, which is connected to each human being's unique perspective on the world – the 'it-seems-to-me' (Arendt, 1981a: 21), while also adhering to a reality that is irreducible to our perspectives on it. Archer's dualism furthermore enables us to avoid tendencies towards reducing plurality to a range of views that either cannot be improved at all, that is, they are all 'relative', or needs to be 'managed' through transcendent principles as visible in the liberal framework of judgement mentioned above.

In relation to debates on structure–agency, I bring into focus Arendt's unique concern with plurality. The discussion on structure–agency has traditionally centred on individuals. More recently, social theory has experienced various turns to relationality, including in the form of relational sociology (Dépelteau, 2018; Donati, 2011). Arendt's pluralism continues to offer key insights that complement formulations of the interplay between structure and agency, due to her unique concern with the political implications of the fact that humans live in the world together. Finally, concerning debates on complicity and responsibility, I develop the conception of social conditioning and judgement further, crucial to rethinking complicity. The book accounts for the ways that judgements on complicity depend on and are strengthened by the interplay of the distinct, yet interpenetrating, causal powers of structure, agency and human plurality. To take responsibility must therefore be to some extent about tackling the reductions that deny the contribution each of them makes to injustice and its transformation.

Book outline

The book consists of six main chapters. Chapters 1 to 4 address the phenomenon of complicity, judgement and social conditioning separately. Chapters 5 and 6 bring the argument together by outlining the improved ethos of reality and illustrating how people can engage with reality in a responsive manner when making judgements on their deeply rooted entanglement in violence and injustice in relation to a case study.

Chapter 1 focuses on complicity and suggests that disagreements between complicity scholars relate to the threefold problem or difficulty of how to identify, attribute and acknowledge complicity. The chapter discusses the different responses to the problem, starting with the dominant framework. It relies on a methodologically individualist conception of society to facilitate moral judgements using pre-given, rigid standards of reason and morality and to ensure that, in theory at least, complicity could be avoided. The social connection model and complicity-as-being foreground the structural processes that produce injustice and violence and combine this vision of society with a broader conception of judgement that attends to both structural injustice and individual responsibility. The chapter concludes with the ethics of responsiveness, focused on ensuring people are able or willing to address the difficulty of judgement in the first place, when faced with deeply rooted structural injustice.

Chapter 2 explores the link between judgement and our engagement with reality, by turning to Arendt as a key thinker on judgement. Arendt suggests that a reflective form of judgement gains in importance following the erosion in modernity of traditional standards as the source of coming to terms with the past and identifying appropriate action for the future. This break in tradition, Arendt argues, is also an opportunity to avoid unwarranted claims to objectivity in favour of recognising, and indeed strengthening, the intersubjective character of our sense of reality. Human plurality thus becomes a central means for improving reflective judgement – I term this the pluralist dimension to the ethos of reality, for which judgement is a key tool.

Chapter 3 weighs the potential and limits of a focus on plurality by engaging with the debate that followed Arendt's conceptualisation of reflective judgement. The debate provides important insights into concepts related to how humans judge politically: the imagination, the affective and unconscious domains, storytelling and common sense. These insights help in providing a more sophisticated conception of political judgement. Contributors also highlight in different ways that a closer look at the issue of social conditioning is key to understanding how we can say that some judgements are better than others without having to rely on narrow standards of validity or rationality. In other words, judgement scholars no longer see an emphasis on judgment's capacity to engage a plurality of perspectives on a world as enough to gain critical purchase on political issues. Instead, scholars seek to say more about the situated agency preceding judgement.

Chapter 4 continues the turn towards social conditioning begun in the previous chapter. I suggest that the critical alternatives on complicity offer an improved approach to social conditioning, but do not fully account for the distinct contributions of structure and agency to injustice and its transformation. In response, the chapter outlines Archer's analytical dualism. Dualism involves a suitable objectivism, by which I mean an orientation towards a multi-layered reality that is independent from our epistemic access to it, yet always socially mediated. Dualism also requires attention to subjectivity, by which I mean a sense of self that is embodied, relational and emotional, but also irreducible to the social or discursive dimensions to reality, and that draws on reflexivity in the form of an internal conversation to mediate between the internal and external context of its agency. Archer thus adds to the conceptualisation of judgements on complicity, and by extension an improved engagement with reality, a focus on both structure and agency alongside plurality.

Chapter 5 hybridises Arendt's and Archer's theories to sketch the key features of an improved ethos of reality. The aim is to reorientate the critical alternatives to the legal-moral paradigm of complicity without giving up on their claims of individual and shared responsibility that arise from structural injustice, or on the insights into the varied ways in which responsiveness could be cultivated. This, I argue, can be achieved by learning to habitually engage with reality in its dualist and pluralist dimension, and by taking into consideration the systemic ways in which the properties and powers of structure, agency and human plurality are denied or strengthened within society. To illustrate the theoretical points made, the chapter utilises the case of consumer complicity in the plastic pollution produced by the food and drink industry.

Finally, Chapter 6 offers an in-depth study of someone making judgements on complicity that are informed by and contribute to an effort to develop an improved ethos of reality. The chosen context, systemic oppression during the 1980s under the Romanian communist dictatorship, is an extreme example and this has two benefits. First, the example prevents drawing quick conclusions for one's own situation as the context will probably be significantly different from the experiences and contexts of most readers of this book. Engaging with an unfamiliar situation can potentially engender critical reflection by allowing readers to evaluate dispositions and long-held assumptions as they orientate themselves in unfamiliar territory while simultaneously reducing the barriers to such critical reflection that can come with the sense of accusation often felt by the privileged when engaging with issues directly related to them. Second, the context heightens the stakes, and this sharpens the contours of the ethos of reality in useful ways. This is visible in Nobel laureate Herta Müller's autofiction, written in response to the terrorisation she faced from the Romanian communist dictatorship leading up to and following her refusal to work as a collaborator. Her essays, novels, interviews and collages enumerate and reflect on a resistant practice of 'living in the detail' that tries to find a place between embrace of one's inevitable complicity and escapism from it. Müller hoped that accounting for concrete action, objects and moments – to live in the detail – could give her life some meaning and stability beyond the uncertainty produced by state terror. The practice is also part of a normative project, which I interpret as exemplary of my proposed ethos of reality: she extends this focus on the concrete through attentiveness to the distinct qualities and interplay of structure, agency and plurality.

Notes

1. Throughout this book, I rely on the first-person plural 'we', 'us', 'our', alongside 'humans' and 'people' to address the subject of this investigation. I am aware of the dangers that come with these descriptors: they obscure differences between people and potentially hide the hierarchies of domination that are central to debates on complicity and responsibility. In relation to issues of complicity and injustice, the term 'we' often refers to the wealthier parts of the global population, who, myself included, disproportionately benefit from injustice and violence and who do too little to contest the status quo. When turning to broader debates about judgement or social conditioning, I follow Hannah Arendt in interpreting 'we' as not a pre-defined category, for example political theorists or citizens of Western society, but as an imagined community that in the process of reading and writing comes into being and is open to contestation.
2. I follow Young's (2011: 45) use of the concept 'structural injustice', which she defines as someone being in a position that they should not be in, as a result of specific social processes. I avoid the term 'structural' in order to capture the contribution both of structures (the system of relationships between social positions or of social wholes, for example MPs and constituents, the state structure, the structure of capitalism) and of human agency (the capacity of humans to act and respond to their context) to injustice. At times, I also use the terms 'political oppression', 'problem' and 'violence' to capture a range of wrongs that go beyond merely being unjust, for example apartheid or climate change, which is not to claim that these concepts can be easily separated. Overall, I wish to capture a wide range of unjust, violent and oppressive practices that are facilitated by entrenched forms of complicity, in full awareness that there are significant differences between for example racism, capitalist exploitation and political violence, and indeed between racism in different countries, for example in South Africa or Japan.
3. The numerous companions and handbooks currently in production and recently published (Baehr and Walsh, 2017; Bernstein, 2018; Gratton and Sari, 2020; Krimstein, 2018) attest to the fact that Arendt's work remains highly relevant for contemporary political theory. At the same time, Arendt scholarship is still assessing the role that she can and cannot play in moving away from a (Western) desire for *a priori* moral principles. Alongside well-known contentious issues in her thought – such as Arendt's (1959) discussion of Little Rock; more on this in Chapter 2 – there are enduring questions about how far she was able to go in distancing herself from a (European) philosophical mind-set, for example in relation to the role of thinking. I contribute to efforts that

balance Arendt's thought through a focus on social theory, without, however, claiming to resolve these important tensions and challenges to her contribution.
4. The full quote reads: 'to put forward a model that is recognisably human; one that retains Arendt's notion of the "Human Condition" as entailing a reflexive "Life of the mind"'. This quote provides a rare example of Archer explicitly acknowledging the affinities and overlap between her own and Arendt's projects. The secondary literature on their thoughts seldom makes the connection between Arendt's and Archer's work, with the exception of Philip Walsh (2015) and Daniel Chernilo (2017). Walsh is primarily concerned with what sociology can learn from Arendt and Chernilo addresses the humanist projects of both Arendt and Archer without seeking their hybridisation. Together with recent scholarship that links Arendt's thought with political theory and international-relations realisms (Klusmeyer, 2011; Owens, 2008; Vogler and Tillyris, 2019), these authors provide an opportunity for a fruitful investigation into the commonalities between various forms of realism, too easily obscured by their different language games. While my argument does not depend on articulating to what extent realisms share a family resemblance, the book draws its strength from a commitment to an attentive facing up to and caring for a world not of our choosing. This commitment is common to political and social forms of realism including Arendt's ethic of reality and Archer's critical realism (but cashed out in various different ways).
5. The terminology 'ethos of reality' intentionally mirrors Patricia Owens, who describes Arendt's focus on a community's collective engagement with reality as an 'ethic of reality' (Owens, 2008).
6. I do not wish to suggest what exactly an active participation entails, for example to what extent it requires intentionality, but the role of human agency should not merely be coincidental and to some extent attributable to a human being.

CHAPTER ONE

Debates on complicity and the problem of responsiveness

This chapter introduces the debate on complicity and its important insights into how people should respond to their complicity. I look at the main disagreements between the dominant framework on complicity and three critical alternative approaches, Young's social connection model, a poststructuralist complicity-as-being and the ethics of responsiveness. My aim is not to resolve these disagreements, although I discuss the benefits of the critical alternatives, but to show how they reveal a fundamental challenge when it comes to judging complicity and responding to it.

There are three dimensions to this challenge and a failure to address any one of them increases the chance that people deflect or disavow their responsibility for injustice. Firstly, there are significant doubts about our capacity to adequately identify our complicity in unjust outcomes. After all, people have fundamental disagreements about what counts as an injustice, and this necessarily affects what they feel responsible for and what they do not. For example, people disagree about whether it is unjust that hiring committees tend to prefer white, middle-class, able-bodied men in their hiring judgements – this of course depends on the context and profession. Those of the view that they are simply hiring the candidate that is most qualified for the job will not feel complicit in unjust hiring practices that discriminate against marginalised groups. Secondly, even where identifying complicity seems straightforward, we face difficult choices about attributing complicity to specific groups or individuals. A focus on the biggest corporations, the richest people, the highest-ranking officers and politicians, risks obscuring the numerous people that have contributed to injustice as consumers, voters and so on; however, a focus on the latter group can mean that the powerful avoid scrutiny. The judgement about who to focus on will largely depend on what the aim is of addressing complicity, which can vary from revenge to engendering positive social change. Lastly, we are forced to judge carefully what it means to acknowledge our entanglement with exploitative and dominating practices. Especially given the first problem of identifying complicity, it is crucial that we ask what motivates us to accept our entanglement in some cases but not in others and whether this means that we are tackling injustice in the most effective way. Each of these challenges highlights how discussions about (responding to) complicity lead to debates about the nature and limitations of human judging capabilities. The dominant and critical approaches to be discussed in this chapter provide different solutions to the threefold problem that shape how they think about complicity and how people should take responsibility for it.

The dominant approach to complicity

My discussion starts with the dominant legal-moral philosophical framework and how it seeks to address the challenge of how to identify, attribute and acknowledge complicity. I have already mentioned in the Introduction that the framework relies on supposedly pregiven standards of moral behaviour and a methodological individualist conception of society to 'resolve' all three problems. Together they lead, as I briefly sketch now, to a narrow conception of complicity that can easily be identified, attributed and acknowledged using reason and morality.

The dominant legal-moral philosophical framework uses the concept of complicity as an analytical tool to identify indirect, but nonetheless potentially important, involvement in wrongdoing that a person could avoid by adhering to widely known legal or moral principles (Ciurria, 2011; Gardner, 2007; Jackson, 2015; Kadish, 1985; Kutz, 2000, 2007, 2011; Lepora and Goodin, 2013; Mellema, 2016). This reading of complicity is individualist in three ways: its subject is an individual, its object the individual's actions and the basis for attributing complicity characteristics of that individual (Kutz, 2000: 4). Other aspects of the situation are treated as background conditions that can shape the individual's motivation and actions but are not themselves involved in the wrongdoing. A classic scenario that typifies this kind of individualist understanding of complicity as wrongdoing is a heist, which involves several people intentionally acting in a morally reprehensible and legally culpable manner; within the scenario, an example of complicity is the getaway driver or a lookout who are not an integral part of the team that organised the heist (Lepora and Goodin, 2013: 53). The image of the heist, as a carefully planned act of criminal wrongdoing, conveys the idea that not being complicit is the norm. The tacit assumption is that 'the accomplice could *avoid* being complicit and walk through life never *failing* to avoid it' (Afxentiou et al., 2016: 2, original emphasis). To judge complicity, we look back at past behaviour to identify whether a person's discrete action, for example looking out for the police, contributed to wrongdoing in important ways. In recent years, theorists have been introducing forward-looking criteria, to move from a strategy of retribution to one of risk reduction, and incorporating collective dimensions to agency (Kutz, 2011: 149), but this does not fundamentally change the underlying assumptions about society and complicity. When focusing on what proponents of the framework describe as collective action problems, for example global poverty or climate change, analysis remains wedded to aggregating individual people's activities and the underlying approach to judging complicity remains in principle the same.

The conception of complicity is part of a broader debate about questions of responsibility and guilt, which has similarly developed a dominant moral and legal framework that upholds a focus on reason, pre-given, rigid moral standards, and methodological individualism. Philosophers belonging to this tradition seek to reduce injustice by attributing moral blameworthiness and/or legal culpability to those who have had a significant influence on legally or morally problematic behaviour. Following Iris Marion Young (2011), we can term it the standard or liability model of responsibility.[1] For those defending the standard model, attributing responsibility to individuals in relation to concrete acts of identifiable moral wrongdoing helps prevent abuses by powerful people, encourages the powerless to seek justice, and morally challenges those who can influence outcomes that harm others. The liability model 'enables us to keep in focus the very question of the difference that agents can make to outcomes and to cast a critical eye on attempts by powerful agents to escape their own responsibilities' (Hayward and Lukes, 2008: 12).

The dominant framework's resolution of the threefold problem of complicity is undoubtedly enticing in its ability to produce simple, clear moral judgements about who is complicit and should be held accountable. It achieves this by limiting judgement in advance to the application of pre-set rules and standards and in connection with an individualist conception of society that allows a primary focus on the thoughts and actions of actors in relative isolation from their context. The 'rigging' of the process of judgement comes, however, at the cost of an insensitivity to the complexity of social reality. To be convincing as an approach, the dominant framework must therefore provide sufficient certainty of judgement to offset the costs of this insensitivity. However, as the debates on complicity clearly show, the approach cannot avoid complex and ambiguous cases altogether. This comes out in both the legal and the moral context.

In the legal context, a central aim is to develop frameworks that identify complicity in such a way as to enable successful prosecution in criminal courts. The legal perspective is thus 'unabashedly "reductionist"' (Osiel, 2009) and there is a strong focus on judgements about complicity by judges. Its doctrine of complicity, known also as the law of aiding and abetting or accessorial liability, commonly describes an accomplice's intentional help with, or influence on, a principal wrongdoing (Kadish, 1985). Accessorial liability was initially an analytical tool in domestic law. It later moved to international law, starting with the Nuremberg trials, and expanded in ad hoc tribunals in Yugoslavia and Rwanda. The move helped respond to the kinds of challenges posed to justice by perpetrators of bureaucratised mass killing such as Adolf Eichmann. Their cases are particularly difficult as they participate in wrongdoing from a great distance; their guilt does not decrease with their distance from the primary wrongdoing, the killing of a human being, but increases as their use of a bureaucratic apparatus allows them to organise and coordinate killings at a mass scale (Aksenova, 2016; Schabas, 2000, 2001). The difficult context consequently demanded a significant departure in international law from the conventional domestic cases of complicity, for example a heist or murder (Clapham, 2003; Osiel, 2005). Nonetheless, international criminal law holds on to complicity as an analytical tool to attribute individual criminal responsibility in the context of collective wrongdoing (Aksenova, 2016).

Complicity in moral terms provides a broader conceptual tool than the one found in legal philosophy (Mellema, 2016). It is possible that we judge someone morally responsible for complicitous behaviour, based on moral-philosophical standards of appropriate behaviour, even if they have not committed a crime. This allows moral philosophy to address a wider array of questionable acts.

The broader reach in turn significantly complicates the attribution and identification of complicity. Moral-philosophical takes on complicity have responded to this challenge by reinforcing their emphasis on causation, intention and/or knowledge as standards for judging someone as complicit. Lepora and Goodin (2013: 42) understand complicity as implication in another's wrongdoing by an actor who should or could have known the primary agent's intentions. Kutz (2011) suggests that a focus on shared intention offers a helpful way to move beyond a narrow focus on causation and to explore the broader context of moral responsibility. Lastly, Gardner (2007) insists that complicity necessarily requires a causal contribution by the accomplice to the principal wrongdoing. In contrast, Kutz (2007) suggests that an accomplice may still be morally blameworthy even if the principal wrongdoer fails to commit the crime, or if the principal actor is able to do wrong with and without the complicitous action.

Both in the legal and moral context, the dominant framework expands the range of people who could be considered culpable or morally blameworthy to more indirect, but nonetheless important, contributors. It also comes with significant conceptual and empirical ambiguity that is not easily resolved. The framework suggests that complicity scholars are left with a difficult trade-off between (a) the desire to incorporate an ever greater range of culpable or morally blameworthy actors and (b) the need to abstract from complex social reality to enable decisive judgements about complicity that could, for instance, succeed in court. The assumption, or hope, is that in developing ever more sophisticated conceptions of complicity, causality and what is sufficient knowledge of wrongdoing, the approach can widen the understanding of complicity without losing out on the simple solution to the threefold problem of judging it.

The structural affirmation of complicity

The alternative accounts of complicity focused on in this book object to the idea that such a trade-off is necessary. The reason is that its representatives interpret injustice primarily in structural terms (Young, 2011). Their alternative solution to the threefold problem of judging complicity begins with a particular sensitivity and attentiveness to the way the world is structured, the social conditions within which people act, and the temporal horizon within which judgements of complicity are made (Mihai, 2019, 2022). Such a sensitivity should lead people to take responsibility even when blame and guilt cannot easily be distributed.

The different approach to complicity is visible in Young's posthumously published *Responsibility for Justice* (2011). In the book, Young considers the challenge of identifying complicity and attributing it to individual people in the context of structural forms of social injustice. By this she means the systematic 'domination or deprivation of the means to develop and exercise' the capacities of a large group of people, which enables 'others to dominate or to have a wide range of opportunities' (Young, 2011: 52). As an example, Young uses the systematic exclusion from the housing market of the economically vulnerable. This structural injustice is irreducible to individuals' choices or the actions of powerful institutions, for example landlords' associations. While individual landlords may act in a greedy manner to exacerbate the suffering of specific vulnerable groups, the unjust distribution of housing cannot be traced back to their actions. Complicity now involves the interaction of a large amount of people that together produce outcomes they would themselves consider to be unjust (Young, 2011: 108). Judgements of complicity must therefore focus on the social processes, institutional organisations and social practices that produce inequality of opportunities amongst social groups (Young, 2001: 16).

Young also alleviates concerns about introducing such social complexity into our judgements about complicity, by developing a different way of thinking about responsibility. *Responsibility for Justice* draws on Hannah Arendt's distinction between guilt and political responsibility. The distinction is related to, but separate from, Arendt's work on judgement, which I address in the following chapter. Arendt (2003) had argued that under the Nazi regime the possibility of claiming neutrality towards the injustices committed decreased significantly, but nonetheless insisted that we should only judge a small group of people guilty and legally culpable. Arendt instead suggested that humans have a political responsibility in relation to crimes against humanity, because of their membership in a political community that is responsible for the wrongdoing. Young has concerns about this broad conception of responsibility: it is 'a mystification to say that people bear responsibility simply because they are members of a political community, and not because of anything at all that they have done or not done' (Young, 2011: 79). However, she finds in Arendt's thought a second, shared notion of responsibility by those who contribute to structural processes with unjust outcomes that demands collective action towards resolving the background conditions of injustice. Her notion of responsibility falls on anyone, by virtue of the

> fact that they are aware moral agents who ought not to be indifferent to the fate of others and the danger that states and other organised institutions often pose to some people. This responsibility is largely unavoidable in the modern world, because we participate in and usually benefit from the operation of these institutions (Young, 2011: 92).

Thus, while not distributing blame, Young insists that 'we can and should be *criticised* for not taking action, not taking enough action, taking ineffective action, or taking action that is counterproductive. We also have a right and an obligation to criticise the others with whom we share responsibility' (Young, 2011: 144, original emphasis).

Young's solution to the threefold problem of identifying, attributing and acknowledging complicity is therefore to foreground the structural nature of injustice and to separate a shared responsibility to transform these unjust processes from any distribution of blame and culpability. The approach ultimately 'avoids' the challenge of judging complicity, by widening the understanding of what complicity and accompanying responsibility entail even as she retains the connection to actual contributions (that are, however, difficult to escape) and suggests that those with greater power and influence have to do more to tackle injustice. Young (2011: 170) acknowledges that there are numerous ways in which people, often legitimately, disavow blame for the unjust outcome. This leads her to reject blame as an ethical foundation and to place hope on our willingness to do good and our ability to criticise each other whenever we seek to deny our responsibility.

The second critical alternative, the complicity-as-being approach, takes similar steps to Young (Applebaum, 2010; Farrell, 2014; Sanders, 2002; Sanyal, 2015; Spivak, 1999). The approach works with the image of complicity in systemic injustice and violence such as genocide or colonialism. In these contexts, complicity can hardly be avoided, and even resistance is imagined within the terms and horizon set by the system of oppression (Sanyal, 2015: 10–11). Therefore, complicity is ill defined in terms of singular acts of complicity in wrongdoing that could be prevented. It requires instead an acknowledgement of the many different, often unintentional ways in which human beings contribute to a system of injustice. This is apparent in the context Mark Sanders devotes himself to, South Africa's apartheid regime. Sanders shows how the apartheid regime relied on a strategy of denying the togetherness of the various South African ethnic groups. In response, he argues (Sanders, 2002: 10) that anti-apartheid intellectuals, in their resistance to the state, necessarily became contaminated by its workings and, indeed, that their resistance depended on acknowledging that complicity.

Proponents of complicity-as-being challenge the necessary link between complicity and legal culpability and the retrospective focus on what people have done. They do not deny that the term 'complicity' can serve an important function in society by condemning reproachable behaviour, but turn attention to a general meaning of complicity, fruitfully deployable in response to systemic injustices (Sanders, 2002: x). This general meaning arises from the fact that we live together and cannot avoid living together. Within poststructuralism, which frames the complicity-as-being approach, this is primarily articulated along the relationship between a self and an Other (Morton, 2003; Probyn-Rapsey, 2010). The approach retains a desire not to be complicit in socio-political wrongs, which, however, must come with an acceptance of this larger complicity, 'etymologically, a folded-together-ness (*com-plic-ity*) – in human-being (or the being of being human)' (Sanders, 2002: 5). Sanders (2002: 11) calls this alternative approach 'responsibility-in-complicity'.

Responsibility-in-complicity has two dimensions. At a general level, acknowledging one's connection to all human affairs becomes the pre-condition of taking up responsibility. It forecloses any attempt to disembed oneself from the unjust system. Responsibility-in-complicity also entails an acceptance that we cannot eliminate acting in complicity, in the narrow sense of contributing to a specific unjust system. Resisting systemic injustice often merely amounts to avoiding the worst excesses of complicity. In separating out complicity in the general sense, which arises from the inevitable interrelationship with the Other, from complicities in the narrow sense of contributing to wrongdoing, the hope is that one's relation to wrongdoing is made visible to us and enables a person to acknowledge and problematise the ways in which they have helped sustain unjust practices. When

> opposition does not free one from complicity, but depends on it as its condition of possibility, responsibility is sharpened. No longer can the intellectual [...] simply proclaim his or her opposition. Complicity is to be acknowledged, and, when a strategy of demarcation is adopted, responsibility assumed for choosing 'between ... terrifying contaminations' (Sanders, 2002: 10, quoting Derrida, 1989: 40).

The brief outline of the poststructuralist position illustrates that the main aim of this conception is to make judgements about complicity along the lines of the dominant framework difficult, because they enable individuals to distance themselves from injustice. Participation alone is 'no basis for judgment. Rather, it is the relationship between actual instances of participation and the possibility of generalising or maximising responsibility from such determinate complicities that calls for judgment' (Sanders, 2002: 23). Similar to Young's social connection model, the approach identifies sensitivity to social reality as a necessary pre-condition for addressing complicity in injustice. Complicity-as-being avoids the concerns that animate the approach of the dominant legal-moral framework, by severing the connection between responding to complicity and culpability and blameworthiness, while retaining the possibility that someone can be held accountable for not responding to their entanglement in injustice and violence.

The two critical alternatives share a focus on structural injustice to attribute complicity to a wide variety of people for their indirect everyday contributions, in relation to which they have a collective, forward-looking responsibility and a duty to change structural oppression. There are also notable differences between the two: Young's social connection model is coloured by Arendt's insights on political responsibility and orientated towards transforming unjust processes. In contrast, poststructuralists emphasise personal responsibility orientated by a self–Other binary. Furthermore, Young and her followers do not accept the totalising, general meaning of complicity-as-being, central to the poststructuralist perspective. Jade Schiff, for example, rejects the overwhelming character of human foldedness as a pre-condition for taking up responsibility. She emphasises that encounters with the Other and the responsibility that arises out of them are always situated, dependent on the context and stories we tell ourselves (Schiff, 2014: 26). The main challenge in utilising this framework is therefore not to privilege an affirmation of the Other over the multi-dimensional responses needed for positive social transformation. Young's approach, in turn, raises concerns that the focus on collective responses to structural injustice overemphasises the potential in coordinated efforts to transform injustice. Both theories nonetheless provide useful ways of conceiving complicity that transcend the shortcomings of conventional, moral-legal philosophical ways of identifying, attributing and acknowledging complicity. They explore different dimensions to how socially embedded humans encounter and participate in pervasive injustice and violence.

An ethics of responsiveness

The ethics of responsiveness argues that Young's social connection model and the poststructuralist affirmation of human foldedness only presuppose rather than address the ability to cultivate responsiveness to complicity. By responsiveness they mean a logically prior problem to taking responsibility that arises when we take the concept of 'responsibility' back to its etymological Latin roots in the verb 'respond' and entails an emphasis on the 'ability to respond to others and oneself' (Beausoleil, 2014, 2017; Oliver, 2004: 83). To give an example, Young fruitfully draws on social theorists Pierre Bourdieu and Anthony Giddens to argue that 'however uniquely individual we think we are, many of our most mundane actions manifest internalised bodily comportments and reactions – the habitus that are typical of people in similar social positions' (Young, 2011: 61). Yet, this insight primarily serves to ward off the individualism of the dominant framework; Young focuses on the person as a moral agent who expects others to be just to them and who wishes to be good, as the motivational force that encourages someone to take up a shared responsibility. However, alongside a 'desire to see the self as ethical', on which Young's model builds, the privileged hold 'an equally powerful desire to avoid relinquishing systematic advantage' (Hayward, 2017: 407).

The desire for disavowal is a product of the dispositional constraints known as bad faith (as defined by Jean-Paul Sartre), misrecognition (as theorised by Pierre Bourdieu), thoughtlessness (as conceptualised by Hannah Arendt) and white ignorance (as captured by Charles Mills). Thoughtlessness provides a distancing mechanism through which we 'either cut ourselves off from others by refusing to acknowledge our implications in their suffering, or else submit to ideological tropes that conceal our implication in it' (Schiff, 2014: 54), bad faith a form of lying to oneself to avoid dealing with the consequences of our freedom to make choices and act, and misrecognition the forgetting of history that conveys to the status quo a sense of endurance and natural status and, in doing so, legitimises the continued existence of privileges and injustice. White ignorance is unlike conventional ignorance, that is, the absence of knowledge: it is 'a non-knowing, that is not contingent, but in which race – white racism and/or white racial domination and their ramifications – plays a crucial causal role' (Mills, 2007: 20). Together these dispositions mean that 'no matter how well-intentioned we are, how conscious of our privilege, how attentive to our implication in suffering, we are all still subject to powerful temptations to disavow those things' (Schiff, 2014: 3). Thoughtlessness, bad faith, misrecognition and ignorance are important dispositions that help humans navigate the complex world. They are highly problematic in that they engender a flight from reality – understood as hiding facts of reality that differ from our vision of the world – and thus from responsibility. These dispositions help naturalise structural oppression so that we forget its contingency, that is, that structural oppression can be transformed. The question therefore is how to disrupt their workings to allow people to become receptive to their complicity and identify ways they can help tackle injustice. In other words, the ethics lays the groundwork for making judgements on complicity.

The ethics of responsiveness emphasises that the difficulty of identifying and acknowledging one's complicity is not simply a matter of insincerity or unwillingness on the part of some people. Instead, we must confront the fact that our unavoidable participation in unjust practices inevitably engenders continued disavowal and that we can never fully grasp our complicity (Schiff, 2014: 39). Behaving as a morally good person could therefore actually contribute to the oppressive system, as Lilie Chouliaraki's (2013) discussion of the media environment dedicated to encouraging solidarity with vulnerable others astutely illustrates. In response to this problem of responsiveness, each proponent offers a different solution that provides a distinct way in which receptivity could be increased and situatedness acknowledged. I will now introduce their approaches in greater detail as each offers an important means to set up adequate preconditions for judging complicity.

Pluralist narratives and heightened vigilance

The first proponent, Jade Schiff, focuses on how bad faith, thoughtlessness and misrecognition undermine the link between the everyday life of the privileged and the suffering of the exploited. In response, Schiff turns to disruptive moments, cataclysmic events that could potentially expose 'conditions of everyday life in which structural injustice *and* crises take root' (Schiff, 2014: 22, original emphasis). Such moments help by showing the contingency of socio-political practices, disturbing our sense of ourselves, and revealing the often hidden ordinary, everyday injustices. Hurricane Katrina or the 2008 financial crisis do not simply make us aware of the systemic injustice – racism, poverty and so on – that we fail to respond to. They also ideally expose us fully to the circumstances of those disadvantaged and our burdens of responsibility for them (Schiff, 2014: 139). Ruptures of everyday certainties could help shatter the barriers to responsibility that arise out of the naturalisation of injustice and violence, which makes them seem objective facts of life for which no one bears responsibility.

How aware people can become of their implication in suffering, depends, for Schiff, on the type of stories we tell about moments of profound crisis. Her work builds on Arendt's scholarship on storytelling (to be explored further in Chapter 3) and draws attention to the fact that narratives can both facilitate responsiveness and further entrench the flight from reality. In order for cataclysmic events to facilitate responsiveness, they require first a suitable disposition towards recognising the potential of crisis for positive social transformation. Schiff directs attention to ironic improvisation in the hope that it might prove a suitable source for nurturing a responsive disposition. Improvisation is ironic when it relies on the past to create something new to face the future. Irony is 'a critical feature of public life because it offers a tentative, improvisatory path forward in and after crises, one that entangles the old with the new – our shared histories with our collective and uncertain futures' (Schiff, 2014: 188). A politics of responsiveness accordingly entails improvised telling of stories that reveals the contingency of current public culture and, at the same time, acknowledges the burdens of living a life (Schiff, 2014: 190). As one such example, Schiff turns to Judith Butler and her emphasis on the experience of a shared vulnerability in the context of 9/11. This experience could serve as a starting point for opening ourselves up to the suffering of others – while acknowledging the limits of our ability to remain receptive amidst the potential for denial in our busy everyday lives.

Moving on to another strand of this ethics, Barbara Applebaum (2010) explores the challenges of complicity and responsibility as part of white pedagogy. The book highlights how education traditionally played a crucial role in reproducing white ignorance and considers her own experience of students struggling with moving beyond the individualist conception of complicity and responsibility, familiar from the dominant legal and moral framework. Applebaum, like Schiff, turns to Butler's account of vulnerability to expand Young's social connection model; however, instead of a focus on ironic narratives about crisis, Applebaum encourages heightened vigilance. This may in part be explained by the poststructuralist influence: while not directly engaging with Sanders's responsibility-in-complicity approach, Applebaum uses Fiona Probyn-Rapsey's (2010) provocative adoption of Sanders – complicity as pre-condition of ethics itself – as the leitmotif of her own argument. In short, Applebaum argues that acknowledgements of one's privilege in the context of systemic injustices and oppression, for example racism, is often characterised by an inability (and unwillingness) to identify any actual complicity, combined with supposedly moral behaviour that helps disavow the need to seriously engage with the question of complicity in the first place (Applebaum, 2010: 31). The scepticism towards a confession of complicity is reminiscent of Arendt's rejection of declarations of guilt by the German public following the Second World War. Where everyone proclaims a diffuse notion of guilt, for example guilt for the terrible crimes committed during the Holocaust, concrete blameworthy acts, specific failures and instances of structural injustices are obscured (Arendt, 2003: 28; cf. Schaap, 2001). The issue seems to raise serious doubts about the responsibility-in-complicity approach and its emphasis on the normative potential identified in embracing complicity as human foldedness. In response, Applebaum maintains that responsibility-in-complicity can move beyond a concern with a morally flawed self by improving our conception of receptivity towards others. Applebaum (2010: 196) expands Young's social connection model through Butler's work to argue that, in the context of white complicity, we should be attentive to how normative violence becomes invisible. Specifically, Butler emphasises that we need to counter the violence inherent in the formation of our (socialised) identity, which emerges from a desire within society to immunise the process of identity formation against any deviation from dominant forms of identity, for example being white, male, middle class, able-bodied, and the possibility that these identities are understood and performed differently. In response, those benefiting from the violence need to cultivate an ethics of non-violence through vigilance, critique, humility and uncertainty that seeks to actively disrupt the closure of how norms are reproduced in society. Ethics becomes a risk we take upon ourselves at the edges of normative frameworks, in challenging even seemingly good action by, for example, becoming more willing to listen to the marginalised.[2]

Disruptive politics and democratic caring

The third representative of an ethics of responsiveness I focus on, Clarissa Hayward (2017, 2020) emphasises that in the context of systemic racism, the ignorance of the privileged presents itself as knowledge and thus forecloses the possibility of seeing white ignorance for what it is. A wide variety of mechanisms and practices secure this false self-perception, including information gatekeeping by powerful members of the dominant groups, internalised beliefs and assumptions, and the desire to seem ethical even when we benefit from asymmetric advantages (Hayward, 2017: 404). In response, Hayward directs attention not to vulnerability or to improvisatory narratives about crisis, but to the potential of the powerless to cause political disruption. The action of, for example, the Black Lives Matter movement provides an important means to challenge self-interested ignorance and bring forth positive transformation. The account seems particularly attuned to the political dimension of injustice. It turns to subversive political acts of protest and moves beyond a narrow focus on cultivating responsive agency. Hayward clarifies that the purpose cannot be to convince the systemically advantaged but to 'make it all but impossible for the privileged to not hear the voices of, to not know the political claims of the oppressed' (Hayward, 2017: 406). Hayward also stresses the partial and temporary effect on white ignorance that disruptive politics is likely to have by undermining racial gatekeeping and disrupting the internalisation of racialised standards and beliefs. Ignorance remains an enduring feature of being human. Disruption must therefore target directly the incentive structures for racialised ignorance, rather than rely on an appeal to a shared responsibility. Disruptive politics must furthermore connect with various other sources of transformation that ensure more widespread changes to unjust processes. These potentials for change include for Hayward the influence that already-motivated sympathetic people in positions of power can take, as well as the constraints that broader socio-political changes – for example in public opinion – might place on actors.

Finally, Ella Myers's *Worldly Ethics* (2013; cf. Myers, 2008) does not engage directly with the theories on complicity central to this chapter, but she offers a sympathetic, critical evaluation of a post-structuralist 'turn to ethics' from which responsibility-in-complicity emerges. Myers juxtaposes her own Arendt-inspired democratic ethos with an ethics of self-care (which also relies on the late writings of Michel Foucault) and charitable care as the infinite responsibility for an Other (associated with Emmanuel Levinas). She argues that the two prioritise the self–Other relationship, which makes their frameworks 'ill-equipped to nourish associative democratic politics. The dyadic relations [. . .] narrow attention to the figures of self and Other and obscure the worldly contexts that are the actual sites and objects of democratic action' (Myers, 2013: 2). A focus on the self or the Other cannot address the political implications of oppression because there 'is little room in these accounts for anything other than human selves and others' (Myers, 2013: 86). The problem with domination is not only the denial of humans' relational character, but the destruction of the possibility of their acting together. The responsibility-in-complicity approach fails to address the 'associative' response needed to make affirming foldedness a viable option. It is 'not an adequate basis' as injustices and domination have an effect 'primarily upon *collectivities*' (Myers, 2008: 140, original emphasis).[3]

Myers's own solution to this problem is the cultivation of a democratic ethos as a care for the world inspired by Arendt's underdeveloped concept of '*amor mundi*' (more on this later) and care ethics. Democratic care for the world is a collaborative effort directed at the things of shared interest and concerns (Myers, 2013: 87). Democratic care does not amount to care for the self and the Other. Indeed, it might even prove antithetical, requiring immediate neglect of a person and their interests. Priority must instead be given to creating and protecting a world that enables people to address their perspective on that world together. Myers also astutely identifies that care for the world entails a recognition that the world is 'a conditioned and conditioning habitat' and that humans are 'of the world and not just in it' (2013: 91). Drawing on Bruno Latour and Jane Bennett, Myers emphasises that a worldly thing is always shorthand for the larger interplay of things and humans at various levels. Care for the world entails an interplay between human agency and other sources of power.

In sum, bad faith, misrecognition, ignorance and thoughtlessness are inevitably part of being human and pose difficult questions about the capacity of privileged people to respond to and experience the suffering of those negatively affected by exploitation and domination. In focusing on four representatives of the ethics of responsiveness, I have shown the multi-faceted insights that a concern with responsiveness offers. Together they bring into dialogue key approaches in contemporary political theory to political problems that, in combination, provide a useful arsenal to overcome constraints on judging complicity.

Concluding thoughts

This chapter has summarised ongoing disagreements within complicity scholarship about how to identify, attribute and acknowledge complicity. First, I show how the dominant framework seeks to solve the problem. It does so by reducing complicity to culpable and blameworthy action of an individual actor that can be judged using pre-given moral standards. The strategy offers an enticing way to make identifying complicity easier, and the attribution of culpability and blame can be a powerful deterrent against wrongful action. The increasing recognition of the complexity and ambiguity of many cases of complicity within the literature, however, points to the fact that the threefold challenge has merely been replaced with an unsatisfying trade-off: between a narrow conception of complicity that is empirically of limited help, and a broader conception for which the tools provided (to identify, attribute and acknowledge complicity) are also of limited help.

In response, the chapter turns to two critical alternatives that stress the structural nature of injustice. They argue that many if not most forms of injustice and violence, from apartheid to rising global inequality, are the outcomes of countless social interactions shaped by (and shaping) social contexts over long periods of time. In other words, the critical approaches address the threefold problem of judging complicity by introducing an improved understanding of social (trans)formation that rejects the suggested trade-off. The different understanding of injustice as pervasive throughout society leads, in turn, to a widening of the meaning of complicity: within modern society, avoiding entanglement in unjust processes is (almost) impossible; complicity is therefore something we all share and is irreducible to acts that are morally or legally wrong. The wider notions of injustice and complicity reduce the negative stigma related to complicity that come with being accused of morally or legally wrong behaviour, which encourages disavowal and denial. The step makes identifying and attributing complicity easier. At the same time, the approaches complicate the responses that we may draw from this complicity, as they demand that one becomes more attuned to the complexity of social reality and takes individual or shared responsibility for involvements in unjust processes even when one's actions do not meet the standard of culpability or blameworthiness.

The chapter concludes by introducing a third alternative, an ethics of responsiveness, and its constructive engagement with the other alternatives. Proponents of the ethics highlight that the social connection model and complicity-as-being approach do not do enough to capture the many ways in which the structures producing injustice also engender disavowal and denial of responsibility. This raises serious doubts about the capacity of those profiting from injustice and violence to identify and attribute, but also most importantly to acknowledge, complicity. The ethics offers several different ways in which greater responsiveness could be cultivated, whether through disruption by the dominated or improvised storytelling following moments of profound crisis. Together they develop an important toolkit that may help increase receptivity and reduce denial and disavowal when faced with one's entanglements in the exploitation, expropriation and destruction of minorities, those deemed different and the planet.

This book supports the insights offered by complicity scholarship, but also seeks to think their theoretical innovations further with regard to judging complicity. In the following chapters I delve more deeply into the process and practice of judgement and what enables us to make appropriate judgements on complicity.

Notes

1. Clarissa Hayward (2017: 397) calls this the 'cause + control' view, where responsibility for harm applies only if the agent was the cause of the harm and that action was under their control. For an extensive critique of the reward-punishment-blame-praise view of moral responsibility, see Waller (2011). For a discussion of the history of the concept of responsibility, see Vogelmann (2017).
2. The focus in democratic theory has traditionally been on diverse perspectives appearing or being heard, while there has been a recent turn towards also the importance of receptivity through forms of listening (cf. Beausoleil, 2014).
3. Myers also points out that such an associative notion of freedom countering disciplinary and biopower can be found in Foucault but not, as theorists, especially Connolly, have sought, in self-care.

CHAPTER TWO

Judgement and the potential in human plurality

The discussion in the last chapter introduced the central role of judgement within complicity scholarship and traced a key divergence on the topic: between those who favour a form of moral judgement reliant on *a priori* standards of reason and morality and an individualist conception of society to make clear judgements on morally or legally wrong behaviour, and those who suggest a form of judgement is needed that accounts for socially embedded agency and structural forms of injustice while retaining notions of individual complicity and responsibility. Sympathetic to the latter, I consider what makes judgement capable of accounting for both unjust processes and individual complicity. As a starting point, I note that disagreements on judgement in complicity scholarship mirror the debate about the difference between moral, determinate and political, reflective judgement, which has found its clearest expression in relation to the thought of Hannah Arendt.

For Arendt, judgements about political issues such as complicity are not (or not primarily) dependent on the object or issue as such. There is nothing in the nature and character of complicity that teaches us how we should judge complicity. Judgements are also not reducible to our rational capacities. While reason can help us challenge more obviously problematic approaches to complicity, it does not, on its own, resolve any of the differences in debates on complicity highlighted in this book. Lastly, judgement is not simply subordinate to relatively fixed ethical and moral principles that we could apply to judge complicity. There is no single standard, for example justice, that provides clear guidance on how we can and should evaluate complicity. As we will see, modernisation and the twentieth century's totalitarianism reveal to Arendt the limitations of each of these approaches. In their place, Arendt highlights the important role played by human plurality, that is, the fact that numerous people live with us in society and that each person brings into the conversation on complicity and injustice their own distinct, but interrelated, perspective.

Judgement on complicity depends on the process of opinion formation, and it does so both in a negative and in a positive sense. Thought negatively, judgements on complicity are only as good as the opinion formation process within society (and the kind of society it produces and reproduces) that has shaped a person's judging capabilities, whether through their education, engagement with (social) media, or direct political involvement and alignment. In other words, our capacity to identify, attribute and acknowledge complicity and in response help tackle injustice depends to a significant extent on the way judgements are formed through the collective opinion formation process. Positively, and this is crucial for Arendt, human plurality can be a source of good judgement, by allowing us to consider an issue from a diversity of perspectives to develop a general, but never perfect or universal, perspective and by creating a world that allows that diversity to be expressed. For this to happen, however, we cannot take plurality for granted and must think about how to strengthen it. Judgement can play an important role for a focus on plurality, because for Arendt judgement is not merely a capacity to adjudicate on issues but 'the ability to say "this is wrong", "this is beautiful"' (Arendt, 1981a: 193), which helps individuals position themselves in relation to particular events, issues and people. Judgement is a practice of world disclosure, to us and others, and this process can strengthen plurality by revealing and incorporating the diversity of perspectives available in society.

Arendt drew on a variety of sources to advance her understanding of judgement and its link to human plurality, especially Kant's conceptualisation of aesthetic judgement (Arendt, 2005a: 332). In his *Critique of the Power of Judgement* (1790), Kant put forward a formalistic account of aesthetic judgement dedicated to theorising the universal conditions, rather than the substance, of judgements of taste. He portrayed judging as subsuming particulars under universals. When dealing with moral issues, judgement becomes a determinate process, where the universals are already given. Aesthetic judgement, in contrast, relies on a reflective process where the universals are found through abstraction from the particular (Kant, 2000). Arendt was attracted to the latter. Judged in the singular, autonomously, reflective judgement is difficult and uncertain – it lacks a universal rule under which to subsume the particular and relies instead on the engagement with others' perspectives for its validation. In a series of posthumously published lectures, Arendt interpreted Kant's *Critique of the Power of Judgement* as providing the political philosophy that he never wrote.[1] This idiosyncratic interpretation helped her displace Kant's focus on reason and his moral and historical philosophy in the earlier *Critiques*. In its place, she emphasised that plurality and an intersubjective engagement with, and constitution of, reality are integral to political judgement.

In short, the key insight that Arendt offers is the close link between human plurality, judgement and our engagement with reality. A reconstruction of her thought on reflective judgement therefore allows me to capture the first dimension to what I called in the introduction to this book an ethos of reality: pluralism. Our capacity to identify, acknowledge and respond to complicity appropriately benefits from a suitable pluralist disposition, ideally combined with the existence of a pluralist public sphere that supports our efforts to come to terms with and address reality together.

Hannah Arendt's political realism founded on human plurality

To begin my discussion of Arendt's insights on reflective judgement, I point to why she thought conventional forms of making judgements within society are inadequate for addressing issues such as complicity. In pre-modernity, (political) communities were able to rely on traditions and customs to provide standards for how to render experiences intelligible. There was therefore little need for independent judgement. The value of tradition is put poignantly in relation to prejudices 'that we share, that we take to be self-evident, that we can toss out in conversation without any lengthy explanations' (Arendt, 2005b: 99). Arendt emphasised that humans

> cannot live without prejudices, and not only because no human being's intelligence or insight would suffice to form an original judgment about everything on which he is asked to pass judgment in the course of his life, but also because such a total lack of prejudice would require a superhuman alertness. This is why in all times and places it is the task of politics to shed light upon and dispel prejudices, which is not to say that its task is to train people to be

unprejudiced or that those who work toward such enlightenment are themselves free of prejudice [. . .] an epoch in which people could not fall back on and trust their prejudices when judging and deciding about major areas of their lives is inconceivable (Arendt, 2005b: 99–100).

The reconciliation with reality is threatened in modernity by a break in tradition, as an expression of the loss of unity between tradition, religion and authority. This unity had offered standards – of ethics and morality – that gave a satisfactory meaning to ongoing occurrences and enabled the community to continue in their set ways. During her time, Arendt argued, the break in tradition had become a fact to be reckoned with. Furthermore, she testified to the fact that, because of this break, the beliefs and traditions and the abstract theories of philosophy offered little protection against the rise of totalitarianism in Germany. Once successfully challenged, these standards of judgement instead quickly turned into systems of thought that were easily amended to justify the crimes against humanity of Nazi Germany (Arendt, 2003: 50). How humans can gain an adequate access to reality thus became a central problem of the twentieth century.[2] We can

> no longer afford to take that which was good in the past and simply call it our heritage, to discard the bad and simply think of it as a dead load which by itself time will bury in oblivion. The subterranean stream of Western history has finally come to the surface and usurped the dignity of our tradition. This is the reality in which we live. And this is why all efforts to escape, from the grimness of the present into nostalgia for a still intact past, or into the anticipated oblivion of a better future, are vain (Arendt, 1973. ix).

To explore the temporal significance of the break in tradition, alluded to in the quote, Arendt returned repeatedly to Franz Kafka's parable 'He' (Arendt, 1981a: 202, 2005a, 2006a). Kafka depicts the individual caught between the antagonistic forces of not yet and no longer, between the future and the past. In Arendt's reinterpretation of the parable, another, irreducible force, the present, emerges out of past and future. The present, however, had little impact on human lives in so far as it was embedded in, and bridged by, the certainty provided through traditions. The break in tradition therefore does not create a gap between the past and future. Instead, it exposes the non-linear movement of time in which the present takes place. This means that the break is not only the origin of a highly problematic existential and epistemic crisis of humanity, but an opportunity for a different, better engagement with reality.

The break in tradition offers an opportunity to challenge the reliance on unreflective and determinate forms of judgement. They are a consequence of projects aimed at establishing standards of meaning and authority outside everyday life and public discussion, through either religion or philosophy. The philosophical project began in Ancient Greece and found its extreme conclusion in totalitarianism.[3] It included a form of teleological progress thinking that denied the present any impact on human development (Arendt, 2005b: 74). Arendt joined an illustrious group of critics, including Kant, Marx, Kierkegaard and Nietzsche, in their attempt to undo this project (Arendt, 1998: 17; cf. Arendt, 2005b, 2006a).[4] Arendt moved beyond them through her focus on how human plurality can serve as an important source for engaging with reality, and by extension for judgement.

Arendt described human plurality as part of her account of different human conditions, that is, constraints on being human that are the product of certain characteristics of the world we inhabit, for example the fact that we will all die at some point. Human conditions can change and are shaped by human activities and relations. Anything that 'enters the human world of its own accord or is drawn into it by human effort becomes part of the human condition' (Arendt, 1998: 9). These two elements to the conditions framing our lives are visible in relation to human plurality. The term 'plurality' refers to the fact that 'men, not Man, live on the earth and inhabit the world' (Arendt, 1998: 7). It also captures the conviction that human existence develops 'only in the shared life of human beings inhabiting a given world common to them all' (Arendt, 2005a: 186). Plurality is thus both an ontological fact to be acknowledged and something that is produced and reproduced through social interaction. There are three elements to this conception of plurality. Firstly, humans, in plural, are characterised by sameness, for they share the same basic constraints on their lives and have a world in common. Sameness enables them to communicate meaningfully with each other and to treat the other members of society as political equals (Arendt, 1998: 175). Secondly, humans are characterised by distinctiveness. Plurality refers to the fact that everybody is human 'in such a way that nobody is ever the same as anyone else who ever lived, lives or will live' (Arendt, 1998: 8). Distinctiveness for Arendt is unlike the kind of otherness that all things share by virtue of their unique location in time and space. Distinctiveness emerges as part of humans' capacity for speech through which to express their perspective on the world as irreducible to any shared characteristics (Arendt, 1998: 176). Thirdly, plurality means that 'a world of things is between those who have it in common, as a table is located between those who sit around it; the world, like every in-between, relates and separates men at the same time' (Arendt, 1998: 52). A thick description of plurality accounts for the common world as an irreducible feature of human plurality alongside an insistence on the sameness and distinctiveness of all human beings.

Arendt saw plurality as under threat from various modern developments that reduce society to inseparable collectives or isolated individuals. Contemporary society 'expects from each of its members a certain kind of behaviour, imposing innumerable rules, all of which tend to "normalize" its members, to make them behave, to exclude spontaneous action or outstanding achievement' (Arendt, 1998: 40). In other words, modern mass society directly attacks the human condition of plurality, because it consists of social processes that are orientated towards a conformity of behaviour. Such conformity denies the possibility of sharing a world from a plurality of different positions, because it prefers sameness at the cost of distinction and a common world in between people. The consequence is an alienation of people from their own unique selves and the world they have in common. Arendt highlighted two variants of this problem, earth and world alienation.

Earth alienation refers to the negative effects of a desire in modernity to escape the confines of human earthly conditions through technological advances. The initial exploration of the earth over the past centuries made much of the formerly distant and unknown (seemingly) familiar. Continued discovery seemed to hinge on an increase in distance between the worldly conditions and the scientist, for example through the artificial conditions of the laboratory experiment or the distance afforded by space exploration (Arendt, 1998: 250–251). Important as such scientific progress may have been, it led to a loss of the connection between humans and their world, in favour of a detached, objective relationship with one's surroundings. World alienation adds to this disconnection the loss of an intersubjectively constituted world. A wide array of developments causes this form of alienation. For instance, it emerged from expropriation and wealth accumulation, which were allowed to develop their own laws, alien, and even hostile, to political practices (Arendt, 1998: 257).

World alienation is furthermore an expression of the modern sense of an increased loss of certainty about the way things are. This sensation led to the tendency in modern philosophy to 'reduce all experiences, with the world as well as with other human beings, to experiences between man and himself' (Arendt, 1998: 254). Such a move, it was hoped, would ground knowledge of the world in the rational processes and logical consistency of the enlightened person. Mathematics and its pure symbolic language became the arbiter of truth and knowledge. Human experience of reality becomes irrelevant or reducible to elements in complex macro-scale formulas. Plurality is undertheorised as research focuses merely on patterns of human behaviour. What humans 'now have in common is not the world but the structure of their minds, and this they cannot have in common, strictly speaking; their faculty of reasoning can only happen to be the same in everybody' (Arendt, 1998: 283).

Both forms of alienation displace the role that plurality plays for human existence. In response, the challenge is how to build and protect a common world that brings together a diversity of distinctive perspectives on shared objects. Here we turn to the third element to Arendt's approach, alongside a break in tradition and human plurality: politics.

Plurality and politics

To begin with, the turn to politics may seem puzzling. After all, the reductive approach to human plurality is similarly visible in conventional associations of politics with instrumental, interest-driven thinking. We might call the orientation a thin[5] conception of plurality, as it reduces plurality and politics to the competing individual interests within a community. Associations of the political with force, authority and sovereignty more generally reduce plurality to the interrelationships between inherently unequal citizens. Politics becomes a matter of control by the strongest – including the state. Arendt tries to recuperate a different way of thinking about politics, which she traces back to Ancient Greece and which focuses on human interaction and speech. She sees the public sphere not merely as a site of domination and violence, but potentially as a space dedicated to the practice of strengthening human plurality. Plurality offers according to Arendt 'the condition [. . .] of all political life' (1998: 7), but it does so only once we discard the dictum of politics 'to rule or be ruled' (1998: 32), in favour of an equal treatment and exchange between members of a political community about ongoing events and common issues. I highlight three elements to her understanding of politics embedded in a thick notion of plurality: the individuals who appear and reveal their unique, partial perspectives on the world by acting together; the spectators who confirm and judge these appearances and give them meaning in relation to their own perspectives on the world; and the common world that exists between all members of the political community. Together they provide the process through which human plurality helps reflective judgement gain a better sense of political phenomena such as complicity.

Firstly, Arendt wished to highlight the 'joy and the gratification that arise out of being in company with our peers, out of acting together and appearing in public, out of inserting ourselves into the world by word and deed' (2006a: 250). Political action is non-instrumental, orientated first and foremost by the freedom we experience in acting together. Arendt separated action from two other, pre-political, human activities: labour to produce consumer goods that help us survive, and fabrication to create durable things like houses or tables that can help make us less vulnerable to our biological condition (Arendt, 1998: 95, 144). Both are embedded in a means–end process that meets the human conditions of biological life – the cyclical movement of the biological process – and worldliness – the fact that humans create things that become new conditions for their lives and beyond. Arendt did not deny the importance of all activities coming together to respond to the various human conditions, as one might infer from her separation of action from the biological demands on our bodies and the need to create a stable and durable world. The distinction also does not mean that Arendt ignored the fact of politics' close relationship with violence and domination. Instead, for the sake of a thick conception of plurality, and against the backdrop of immense violence destroying the public sphere in Nazi Germany, Arendt rejected the idea that politics must be about violence and authority, or issues of labour and fabrication. The purpose of politics is to enable the public manifestation of plurality by providing a platform on which to express the distinctive 'who' of a person. Political action is a form of collective self-disclosure. The individual enters the public stage and presents their unique socio-political position towards the world – how it appears to me – in relation to others (Arendt, 2003: 12–13).

A second way in which Arendt captures plurality in politics is her insight that action depends, as a form of world disclosure, on an audience. Action is in some sense short-lived because it does not leave anything physical behind. Instead, to last, actions need to be heard, seen and remembered – action continues to exist only through its acknowledgment. For this reason, action has a close connection to communicating through speech.[6] Alongside the plurality of actors who act together, Arendt thus adds a second plurality: the judging spectators, to whom action speaks and who in turn give it enduring meaning. Crucially, this communication goes both ways. Through judgement, humans disclose something of themselves and of the world as they see it, they reveal differences and communalities between themselves and others (Arendt, 2006a: 220). Both action and judgement require taking a position within the world and, in so doing, enable people to get a sense of the world.

A thicker conception of plurality refers additionally to the in-between of people. Politics is according to Arendt not 'so much about human beings as it is about the world that comes into being between them and endures beyond them' (2005b: 175). A suitable common world – that is, an 'ever-changing and fragmented web of relations and built environments that people draw on and reproduce as they reveal their differences and commonalities in speech and action' (Vogler, 2020: 84) – must accommodate both sufficient separation, so that each person provides a distinct perspective on an object, and connection, which ensures that the perspectives remain communicable and related to the same object. Action contributes to this common world by producing the 'fabric of human relationships and affairs' (Arendt, 1998: 95) between those that disclose and those that judge and confirm that appearance. Action and judgement must therefore entail a consideration of the implications of human endeavours for a common world and its continued existence beyond one's own generation.

The connection between plurality and politics brings with it specific frustrations that shape the way we should approach political problems including complicity. Action is characterised by the 'unpredictability of its outcome, the irreversibility of the process, and the anonymity of its authors' (Arendt, 1998: 220). Politics is always exercised in a pre-existing web of human relations, which is likely to feature numerous conflicting interests, so that action's effects are seldom controllable; on the contrary, the outcome of action is often unintentional and almost never fulfils its original purpose

(Arendt, 1998: 184). Embedded in complex processes, action is also the activity with the closest connection to the human condition of natality. Arendt emphasised the political freedom that arises from a human affirmation of the capacity to begin something new (Arendt, 2006a: 151). It is action's power 'to break through the commonly accepted and reach into the extraordinary, where [. . .] everything that exists is unique' (Arendt, 1998: 205). In light of the frustrations that come with political practices, their unpredictability and capacity to begin anew, people constantly attempt to constrain action or to replace it with labour and fabrication. Individuals are tempted to instrumentalise politics for their specific ends in an endeavour to control the effects of one's actions and avoid the frustrations that come with it. However, to displace acting together in such a way is to take away its ability to produce meaning, which reveals itself only through the unique direction that interaction takes (Arendt, 1998: 179–180). Such a reduction of politics and its uncontrollable, unpredictable qualities misconstrues the plurality that is intrinsic to political practices. Political action is always contingent, complex and open-ended. It is non-instrumental, a practice of freedom to begin anew and to disclose amongst equal peers how the world appears to me. Politics is instead at its best when it makes human existence memorable in unprecedented ways and, in so doing, expands the sense that humans have of the kind of shared reality that they live in.

We can take from these reflections on politics that the human condition of plurality, in its thick description, necessitates a public sphere, in which to express a diversity of views on a shared reality. Arendt understood that in a world inhabited by human beings, reality is inextricably linked with the political sphere and its mediation of individual, partial perspectives on the world. Without the testimony by others on the realness of an appearance, reality 'comes and passes away like a dream, intimately and exclusively our own but without reality' (Arendt, 1998: 199). A strong (sense of) reality is thus only achievable as part of a judging and acting community that recognises and engages with how things appear to different people.

Arendt's political realism

Given the dangers that remain from the break in tradition, in the form of alienation and instrumentalist thinking about politics, it is not enough to make the case for a different approach to engaging with reality that is dependent on human plurality. Such an approach must also be protected and cared for. With this in mind, Arendt articulated a unique 'realist' position that is encapsulated by the concept '*amor mundi*', love of the world. Arendt asked whether 'one was capable of loving the world more than one's own self. And the decision indeed has always been the crucial decision for all who devoted their lives to politics' (2006c: 286). She opposed *amor mundi* to any nihilistic thoughts and desire to deny the political realities of one's time. While it is understandable that people may wish to suppress reality during dark times, such attempts are only acceptable, according to Arendt, if they are connected with an honest acknowledgement of one's escapism (Arendt, 2005b: 203). Arendtian love of the world properly sets in when we have to come to terms with facts and events that we accept as being real even if we do not wish them to be so. Arendt encouraged an 'attentive facing up to, and resisting of, reality – whatever that may be' (1973: viii). Coming to terms with reality does not simply mean that we normalise extreme phenomena such as totalitarianism. Instead, Arendt suggests that we seek to understand – that is, by making our knowledge of its unique reality meaningful.

A commitment to love the world led Arendt to be highly sceptical of any attempt to resolve political problems by applying frameworks with only limited attentiveness to the particularities of politics and reality. This scepticism expressed itself in several ways. Arendt questioned the traditional role of ethics in politics, which she identified as providing a framework for judgement that, in moments of crisis, turns too easily into mere customs. She rejected a reduction of politics to conflict but was similarly critical of the liberal belief in progress as the peaceful resolution of the interrelationship between violence and politics. Her thought aligned with Carl Schmitt and Hans Morgenthau in suggesting that moralism and fighting wars on behalf of political ideals, for example equality, liberty or justice, would only lead to a worsening of war's brutality (Arendt, 2005b: 3; cf. Owens, 2008: 108). Finally, she rejected any reference to 'lesser evils' because it opened the door to seeing evil doing as an acceptable and legitimate course of action (Arendt, 2003: 36). In short, her bet, as Rei Terada puts it, was that

> an empirical scepticism that asks, 'Is that the way things really are?' is more likely to support a tolerable world, and less likely to support an intolerable one, than affirmative fidelity to anything else, no matter how universally or

singularly good. There are more politicians whose imperial fantasies could be corrected by realism than there are ones who could be corrected by ethics (Terada, 2008: 103).

Ethics and reality are no longer opposites, as conventional approaches that measure reality against external principles would have it. Instead, coming to terms with reality together is the foundation of ethics. Arendt emphasised that the need to engage with reality can be a normative project in and of itself – this insight is key to the argument in this book.

Arendt's practice of *amor mundi* consisted in a continuous engagement with the political events of her time, including totalitarianism, the student demonstrations of the 1960s and American foreign policy. Commentators often (rightly) received her political interventions critically, an infamous example being the angry responses that followed her report on the Eichmann trial. Adolf Eichmann had been responsible for the mass deportation and extermination of Jews in Nazi Germany, and Arendt stood accused of seeking to understand and judge Eichmann in isolation from the effects that such a desire to understand might have on others (Arendt, 2006b; cf. Rabinbach, 2004). I return to the limitations of Arendt's practical approach in the conclusion of this chapter; for now, I note that, in her response to the controversy surrounding the report, Arendt asked 'what kind of reality does truth possess if it is powerless in the public realm, which more than any other sphere of human life guarantees reality of existence to natal and moral men' (2006a: 223). Her response deepens the connection she provides for judgement between plurality, reality and politics.

Factual truth for Arendt is central to politics and emerges out of the partial perspectives of a political community. It is susceptible to power and interest conflicts in the public sphere, and can even be lost permanently, due to its dependence on experience and agreement. Factual truths can nonetheless prove sufficiently stable; take Arendt's example of the enduring factual truth that Germany invaded Belgium and not the other way around (Arendt, 2006a: 245). In contrast, philosophical truths that enter the political sphere are much more at risk, as they move from one part of human existence to a radically different one. Rational truth, like all truths, is turned into one opinion amongst many, and its unique qualities, which make rational truth so valuable for contemplation and theorising, provide no privileged status in a public debate (Arendt, 2006a: 233). In modernity, fraught with the break in tradition, factual truths became increasingly undermined and no longer found widespread acceptance. At stake is therefore the 'common and factual reality itself, and this is indeed a political problem of the first order' (Arendt, 2006a: 232). In response, Arendt insisted that it is not a problem that factual truth depends on appearance and witnesses, and that it is bound up with opinions, interests and passions. On the contrary, in light of the threats to plurality outlined in the previous section, contemporary society is dependent on factual truth and its ability to engender a diversity of perspectives that, crucially, remain connected to concrete objects and events. Factual truth is important for politics because it provides the dynamic confines in which politics occurs, defining what at any point is seen as an unchangeable foundation on which to begin something new, to act together and give reality new meaning (Arendt, 2006a: 259). To ensure that factual truth continues to hold this role for humans, Arendt suggested that we replace its connection to tradition, by embedding facts in action-in-concert and political judgement.

The exemplary person who for Arendt cultivated *amor mundi* in relation to factual truth is Gotthold Ephraim Lessing (cf. Vogler, 2020). Lessing, in Arendt's reading, cared about people 'humanising' truths by speaking about them, that is, revealing both how things are and what they tell us about who we are as human beings (Arendt, 1968: 25). This is 'not an activity in fact-checking' but in 'expressing our understanding of' an issue and 'advancing that understanding as we listen to those for whom that fact' is more than 'mere data or opinion, but who can imbue it with experiential insight' (Vogler, 2020: 101). Lessing embraced the contingency of factual truths and was not concerned with proving that something was right (Arendt, 1968: 27). As a political actor he cared not simply about facts themselves but about opinions that are articulated in an open way that cares for the world and its capacity to enable people to see an issue from different perspectives and to explore their commonalities and differences together. I expand on this understanding of *amor mundi* and orientation towards the world in Chapter 5.

Reconciling withdrawal and action through reflective judgement

To conclude this chapter, I show how Arendt addressed a tension that inevitably emerges by placing judgement central to politics, and in connecting judgement, our engagement with reality and human plurality: judgement is, first and foremost, a mental capacity that relies on and benefits from withdrawal from action. But how can reflective judgement withdraw from action and yet contribute to political practices without being a coercive, outside force? Only by overcoming this tension can judgement become a reflective tool that does not view human plurality as a hindrance to making appropriate judgement that needs to be managed through pre-given standards.

My analysis identifies three ways in which Arendt overcomes this tension between plurality and judgement, starting with judgement's role as part of the mental activities that Arendt discussed in *The Life of the Mind*. I further look at Arendt's reformulation of the actor–spectator dichotomy and common sense. Commentators traditionally turn to both in search of Arendt's unfinished theory of political judgement – more on Arendt judgement scholarship in Chapter 3.

The faculties of the mind

Arendt complemented her reorientation of politics towards a thicker conception of plurality, by developing a trilogy on three mental activities, thinking, willing and judging, called *The Life of the Mind* (1981a, 1981b). She never wrote the final book, on judgement, due to her death in 1975, and commentators have instead relied on earlier and unpublished work to debate what Arendt might have written. This suggestive theory of judgement must be read in relation to the challenge central to *The Life of the Mind*: how to bring together mental activities, which are uniquely characterised by a '*withdrawal from the world as it appears and a bending back toward the self*' (Arendt, 1981a: 22, original emphasis), and to reconcile these activities with a prioritisation of pluralist politics and the creation of a hospitable world? Arendt's remarks on judgement also form part of her investigation into the complex relationship between mental activities and evil that she concentrated on following the Eichmann trial. In response to both puzzles, Arendt acknowledged that judging, willing and thinking are all dependent on some form of withdrawal from the space of appearance. She also addressed the importance of plurality for the life of the mind and denied any attempt to detach the functioning of mental activities from their effects on politics. *The Life of the Mind* thus offers an initial insight into the connection between judgement as a mental, detached activity and a plurality strengthened through politics.

The first book of *The Life of the Mind* deals with the faculty of thinking. Of interest for the present investigation is that Arendt saw judgement as connecting thought with the space of appearance: judgement is the 'by-product of the liberating effect of thinking, [it] realizes thinking, makes it manifest in the world of appearances, where I am never alone and always too busy to think' (Arendt, 1981a: 193). Thought helps judgement break from the immediate worldly activities to gain critical purchase on the world, and provides the means of memory and imagination. The connection between judgement and thought gains in importance in relation to two dangers to thought in modernity: thoughtlessness and the ever-present nihilistic tendencies inherent in all forms of thinking. Thoughtlessness describes the failure of the internal conversation through which humans deliberate about themselves and the world and decide upon the right actions to take. It may also refer to a troublesome desire for rules that can be applied automatically with little need for independent thought (Arendt, 1981a: 177; cf. Schiff, 2013). Such a thoughtless disposition could prove disastrous for a society, because the thoughtless person shows little concern for the effect that the application of rules has on other people and the common world. This was, Arendt argued, Eichmann's main shortcoming, leading to a devastating failure of judgement. She noted his constant references to clichés, 'stock phrases, [his] adherence to conventional, standardised codes of expression and conduct' which provide 'the socially recognised function of protecting us against reality, that is, against the claim on our thinking attention that all events and facts make by virtue of their existence' (Arendt, 1981a: 4, 2006b).

Thought can similarly be dangerous as it lacks a precise end goal, disrupts other activities and occurrences, and seeks withdrawal from the world (cf. Arendt, 1981a: 176). Arendt identified such problematic tendencies in the projects of professional thinkers. She accused philosophers, including Heidegger and Descartes, of committing metaphysical fallacies that are the result of a struggle of the thinking ego with the world of appearance. Drawn to contemplation as the maxim of their lives, they seek to close the 'abyss of pure spontaneity' (Arendt, 1981b: 215) of action, by reducing new appearances to what is already known or knowable through thought.

Philosophers share with social scientists a thirst for objective knowledge via an Archimedean point, which requires the withdrawal from human affairs but nonetheless claims coercive power in that sphere. Arendt was especially averse to the Marxist-sociological strategy of unmasking – which she later condemned as naïve, sinister and cruel – and showed contempt for 'functionalism' (Arendt, 1981a: 27; Baehr, 2007: 343). By constantly perceiving something as a façade with an underlying 'real', phenomena are reduced to their function (Arendt, 2005a: 374–375). Thus, functionalism allows the researcher simply to ignore what is actually being said or done.

Judgement offered Arendt a hopeful response to both allures, thoughtlessness and the dangers of thoughtfulness, in so far as it manifests thought in a pluralist politics. Judgement links the continuous critical investigation back to action and the appearances that caused humans to think in the first place (cf. Arendt, 1981a: 193). By anchoring thought in the space of appearance, political judgement denies a withdrawal from sense experiences and the engagement with others. Judgement prevents a flight into thoughtlessness by ensuring that one's thoughts encounter potential opposition and the kind of contradiction in views which is likely to be found in other people's perspectives. Arendt framed thought, in turn, as the negative pre-condition of judgement. Thought frees judgement from habitual processes of non-thinking. In addition, the foundation of judgement in thought extends to judgement the capacity for memory and imagination, through which the mind can represent that which is no longer present. Together, imagination and memory enable thought – and by extension judgement – to transcend temporal and spatial distances. They help 'anticipate the future, think of it as though it were already present [. . .] [and] remember the past as though it had not disappeared' (Arendt, 1981a: 85). In the context of the break in tradition, which disrupted the flow between past and future, the ability of imagination and memory to invoke the past, present and future is a vital tool for judging politically.

In the second book of *The Life of the Mind*, which remained less developed than the first, Arendt considered the activity of willing. The faculty of the will has become an essential part of modern moral theorising in the form of free will and as the source of choice, new beginning, freedom, individual sovereignty and responsibility. Arendt challenged this role because she identified a troublesome tension at the heart of willing. Whereas thought largely deals with the past, the activity of willing is orientated to the future, dealing with things that never actually existed; the projects produced by a person's will are therefore inherently uncertain and constantly challenge the will as humans cannot stop willing (Arendt, 1981b: 37). For this reason, the activity is caught in a conflict between the individual freedom of 'I will' and the constraints that arise from one's past and present context and shape the 'I can'. Arendt concluded the book with the insight that the faculty of willing, as understood in modernity, left her investigation into mental activities at an impasse to be resolved by judgement (1981b: 217).

Arendt identified in willing a capacity to start something unpredictably new, which links free will with action (1981b: 29, 158). Willing helps judgement move from an impulse of withdrawal to a motivation to act upon the world. However, the freedom that Arendt was after is not one of free will, which is orientated towards the individual, domination, sovereignty and the future. Instead, political freedom expresses itself in the practice of acting-in-concert. We can thus read the role of judgement in resolving the impasse of willing as follows: judgement, as a capacity to make sense of events in their irrevocable and contingent character, could help willing by providing reconciliation with the past as a starting point for new forms of action in the present. Judgement connects the backwards glance of thinking with the future-centrism of the will to be brought to bear in the present through acting and judging in concert.

This brief introduction of *The Life of the Mind* gives us a sense of the context in which Arendt sought to formulate the second crucial activity for her focus on plurality alongside action, judgement. The incomplete state of the trilogy marred Arendt's insights into judgement; nonetheless, my discussion has delineated some important points. Thought helps judgement withdraw from immediate worldly activities and willing reconnects it with the world. Judgement in turn links the two capacities of thinking and willing to political practices. It anchors their focus on the past and future in the freedom found in acting together and the meaning that emerges from evaluating public appearances. The discussion shows that the pluralist potential of judgement also emerges out of a complex interplay between different mental activities, including their often-strained relationship to politics. The question remains how judgement, as an ultimately individual, detached act, can tie mental processes to pluralist practices.

The judging spectator

The binary of actor and spectator in Arendt's theorising on judgement has been hotly debated in the past (cf. Yar, 2000). Richard Bernstein, for example, argued that Arendt's interpretation offers a 'flagrant contradiction' (1986: 230) and more questions than answers. The discussion centred on how she brings together Aristotle's conception of practical wisdom with the Kantian formulation of aesthetic judgement. It is not my intention to locate Arendt, once more, between Kant and Aristotle, for her contribution is precisely to move beyond the two (cf. Disch 1994: 142–143). Arendt reformulates the relationship between actor and spectator to accommodate her understanding of plurality and reconcile the urges for withdrawal and public appearance. I highlight two features of Arendt's reinterpretation of the actor–spectator binary. Firstly, she connects political judgement to taste rather than objective knowledge. Arendt attributes judgement to a spectator who experiences an appearance and is affected by it, and who enlarges their view on the matter by incorporating other perspectives on the object to be judged.

The binary spectator and actor emerged in Arendt's thought as part of the critique of professional thinkers addressed in the last section. She was particularly concerned with the role of the detached observer, familiar from logical positivism, who relies on a strict object–subject distinction and puts an unwarranted emphasis on objectivity. Her own spectator is closer to what usually comes to mind when we talk about spectators, a crowd that, for example, attends a football game (Arendt, 1981a: 94). This spectator exists in the plural (fans, commentators, pundits) and is part of the appearances without being directly involved in the action, that is playing football. Their observations are not orientated towards objectivity, but the production of meaning, for example which team deserved to win. Spectators, as judges who are not distant observers, do not escape the political partiality of their role (Bilsky, 1996: 138). Kant provided Arendt with the image of a judging spectator who looks for the enjoyment of the aesthetically pleasing, as an alternative to the philosopher who searches for truth and objectivity. The relationship between politics and aesthetics is complex, but Arendt drew on judgements of taste because they share with politics the quality that they are largely concerned with the unique and particular. Taste and smell are 'discriminatory by their very nature and [. . .] only these senses relate to the particular *qua* particular' (Arendt, 1982: 66). The 'point of the matter is: I am directly affected. For this reason there can be no dispute about right or wrong here' (Arendt, 1982: 66). Taste triggers our sense of what is meaningful in the world and mobilises us to take up a position towards it – whether we consider it beautiful, right or good.

The question is how to move from a sensation of the particular to the pluralist politics that Arendt had in mind as the source of coming to terms with reality. After all, it is difficult to communicate and discuss one's experience of this extremely subjective and private sense. To move from the private to the political, Arendt drew on Kant's emphasis on disinterestedness, the transcendence of 'what we usually call self-interest, which, according to Kant, is not enlightened or capable of enlightenment but is in fact limiting' (Arendt, 1982: 43). The transformation of a personal sense of taste succeeds with the help of imagination, through what Kant terms an 'operation of reflection' (Kant, 2000: §40, 294b). Disinterestedness means that judgements withdraw from the direct perception of an object that has caught our interest towards a contemplation of the image of an object which may attract our approval or disapproval (Arendt, 1982: 65). This process allows judgements to include further parameters of evaluation alongside the immediate sensation.

Disinterestedness culminates in Kant's notion of enlarged mentality. By 'enlarged mentality' Kant means the general perspective that emerges when the object is viewed from different standpoints (Kant, 2000: §40; cf. Arendt, 1982: 55–56). However, enlarging one's mentality remains for Kant a theoretical, mental adoption of other people's perspectives to gain general standards for one's judgement. Arendt replaces his desire for *a priori* agreement on one's judgement with her emphasis on plurality. Arendt is here informed by a form of impartiality which she attributes to the Ancient Greeks, who learned to 'look upon the same world from one another's standpoint, to see the same in very different and frequently opposing aspects' (Arendt, 2006a: 51). Going 'visiting' (Arendt, 1982: 43), or 'representative thinking' (Arendt, 2006a: 237), transcends the subjective experience by anticipating the future communication with other members of society and their distinctive perspectives on the world. Having moved beyond self-interest, it helps look at an object from many different standpoints, without simply adopting them – representative thought is orientated towards the world and does not require us to share another person's perspective. The establishment of an enlarged perspective is meant to provide 'a viewpoint from which to look upon, to watch, to form judgments, or [. . .] to reflect upon human affairs' (Arendt, 1982: 44). The incorporation of an affective and representative dimension to judgement has become known, following Arendt scholar Lisa Disch, as 'situated impartiality' (Disch, 1993: 666) – the critical vantage point from within a community and plurality.

One way in which judgement can express this situated impartiality is through the telling of a story about an event open to judgement. Storytelling, for Arendt, could help judgement by representing a 'dilemma as contingent and unprecedented and [. . .] [by pushing] its audience to think from within that dilemma. It invites the kind of situated critical thinking that is necessary' (Disch, 1993: 669) to judge in modernity. Arendt's use of storytelling is indebted to Walter Benjamin and his rejection of a linear conception of time, particularly of history as progress (Arendt, 1968: 165; cf. Benhabib, 1990; Herzog, 2000). Arendt followed Benjamin as she identified in storytelling the capacity to give meaning to information without reducing it to that information. Exemplary stories avoid providing definitive interpretations of events and facts, that is they avoid defining the meaning of their content and open it up to a plurality of interpretations.[7] Arendt's use of storytelling was further informed by Ancient Greece, particularly the way stories were told by Thucydides and Homer (Arendt, 1982: 5, 56). They, too, faced extreme forms of violence and showed Arendt how to judge through telling a story from a second-person perspective that avoids reducing judgement to empathy for the 'victims of history'.

This concludes my investigation into the first feature of Arendt's reformulation of the actor–spectator binary, the connection that Arendt put forward between a spectator who goes visiting and tells representative stories, and pluralist politics. The second feature concerns the interrelationship between spectator and actor. As I highlighted, spectators have a much more active part to play in politics, but Arendt at the same time clearly separated their judgements from action; reflective judgement is linked to certain features of the spectator, in particular the capacity for withdrawal from the world of appearances. She emphasised that the actor who 'acts never quite knows what he is doing' (Arendt, 1998: 233), in part as action leads to irreparable and unforeseen consequences. Arendt also clarified that all actors have to take up the position of spectator from time to time to avoid acting foolishly and unaware of action's consequences. The spectator and actor are ideal types of the judging and acting capacity in every human, and all humans deploy a mixture of both positions in their everyday lives. In Arendt's words, 'this critic and spectator sits in every actor' (Arendt, 1982: 63).

The interrelationship between actor and spectator expresses itself in politics as follows: while action provides the content and origin of politics, which emerges out of humans inserting themselves into the world and engaging with each other (Arendt, 1998: 199), the spectators constitute the public realm and give the appearance in it meaning (Arendt, 1982: 63). Arendt therefore points readers towards the need to acknowledge both the spectator and the actor. The quality of political judgement depends on a moving back and forth between them. Action cannot fulfil its role without judgements that give it meaning, that define what of the appearance is relevant and important. Similarly, the spectator's political judgement relies on the possibility of its communication and translation into action. Otherwise, it returns to the untenable position of the detached observer. As Arendt emphasised, the 'condition *sine qua non* for the existence of beautiful objects is communicability' (Arendt, 1982: 63). The spectator only opens up the public space through their ability to judge and give meaning, if their judgement is communicable.

A return to Arendt's use of storytelling illustrates this point. Storytelling provided Arendt with the modus operandi of the political sphere that brings together actor and spectator. Political actors take to the public stage and reveal their own story. Action, with its capacity for natality and unpredictability, continuously produces unforeseen stories (Arendt, 1998: 184). The judge, in turn, delineates the political by stating what is relevant and meaningful in action. The meaning is only fully revealed at the end of the story and only to the storyteller, 'that is, to the backward glance of the historian, who indeed always knows better what it was all about than the participants' (Arendt, 1998: 192). As I suggested above, the historian for Arendt is a storyteller and judging spectator that aims for a second-person perspective and for situated impartiality. In telling a story the judge also becomes once again an actor, inserting their view into the world and continuing the movement between judging spectator and actor.

In sum, in her interpretation of the role of actors and spectators, Arendt fruitfully shows that the capacity of judgement to make sense of reality depends on the interplay between spectator and actor. Political judgement is always negotiated between the particular and the universal, impartiality and partiality. Fully aware of this fact, Arendt insisted on tying judgement to a plurality of spectators and on anchoring the spectator in experience and the political community. For judgement to move beyond mere affectedness and a partial perspective on the world, it must become political, and this means to think representatively, to take into account other spectators and to communicate with fellow political actors. To judge politically is, however, also to consider the world from a diverse range of perspectives without losing focus on the 'it appears to me'.

Community sense

This section deals with a third way in which plurality comes into play for judgement to combine withdrawal and appearance: community sense. Community sense refers to the connection between judgement and the community in which judgements are embedded. Judgement simultaneously draws on a shared world as a framework of reference to evaluate political problems and helps reproduce and strengthen the common world for future action and judgement. I focus on how Arendt formulates common, or community, sense as a point of reference that never transcends the context and the individual's position, but neither makes judgement merely subjective, contextual. Instead, community sense is the product of a continuous, open-ended practice of creating a world in which to judge through engagement with a diversity of perspectives on a shared object.

Common sense describes the relation between humans and their common world. From Plato's cave myth onwards, philosophers have looked down upon common sense and the philosopher has sought to escape from its constraints to access transcendental knowledge. In contrast, Arendt valued common sense. She identified the originality of totalitarianism in the loneliness it caused by succeeding in separating people from their common world, their common sense and thereby, each other (Arendt, 1973: 475). Modern mass society brings with it a lack of common sense, as people communicate with only limited references to their common world (Arendt, 2006a: 89–90). Common sense is thus both a necessary pre-condition of modern political judgement and uniquely under threat from the effects of modernisation.

There are two uses of common sense in Arendt's work: common sense and community sense. Both rely for their functioning on the commonality of the world, and I discuss them briefly to show what role they play for Arendt's theory of reflective judgement. Common sense, in French '*le bon sens*', refers to a cognitive capacity for truth and knowledge. Arendt considers its contribution in the first volume of *The Life of the Mind*. Common sense responds to the worldly context of perception, the feeling of its realness. It builds on a

> threefold commonness: the five senses, utterly different from each other, have the same object in common; members of the same species have the context in common that endows every single object with its particular meaning; and all other sense-endowed beings, though perceiving this object from utterly different perspectives, agree on its identity. Out of this three-fold commonness arises the *sensation* of reality (Arendt, 1981a: 50, original emphasis).

Common sense enables the unification of different sensual frameworks (the object I see is experienced as image, the object I hear as sound), because it allows us to trace their communality to the same object. Given this role, common sense is incomparable to the experience of the other senses. It can also not simply be reconstructed by thinking, as the sense of realness that comes with common sense is outside the grasp of thinking (Arendt, 1981a: 51–52). Indeed, for Arendt, there is a natural tension between thinking and common sense, for thought aims to withdraw from the use of sense data and the common world. In contrast, the sixth sense offers the bridge between private and public spheres, linking up our private sensations, which are by nature difficult to communicate, with the commonness of object and context. Common sense is therefore a necessary and important foundation of judgement, without which representative thinking could not get off the ground.

The second use of common sense by Arendt, community sense, refers to a capacity for judgement and meaning which Arendt discussed in her lectures on, and idiosyncratic reading of, Kant's political philosophy. Arendt drew on Kant's *gemeinschaftlicher Sinn*, which refers to an ability to judge the communicability of sensations and to gain validation by appealing to others (Arendt, 1982: 71–72). Community sense relies on communicability and enlarged mentality as the foundation for good judgement. It is neither objective nor arbitrary but is called upon by reflective judgement, through which one can only reach agreement if one manages 'to "woo" or "court" the agreement of everyone else. And in this persuasive activity one actually appeals to the "community sense". In other words, when one judges, one judges as a member of a community' (Arendt, 1982: 72). The possibility to refer to a community of peers, Arendt realised, is vital to judgement in politics, where the standards of judgement are often obscure and changing.

Although Arendt embedded judgement in a community, she did not reduce it to what is culturally accepted. Membership of a political community does not mean that political judgements must trigger an actual public acceptance of one's perspective on the world. Neither did she make the quality of judgement dependent on characteristics of the judging person, or seek a transcendental, *a priori* process of agreement, as visible in parts of Kant's third *Critique*. Instead, Arendt's community sense is concerned with the coming together of a plurality of differing views on shared objects: Arendt shows how action and judgement are embedded in a common world, but also create and maintain that world by exploring new ways of giving meaning to experiences together (cf. Borren, 2013; Degryse, 2011). Community sense is given concreteness by two further qualifications. Firstly, community sense does not demand that one consider all perspectives in one's society but appeals according to Arendt to the community of judges who have similarly gone through a process of affectedness and representative thinking upon the matter to be judged (Arendt, 2006a: 221). Community sense is limited to incorporating the perspectives of those who have judged, those who one relates to in judging, and those to whom the phenomenon to be judged has appeared and matters. Secondly, far from an abstract ideal held in society, community sense is a product of cultivating a practice of judgement in interaction with other members of the community. The community sense that a person refers to is characterised by the different perspectives one has encountered throughout one's life, and the perspectives and judgements one relies on in making one's own judgement. The quality of judgement is therefore largely dependent on the kind of company we keep (Arendt, 2006a: 226).

These qualifications find their expression in the key mechanism through which community sense links the common world and judgement, exemplarity. Exemplarity was Arendt's 'favoured means of improving judgment' (La Caze, 2010: 78) and refers to 'a particular that in its very particularity reveals the generality that otherwise could not be defined' (Arendt, 1982: 77). Arendt identified exemplars as bestowing judgement with a general validity, by capturing characteristics of many particulars and by often being held by a large number of people (Arendt, 1982: 83). Examples, such as Achilles' courage or Jesus' kindness, lend judgement 'exemplary validity' to the extent that they are adequate for the particular and contain a concept or general rule of relevance for this particular. They do not gain universal validity: the moment 'I speak about Bonapartism I have made an example of him. The validity of this example will be restricted to those who possess the particular experience of Napoleon, either as his contemporaries or as the heirs to this particular historical tradition' (Arendt, 1982: 84–85). Exemplarity thus provides illustrative cases as standards to follow in judging and acting, but it also links judgement to shared meanings of a political community. Furthermore, judgement and action continuously create new exemplars to follow and, in doing so, expand our community sense.

This concludes my discussion of how Arendt addressed the tension between a focus on human plurality and our collective engagement with reality, on the one hand, and judgement as an individual mental activity dedicated to identifying what is right and wrong, good and bad, just and unjust, on the other. The tension between the two, Arendt showed, is beneficial to judgement and allows it to bring together the best of both the active and the contemplative life to avoid the worst features of thought and action. For this to happen, however, we need to overcome the hierarchy that values contemplation above the potential in public appearance. We also need to address how the mental activities are always already embedded in and a part of the process of public opinion formation, from which, in part, they gain their strength.

Concluding thoughts

Before concluding my investigation into judging complicity and the first dimension to the ethos of reality, pluralism, I reflect on one important challenge to Arendt's thought. Commentators have highlighted Arendt's repeated reproduction of racial prejudice towards Black and Asian people in her writing, and her inability to engage with this prejudice in the way she did with totalitarianism, racism and imperialism in other contexts (Bernstein, 2018; Gines, 2014; Owens, 2017). Both inclinations are visible in passages in most of her key works, from *Origins of Totalitarianism* to *Eichmann in*

Jerusalem, as well as in the way she used her conceptual distinctions rigidly to articulate highly problematic interventions in debates on racism in the US, most famously in the case of Little Rock surrounding educational segregation (Arendt, 1959).

A source of these failings in her work and thought is probably the fact that Arendt was educated in and part of a European tradition and cultural elite that assumes European superiority and non-European inferiority and the neutrality of their own conceptual analysis and tools (Owens, 2017). This fact offers a reminder that political thinkers should not be put on a pedestal and their work, too, is only as good as the opinion formation process in which they participate (and which Arendt heavily criticised in the context of the ascent of the Nazis in Germany). In Arendt's case, this means interrogating the empirical claims she sought to make in different cases, but also the way that the distinctions she made to develop a distinct notion of action and judgement ultimately produce a highly exclusionary understanding of politics. What then can we retain from Arendt's theoretical insights considering these serious shortcomings? My answer to this is (a) an emphasis on inconsistency in her writings – that for instance the distinctions she made between violence and politics and the social and political are analytical in nature and I would therefore reject her failure to engage reflectively with them in her discussion of specific contexts, which flies in the face of her theorising in the way I articulated it in this chapter; which (b) lead me to highlight the tools in Arendt's work (her emphasis on equality, on addressing prejudice vigorously) that help us counter these failings. I furthermore stress that any approach necessarily comes with costs – by the way it precludes other ways of thinking – and it is Arendt's mistake that she did not sufficiently explore the costs that her distinctions have (and her ability to evaluate the costs and benefits). Thus, a separation of the political must always come with a continuous concern with what is left out by defining what is political and what isn't.

At the same time, I do not wish to discard Arendt's account fully. I specifically chose to provide this reflection on racism and Arendt after introducing her work, because this approach allows us to understand the motivations within her framework that led Arendt down this problematic road – beyond the simple fact that she could not escape the Eurocentrism of her context and upbringing. Her need to separate out and protect politics and action in the middle of extreme violence and the complete demolition of the public sphere comes at the cost of her tendency to overly idealise particular elements of the public sphere, whether in relation to Ancient Greece or the United States, and which led her to ignore the way that such a political sphere excludes different oppressed minorities. I don't think it invalidates her fundamental concern with protecting pluralism and politics, which is shaped by her own experience of violence and oppression, but there is a need to read oppression and violence more explicitly back into her conception of plurality and judgement. In reading Arendt against Arendt, we may therefore expand on Kathryn Gines's (2014: 128–9) potent analysis of how Arendt consistently failed to develop a representative thinking that accounts for Black people's perspectives. Representative thinking for Arendt is precisely not just about enlarging one's mentality, but part of a political process. Once we accept that this process at her time was deeply shaped by racism (and still is), then it is especially important to recover and strengthen an appropriate public sphere by attending to the perspectives of those excluded by it. This is something that Arendt failed to attend to as she merely reinforces the separation between the social and the political. As Gines's analysis of Arendt's thought exemplifies, there is always a danger when attempting to engage with and strengthen plurality that we end up reproducing an exclusionary conception of plurality, and that in trying to account for this plurality we end up simply projecting our own way of thinking on to other perspectives. These problems cannot easily be resolved, due to the structural nature of violence and injustice, and it is not to Arendt but to the ethics of responsiveness that readers should turn to try to address this problem. Crucially, then, Arendt's own case reveals that a focus on plurality, politics and judgement is not a panacea on its own for a person failing to judge politically. But a different, better public opinion formation process together with a greater willingness to interrogate her own prejudices might have helped Arendt identify and acknowledge how her frame of reference is vulnerable to reproducing racism.

With these important reflections in place, it is time to summarise the insights we can take with us from the discussion of Arendt on human plurality and reflective judgement. This chapter has addressed how people can judge their complicity in a way that takes a clear position on complicity but does not rely on supposedly predeterminate standards of blame and culpability. The answer, according to Arendt, lies in human plurality: whereas an impoverished notion of plurality can endanger our capacity to make appropriate judgements, a thicker notion can be a powerful source of judgements on issues such as complicity.

In addition to this key message, the chapter has highlighted that Arendt defines judgement as a capacity to make sense of reality, to process meaning and to situate humans in relation to events, issues and other people. It is therefore one of the key practices and processes of our ethos of reality. Judgement gains in importance in modernity, with a break in tradition that undermines conventional ways of reconciling with reality. The break also creates the opportunity to explore better ways of engaging with reality as a community. People now have to make reflective judgements that lack pre-given, universal standards under which to subsume events and issues and instead rely on looking at an object from different perspectives to develop a form of situated impartiality. In other words, Arendt links the potential of judgement for making sense of reality to human plurality, that is, the sameness and at the same time distinctiveness of individual people, and the fact that they share a world in common that they can only make hospitable together. This dependence on human plurality should, however, be interpreted not as its limitation but its strength, as Arendt shows that universal standards are easily overturned and inverted. Yet, human plurality too is under threat in modernity and in response Arendt suggests that we protect politics as a space in which actors and judges can come together to discuss events and issues and act together to shape their future – although, as I have just pointed out, this process is plagued by problems of exclusion and oppression and we must continuously challenge ideas about what is and isn't political and what qualifies as 'human plurality'.

Our ability to be responsive and respond to complicity is dependent on two factors that are inherently interrelated: on our capacity and contributions as judges and actors and on the public opinion formation process in which we participate. There is little we can do against the way our judgements and responses to complicity are shaped in the present by these two factors, but Arendt also tells us that there is always the possibility to improve this situation: (a) by developing a love of the world that encourages us to cherish and reproduce the pluralist dimension to human existence in our judgements and actions, by asking ourselves whether our judgements and actions enable the world, as it appears to us, to appear to others, while simultaneously helping ensure that those voices and actions are foregrounded that speak directly to the topic and that both enable a diversity of perspectives to be heard and may have been excluded from the conversation in the past (but not for their tendency to threaten such plurality); and (b) by participating in a pluralist public sphere in which differences and communalities can appear, whereby we come to terms with the objects that appear before us, and work together to strengthen the pluralist dimension to the shared opinion-formation process, using our *amor mundi*. Put together, these two features are core elements of what, in this book, I call the pluralist dimension to an improved ethos of reality.

NOTES

1. Ronald Beiner later published a series of lectures on Kant's political philosophy. In his accompanying interpretive essay (Beiner, 1982), he maintains that these lectures can provide an appropriate interpretation of what Arendt would have written as the final book of her unfinished trilogy *Life of the Mind*. Because the interpretation of Arendt's theory relies on a reading of her lectures on Kant, it is difficult to criticise Arendt for not separating sufficiently her own standpoint (cf. Borren, 2013: 226).
2. The centrality of the break in tradition in Arendt's thought, and the role totalitarianism plays in it, is widely accepted (cf. Birmingham, 2006; Canovan, 1992; Villa, 1999).
3. We should not read Arendt's analysis of this project as embedded in a continuous historical narrative. Arendt was averse to causal historical narratives, preferring an analysis of the elements, or the conditions that under certain circumstances may or may not come together to form certain outcomes (Arendt, 1973; cf. Disch, 1993).
4. Arendt's appreciation for the Greek and Roman *polis* has been read as making her a 'reluctant modernist' (Benhabib, 2003) who turns to ancient political thought to flee from reality. I suggest such a reading underestimates her attempt to formulate a distinctly modern political project that responds directly to the threat in modernity to plurality.
5. The terms 'thin' and 'thick' have been used by scholars in various ways, for example by Michael Walzer (1994) to distinguish two types of moral arguments, but any similarity between my use and theirs is coincidental and does not bear on my argument.
6. Scholars have struggled with the seemingly empty character of Arendtian politics as speaking void of interests (cf. Pitkin, 1981). This tension cannot be resolved as Arendt's conception remained fragmented and incorporated Homeric, Athenian, Roman, Christian and revolutionary

elements. However, Canovan (1992: 137ff.) builds on unpublished lectures to identify Arendt as even critical of an overemphasis on action as speech. I suggest that it is therefore more helpful to think of her separation of action from instrumentalist projects not in absolute terms but as an attempt to show that politics is more than mere zero-sum games of domination and violence.

7. Arendt also emphasised the role of the theorist as storyteller who 'dives for pearls', especially when the political sphere is lost. To dive for pearls means to turn to the past not to reminisce and resuscitate it, but to find what over time crystallised, survived and has turned into something worth saving (Arendt, 1968: 205; cf. Herzog, 2000: 3).

CHAPTER THREE

Judgement following Arendt: from pluralism to social conditioning

Building on the discussion of the phenomena of complicity and judgement, this chapter initially serves a more technical purpose. At the time of her death, Hannah Arendt had hardly begun the book on judgement that was to form the final part of the trilogy on the life of the mind. Her conceptualisation of this faculty is therefore (possibly more than with any other concept in her thought) about its reception, that is, about how scholars use her unfinished remarks to articulate what would have likely been her theory of (reflective) judgement. This chapter provides an outline of the developments in the debate on political judgement that followed Arendt. I identify two loose phases to the debate and introduce four projects related to the second phase. My investigation, however, does not seek to contribute directly to the debates surrounding these two phases. Instead, their introduction helps move my overall argument about judging complicity forward in two important ways.

Firstly, I highlight that judgement scholars move further away from concerns with reason and validity in making judgements. The introduction of this book mentioned that late twentieth-century political theory identified increasingly pluralist liberal democracies as potentially inhibiting moral judgement (for, without an overlapping moral framework it is no longer possible to say which worldview is the correct one). In response, theorists sought to mediate the impact of pluralism through reliance on pre-given procedural standards or substantive principles (Azmanova, 2012: 120). The dominant framework of complicity similarly relies on *a priori* moral standards and a reductive conception of social processes to facilitate judgements about whether a person is blameworthy. In contrast, Arendt scholarship argues that any notion of objectivity or suitability necessarily emerges from the interaction of a plurality of judges and actors.

They articulate different means for judgement to gain critical purchase on issues such as complicity in injustice without reliance on preceding standards that seek to limit what is open to judgement and without falling back into relativism. Secondly, Arendt scholars turn to the issue of social conditioning (and transformation) that underpins plurality and argue that an emphasis on the intersubjective capacities of judgement is not enough to gain critical purchase on reality. Instead, scholars seek to clarify further the relationship between subjectivity and objectivity in judgement that frames the pluralist potential, by turning to imagination, emotions, the unconscious, storytelling, and the pre-discursive structuring of judgement. My interest in these debates is therefore an indirect one: I am interested in how they see the situated character of pluralist judgement as a potential for, rather than primarily an obstacle to, judgement.

The two phases of the debate on political judgement

The first response to Arendt's conception of judgement was to weigh the benefits of her idiosyncratic theory against what commentators considered its significant limitations.[1] It is not my intention here to respond to their concerns directly. The initial reception of Arendt's unfinished theory tended to read her through a Kantian lens, by which I mean that it focused on how judgement relates to validity and truth. This approach failed to capture fully the centrality of freedom and plurality in judgement that Arendt had in mind. The insights of early commentators nonetheless warrant a brief introduction, because they continue to shape the ongoing debates on Arendt's project that I address in this chapter.

From the perspective of the early commentators, Arendt provides an important contribution to conceptualising political judgement. At the same time, these scholars were concerned that her idiosyncratic reading provides such a problematic reinterpretation of Kant that it is no longer supported by his insights and concepts. A transformation of his aesthetic judgement into a political one, so the argument goes, only leads to confusion about what her own position entails. The scholars claimed that, ultimately, this confusion severely undermines the potential of Arendt's innovative contribution to the debate.

One of the triggers of the first attempts at piecing together and evaluating Arendt's theory of judgement lies in Jürgen Habermas's article (1977) on Arendt's communicative concept of power.

The article created a particular, paradigmatic reading of Arendt (Benhabib, 2003). Habermas points to Arendt as a source for a revival of practical philosophy and especially to her account of communicative action. However, he criticises her for idealising the Greek *polis* in opposition to modern polities, which Arendt saw as pathologies of modernity. Habermas also identifies her as undermining the value of rational discourse. Of particular concern to the first phase of commentators was Arendt's use of aesthetic judgements for politics and its detrimental effect on rational discourse and truth claims in politics. Arendt seemed to share Kant's concern with how a consensus secured through judgement can gain validity (Arendt, 2006a: 217). Kant's *Critique of the Power of Judgement* assumes that judgements of beauty, for example 'This rose is beautiful', are not simply statements of preferences of the kind 'I like wine'. Instead, these judgements entail an *a priori* premise of assent as they go beyond individual preferences (Kant, 2000: §22). In making a judgement that the 'rose is beautiful', I expect others to come to similar conclusions given similar conditions and deliberation. Aesthetic judgements can thus gain a general validity. Yet, according to Kant, they cannot become universally valid, because the principle 'beauty' does not exhaustively describe whether a rose is beautiful or not, that is, there is no universal rule to subsume the particular rose under. Arendt, in contrast to Kant, extended the limited validity of aesthetic claims to political judgement and emphasised furthermore its intersubjective quality. This move led Ronald Beiner (1982: 136–137) and Habermas to claim that Arendt ultimately left behind a 'yawning abyss between knowledge and opinion' (Habermas, 1977: 23), because she did not wish rational arguments to close that gap in politics between 'mere' opinion and 'undisputed' knowledge.

In parallel with this challenge to Arendt's reading of Kant, interpreters also worried about her decreasing concern with public life. As Arendt emphasised the spectator in her later work, judgement became seemingly more retrospective and moral: it ironically 'now seems to be the faculty that comes into play when politics breaks down' (Bernstein, 1986: 233). The interpreters took issue with the increasingly historic, distant character of judgement in Arendt's later work, because Arendt at the same time continued to object to the transcendental arguments found in Kant's moral and political philosophy. What grounds the spectators' judgements, they asked, if they can no longer rely on Arendt's commitment to pluralism?

As I suggested at the beginning of the section, this reading remains too focused on concerns with validity and truth. In reading Arendt through Kant's formulation of reflective judgement, they miss the reformulation of his theory towards plurality that I have outlined in Chapter 2 and which a second phase of political judgement scholarship helped clarify.

The second phase from the 1990s onwards showed the virtues of Arendt's account contra these earlier criticisms and responded through various attempts at extending her theory of judgement. Exegetes belonging to this phase reread Arendt's work, incorporated archival material and previously unpublished work, and even re-examined her theoretical sources – especially Aristotle, Heidegger and Kant – to provide a more nuanced understanding of her contribution.[2] From this literature emerges an emphasis on how judgement is a key capacity that is present throughout Arendt's thought of the 1940s to the 1970s. Arendt is read as purposefully defining judgement both from a political perspective and from within the life of the mind. Her theory gains its value precisely through the tension between the two, as they have to work together in order to maintain a strong political sphere (Meints, 2014). My reading of Arendt in Chapter 2 is indebted to this interpretation and has additionally brought the connection between reality, plurality and judgement to the fore.

The second phase furthermore includes various projects aimed at the extension of Arendt's theory.[3] For example, commentators such as Linda Zerilli (2012) attempt to show the value of liberating judgement from current concerns with validity in political theory. In place of this focus, they are concerned with what gives judgement the potential to be world-building and freedom-affirming. Others have turned to social theorists, notably Pierre Bourdieu, to substantiate or balance Arendt's focus on reflection in judgement (Azmanova, 2012; Kornprobst, 2011, 2014; Mihai, 2016b). The focus risks overemphasising the contribution of consciousness to judgement and undervalues or underestimates the role of the unconscious. A large part of the scholarship has also explored specific concepts from Arendt's theory, especially the spectator, exemplarity, common sense and storytelling, to make sense of contemporary political issues. In what follows, I engage with four representative approaches that take forward Arendtian insights in ways relevant for my overall project on judging complicity.

Before I turn to these, one caveat: the ability to judge politically should not be romanticised. Robert Fine (2008) notes that judgement has become a philosopher's stone of Arendtian political theory. The sole focus on the mental activity obscures the various other aspects of her work. Some judgement scholars (Bourke and Geuss, 2009; Krause, 2008; Weidenfeld, 2011) instead choose to avoid Arendt's contribution altogether, generally arguing that the influence of her unfinished work can be a hindrance to moving the debate on (political) judgement further. I take these concerns seriously, but they are problematic in so far as they implicitly rely on the image of Arendt's theory that emerged from the first phase of scholarship. In contrast, I suggest that the various extensions and revalorisations of Arendt's account can offer a suitable point of departure for current and future scholarship on political judgement and politics more generally.

JUDGEMENT USING THE IMAGINATION AND STORYTELLING

For the first two projects that extend Arendt's theory, I turn to Zerilli's work on the imagination, followed by engagement with Arendt scholars on storytelling.[4] Both projects deepen Arendt's insights into the pluralist dimension to judgement. At the same time, they reveal a shift in the literature towards viewing different elements of the relationship between judge and context as critical to the potential in judgement. The projects look at this relationship with an emphasis on the judge side of it.

Zerilli deepens our understanding of the role played by the imagination in reflective judgement. To this end, she makes two movements. To begin with, Zerilli moves Arendt further away from elements of Kant's theorising on judgement and from what she terms the epistemological problem of the political judgement debate. Arendt, according to Zerilli, undermined her focus on plurality in theorising judgement by holding on to the distinction between reflective and determinate judgement. Arendt upheld the possibility of pure determinate judgement, in the form of logic judgements, for example that two plus two must be four, which automatically compel us (Arendt, 1982: 72). Thus, only reflective judgement is for her truly political. She then went on to adopt aesthetic judgement for politics, which led to accusations that she left behind a yawning abyss between knowledge and opinion and failed to account for how rational standards may help validate judgements and differentiate between good and bad judgements in a meaningful way. Both decisions hide Arendt's crucial contribution in capturing the political qualities of judgement through a thicker conception of plurality. They position reflective judgement as an incomplete rational process that must rely on other means, that is, a turn to the potential for deliberating with others, to ensure adequate judgement.

Building on Wittgenstein, Zerilli (2016b) questions whether distinguishing between purely determinate and purely reflective judgement is possible. Wittgenstein offers, in Zerilli's reading, a way to break the stronghold of logic on judgement, by questioning why something must be a certain way, for example why two plus two must always lead to four. He helps shed light on what happens if we imagine that someone simply does not follow our logic, which we assume to be so intuitively reasonable. What instead seems to play a crucial role as to whether we follow a rule and whether it has a compelling, logical character, is its acknowledgement. Because logic is generally compelling – 'obvious' to humans, what seems to characterise these forms of determinate judgements is their unique ability to combine its compelling character with a lack of reasons for it: four must be the answer. Judgements of a particular issue or object gain their compelling character not from their cognitive compulsion, but from 'finding the right expression, one that I accept because it satisfies me' (Zerilli, 2016b: 142). This means that all judgements, even more determinate ones, presuppose aesthetic values about what ought to be. Validity arises out of persuasion, that is, giving facts the appropriate, satisfactory meaning according to these values. To judge compellingly, Zerilli concludes, is possible because of, and not despite, the aesthetic character of judgement (Zerilli, 2016b: 130–131). Zerilli turns Beiner's and Habermas's 'yawning abyss' on its head: it is not the case that Arendt failed to account for the need for rational standards in politics because she turned to aesthetics. Instead, Beiner and Habermas neglected the necessarily aesthetic dimension to the functioning of rational standards, and with it the important role played by persuasion.

Alongside persuasion, Zerilli in a second movement criticises Arendt for her failure to utilise imagination beyond its reproductive contribution as a faculty that enables humans to make present what is absent and to view an issue from different perspectives (2005b: 163). This capacity 'to go visiting' allows judgement to move beyond the limitations of subjectivity. Zerilli suggests that the use of the imagination in Arendt's thought does not explain how 'members of democratic communities, can affirm human freedom as a political reality', that is, their ability to respond to events and issues in novel ways, in a 'world of objects and events whose causes and effects we can neither control nor predict with certainty' (Zerilli, 2005b: 162). For this project, a notion of imagination is needed that is not reproductive but generative and spontaneous, and thus able to extend the reference of judgement beyond its original meaning (Zerilli, 2005b: 163). Building on Cornelius Castoriadis, Zerilli terms this notion 'radical imagination' (2005b: 174, 2005a). Radical imagination opens the public space to 'values that have not yet found expression in the sense of a determinate concept'; through imagination, humans 'hold to an imaginative extension of a concept beyond its ordinary use in cognitive judgments and affirm freedom' (Zerilli, 2005b: 171). Judgement that exercises this radical imagination can help create new connections in the shared world and give them meaning without returning to an application of existing rules or pre-given concepts. The spectators' judgement creates 'the space in which the objects of political judgement, the actor and actions themselves, can appear, and thus alter our sense of what belongs in the common world' (Zerilli, 2005b: 179).

To illustrate what radical imagination entails, Zerilli turns to Frederick Douglass's famous speech 'The Meaning of July Fourth for the Negro', from 1852, as exemplary political judgement at the boundaries of deliberative discourses. She shows how the aim of the speech is not to convey the rational character of anti-slavery argumentation. Instead, Douglass attempts to reveal the hypocrisy of claims to rationality, through various means of rhetoric, including sarcasm and irony. The aim is not to convince his audience by reference to shared beliefs, but to 'gain critical purchase on what each takes for granted' (Zerilli, 2012: 18). Our responsibility as theorists and listeners therefore cannot be to redeem Douglass's public unreason as public reason, but to acknowledge the political, transformative force of 'a form of speaking and judging that unsettles how we understand those principles and the apparent coherence of the "we" that denies its contingent and exclusionary character' (Zerilli, 2012: 19).

Zerilli's emphasis on persuasion and imagination also raises difficult questions: what makes persuasion and radical imagination a medium that contributes to democracy rather than one that simply manipulates? Put differently, what can we say about the social practices from which they emerge and how can we ensure that judgement helps affirm freedom and strengthens a community's sense of reality – without returning us to a concern with validity and epistemology? Zerilli's work is attentive to this issue of social conditioning, including through her contribution to feminist debates, but challenges feminists' overwhelming concern with the 'subject question' (Zerilli, 2005a: 10). By this Zerilli means a concern with the formation of a subject, and the internal and external forces hindering freedom. The concern fails to recognise the political freedom that emerges from acting together as an alternative to the freedom associated with free will, which feminists criticise. Amongst others, Lois McNay, in turn, raises doubt about Zerilli's capacity to evade the problem of the 'subject question', which is considered pivotal to the issue of social conditioning. The 'emergence of the radically new is almost always mediated through, and therefore constrained by, the confines of embodied existence and understanding'; a conception of politics that seeks to transcend these 'confines in order to intervene more creatively in the world' must account for 'their limiting effects' rather than dismissing the effects 'in favour of the postulation of an inchoate potentiality' (McNay, 2014: 16).[5] I share Zerilli's commitment to Arendt's thicker conception of plurality, which I take to be irreducible to the issue of subject formation, or social conditioning more generally. The challenge that arises out of Zerilli's contribution, as I see it, is therefore how to uphold the human capacity for radical imagination and persuasion (that is, plurality) without falling back on an intellectualist account that obscures the embeddedness of imagination and persuasion in the interrelationship between judge and context. In other words, reflection on both persuasion and imagination in relation to judgement has opened the space to discuss further the issue of social conditioning that inevitably confronts us following a departure from a search for transcendental validity.

The situated impartiality of storytelling

The second direction in which Arendt scholars have fruitfully extended her theorising on judgement is in relation to storytelling. Chapter 2 discussed the fact that the Arendtian practice of action and judgement together form an activity of world disclosure, that is, how the world seems to a community, and that this activity entails telling a story (about the world) and giving it meaning. Arendt scholars have engaged with the practice in a variety of different contexts.

Each setting comes with new insights, but also reproduces the central movement from pluralism towards the second dimension to judgement.

Lisa Disch (1994) situates Arendt's innovative approach to storytelling and judgement in the context of the postmodernism–modernism divide. The modernist position is concerned with legitimacy gained through rational discourse and was mentioned in relation to twentieth-century political theory's concern with pluralism at the beginning of this chapter. While its proponents acknowledge the failures of the Enlightenment, they nonetheless continue to hold on to the central belief in the possibility of progress. They accommodate the limits of the main narratives in society that too easily become instruments of power and domination and turn instead to the critical potential found in the stories told that capture marginalised voices. Postmodernism opposes this perspective through a radical scepticism towards collective agreement. Its exegetes emphasise storytelling's capacity to reveal the constructed character of any claims in society and find emancipatory potential in fragmentation and discontinuity (Disch, 1994: 9). Disch searches for an alternative to the two sides, which falls for neither dogmatism, attributed to modernism, nor scepticism, identified in postmodernism. For Disch, Arendt's most provocative contribution is her notion of 'visiting', which proposes to combine impartiality and situated interestedness by looking at an issue from different perspectives. Visiting involves 'imagining the story of an event from a plurality of contesting positions not to reconcile them in a general statement of principle but to arrive at a public interpretation of the event's meaning. Such a judgement is only provisional, and defending it does not involve proving it is right' (Disch, 1994: 208). Storytelling departs from the 'premise that it is precisely because they [stories] call for interpretation – that they cannot be taken literally' (Disch, 1994: 9). Pluralist stories help capture 'the ambiguities of a social reality that is never linear but many-sided and multidimensional' (Disch, 1994: 9). Storytelling thus encapsulates a form of judgement that accepts that its content is not self-evident and conclusive, and refrains 'from the rhetorical moves that would give one's position the appearance of unquestionability' (Disch, 1994: 4). Visiting, or representative thought, proposes to find a middle ground between an embrace of telling the stories of the marginalised, who are said to provide particularly 'objective' insights (fundamental to modernist literature), and the absolute rejection of any form of objectivity in storytelling (defended by postmodernists) by turning to public engagement with perspectives.

The extension of Arendt's thought on storytelling to the modernism–postmodernism debate also reveals the limitations of a focus on plurality for judgement and storytelling. Disch concludes that Arendt cannot answer fundamental questions surrounding the need for storytelling: how 'to find a way to speak critically from experience without the dogmatic parochialism that asserts my experience as an unquestionable ground of my authority'? And, how to 'hold various claims to experience open to question without the reluctant scepticism that postpones decision making to the point where it becomes politically paralysing' (Disch, 1994: 209)? These kinds of questions remain unanswered by a focus on plurality alone and require the theorisation of a second dimension that responds directly to the situated character of judgement.

While not resolving Disch's concerns about Arendt's approach, the second scholar I turn to, Maria Pia Lara (1998, 2007), captures the critical potential in stories of the past. In connection with Arendt's discussion of Rahel Varnhagen, Lara considers the contribution of feminist narratives in revealing 'the concrete nature of personal struggles' (1998: 46) of women in modernity. The telling of stories by writers such as Jane Austen helped women gain knowledge about their identities and position in society; narrative 'identities are achievements, they are guided by a cognitive role – a "praxis-oriented" discernment and understanding of the agents of action in becoming selves through narrative clarification and grasping for consistence in one's own life' (Lara, 1998: 71). Furthermore, by recovering the ways that women in the past conceived their lives as struggles for 'self-clarification', contemporary feminism can articulate new stories that help not only 'to increase women's self-esteem, but to alter the conception of who women are' (Lara, 1998: 77).[6] Lara thus reads storytelling as 'the articulate social weaving of memories, the recovery of fragments of the past, the exercise of collective judgment, the duty to "go against the grain" and promote, with the retelling, a performative frame for a "new beginning"' (1998: 40). She offers an Arendtian reading of storytelling that sees the past context not as a fixed background for political action but as central to it: the continuous refiguration of the past through stories allows a community to tackle past injustices and give meaning and a potential of renewal to the present (Lara, 1998: 36).

Lastly, Jade Schiff, as we saw in Chapter 1, considers storytelling in relation to the failure of affluent societies to respond to global poverty (2014: 10). Schiff's work denies any desire for an easy solution achieved through the one-sided search for the critical potential of narratives, for instance in relation to situated impartiality and the feminist retelling of women's stories. Stories can undoubtedly help illuminate suffering, but they can just as well obscure it, depending on their production and reception. Schiff suggests that, in light of this dual contribution of stories, Arendt failed to ask a crucial question: why we choose to tell stories that obscure our ability and responsibility for transforming injustice (Schiff, 2014: 23). Awareness of the dispositions that encourage us to tell obscuring stories – that facilitate our incapacity to think, our choice to lie to ourselves and our forgetfulness of the contingency of social formations – is a precondition for an affirmative theory of human responsiveness. In other words, only following such a step, that is, the investigation into the issue of social conditioning, can we provide a rounded conception of reflective judgement in which storytelling can prove invaluable as a creative, world-building capacity, as opposed to the facilitating role in relation to practices of complicity in systemic injustice.

The second project aligns with the first in combining an embrace of pluralism with questions of social conditioning, and in viewing these questions not merely as obstacles and constraints on a pluralist politics, but as giving judgement and action their distinct qualities. The hope that Schiff, Lara and Disch seem to share is that, through the turn to 'situatedness', we can begin to understand why certain narratives and not others gain situated impartiality, transform identity claims and inequality, and cultivate responsiveness.

The affective and pre-discursive structuring of judgement

My discussion turns to two further projects aimed at extending Arendt's conception of judgement in relation to the unconscious and affective and to common sense. The projects look at the relationship between judge and context from the other side, placing an emphasis on the context rather than the judge.

The role of the non-/sub-/unconscious in the process of judging politically remains heavily contested. One explanation for this is that judgement provides an unusual case of belief formation. We can only speak of judgement if it is made intentionally, has arisen out of at least some degree of reflection, and builds on some form of evidence. At the same time, judgements have drag effects similar to perception, which elude awareness. They are 'subject to silent forces that are as powerful and unrelenting as gravity and that curve the space of reason in ways that is difficult for us to detect' (McGeer and Pettit, 2009: 64). Human beings are therefore not by nature 'the enlightened masters of where our judgement goes; having been selected for survival, not for insight, our natural instinct is a wayward ally in the struggle for truth' (McGeer and Pettit, 2009: 65). The source of many of the disagreements about conceptualising judgement, as well as the motivation for the rationalist projects that turn to transcendental and logical reasoning to strengthen the 'intentional side' to judging politically, can be traced back to this inherent tension between intentionality and 'drag effects'.

Psychology and neuroscience have provided various insights into these drag effects (Hibbing et al., 2014; Thiele, 2006: 60).[7] Historically, psychology dealt with judgements through decision theory, which reduced judgements to models of efficient information processing and probabilistic reasoning (cf. Thiele, 2006: 60). This mind-as-machine approach is problematic and contemporary decision theory has instead shown that to judge successfully, human beings rely on mechanisms that help avoid the infinite regress of exhaustive reasoning.[8] These mechanisms consist in mental short cuts known as heuristics, for instance the sunk-cost effect (past investments encourage non-beneficial future investments), or the rationalisation effect (only reasons supportive of pre-judgements considered). They provide quick 'dirty' judgement, but may also lead to systematic errors, in which case the mental short cuts are defined as biases (Thiele, 2006: 63). Biases are not inherently bad or wrong, keeping us from fulfilling an ideal of enlightened beings. Instead, while attempts to decrease common biases are important, mental shortcuts are indispensable to navigating our complex world efficiently and effectively.

These neuroscientific and psychological insights gain in importance for the present investigation with efforts to utilise the scientific evidence on the non-conscious for political theorising (cf. Bennett, 2009; Connolly, 2002; Gunnell, 2007, 2013; Zerilli, 2015). The various positions on 'neuropolitics' (Connolly, 2002) argue that theories about the role of deliberation in politics have not accounted sufficiently for the visceral dimensions to political action and decision making (Connolly, 2002; Massumi, 2015). This insightful literature has provoked cautious voices, including from Arendt scholars who challenge the underlying empirical evidence and ideological commitments. These voices do not deny 'that many bodily (and mental) processes take place subliminally, below the threshold of awareness. Who would dream of doubting that they do?' (Leys, 2011: 456). Instead, they point out that the embrace of habituation and sub-threshold automatic processes, for example the movement of fingers to play a piano, often retain the distorted vision of the mind as a disembodied consciousness. The unreflective engagement with the rationalist framework then leads too easily to a complete rejection of the role of cognitive capacities, which opens up the space for a 'pyrrhic victory' of the unconscious in politics and political theory. It raises serious concerns at a theoretical and practical level in relation to political judgement.

Theoretically, scholars including Zerilli (2013), challenge the fruitfulness of approaching political problems through a focus on different brain functions. Such a focus inevitably misconstrues socio-political phenomena in their complex intersubjective character and the import of psychology/science. The theory of nudging and other popular approaches to steering human behaviour may seem particularly powerful as they target the immediate reactions of humans and have a direct impact on mass behaviour, but the multi-layered character of social processes significantly narrows their impact. Practically, the all too enthusiastic turn to visceral, embodied contributions to decision making comes with significant dangers for politics. The embrace of neuroscience in political theory is a reaction to right-wing strategies of tapping into xeno- and homophobic, sexist and other problematic sentiments in Western democracies at the sub-threshold, that is, visceral, level. In response, progressive politics is ultimately encouraged to open the doors to a race to the bottom of (unpredictable) manipulation schemes. This strategy turns critical judgement into an epiphenomenon, an irrelevant afterthought of non-conscious processes. Both at a theoretical and practical level of politics, there is thus a problematic tendency to give up too easily on the potential of public spheres and on the difficult project of freeing politics from intellectualist approaches to deliberative democracy (cf. Livingston, 2012).

The non-conscious contributions to judgements play an important role as a part of the processes of making sense of social reality, for the relationship between deliberation and the visceral in politics is not a zero-sum game; rather, they complement each other (Vogler, 2021). Good judgements put a 'panoply of deliberative and intuitive faculties to work in the perception and appraisal of multi-faceted problems' (Thiele, 2006: 152). After all, moral judgements are for most people 'a product of intuitions that have been shaped through active participation in socio-cultural environments, and occasionally refined by propositional discussions' (Thiele, 2006: 136). Judgement is reducible neither to rationality, retrospectively fully reconstructed by it, nor to a mere unconscious bias. In short, in terms of the approach I am developing in this book, we must account for unconscious contributions to our 'making sense of reality' that are part of complex socio-political processes and practices and cannot – nor should they – easily be disentangled from them.

The affective dimension to judgement

Following on from the discussion of the non-conscious contributions to judging, I now turn to the interrelated and equally hotly debated issue of the affective dimension to judging politically. Since at least the 1990s scholars across the humanities, psychology and the social sciences have worked to challenge the belief in rational progress, that is, in enlightened reason replacing 'irrational' emotions. They 'hesitate to conceptualize emotion and rationality as different beasts entirely, and they hesitate even more to map these faculties onto different categories of people (masses vs. elites, western vs. non-western publics, and so on)' (Heins, 2007: 715–716; see also Bickford, 2011; Clore and Huntsinger, 2007; Clough, 2009; Clough and Halley, 2007; Protevi, 2009). In contemporary political theory, the foundation of the current debate on emotions for judgement lies in neo-Kantian reason, as expressed in the thought of Habermas and Rawls and their heirs, which displaces emotions (cf. Bickford, 2011; Krause, 2008; Liljeström, 2016). While these accounts may accept the importance of emotions as motivating force, they wish to downplay affect's role in their thought to present people as autonomous, rational and with a strong sense of justice. In doing so their approach fails to account for emotions' imbrication with reason. This shortcoming has resulted in the postulation of a wide variety of alternatives to rationalism, from virtue theory and the communitarian critique of Rawls, care ethics and Martha Nussbaum's work on political emotions, to various Humean approaches.[9]

Of note is that the affective and emotional turn has at times reproduced the traditional dichotomy between emotions and reason by overemphasising the embodied, non-cognitive nature of affect (Zerilli, 2015, 2016a). In affect theory affect is viewed as pre-personal and as distinct from emotions, which are social (Shouse, 2005). The term 'affect' describes the 'bodily capacities to affect and be affected' (Clough and Halley, 2007: 2) and the 'persistent proof of a body's never less than ongoing immersion in and among the world's obstinacies and rhythms, its refusals as much as its invitations' (Seigworth and Gregg, 2009: 1). Affect theorists highlight that an emphasis on affect's pre-personal qualities does not mean that affects are not mediated through the various regimes ordering our body and everyday lives (Grossberg, 2009: 316). Nonetheless, they clearly separate out emotions as at least a 'minimally interpretive experience whose physiological aspect is affect' (Terada, 2003: 4). The affective turn thus holds on to a problematic dichotomy between the conscious 'signifying ("emotional" and intellectual) processes held to be captive to the fixity of received meanings and categories' and, on the other hand, the 'non-conscious affective processes of intensity held to be autonomous from signification' (Leys, 2011: 450).

I have already addressed the problems with this strategy in relation to the unconscious and will not repeat them here. Instead, I take up the crucial cue that emerges from their embrace of a more sustained engagement with how humans really make judgements. I put forward assumptions that add to the insights by Leslie Thiele and Zerilli on the unconscious and maintain the balance between reason and affect.

Firstly, emotions are affective states and to some extent conscious feelings that motivate humans to judge their context. Emotions provide a commentary on circumstances that helps prioritise information and supports appropriate reaction. Without these affective contributions, rational judgement would have no direction, no interests to judge in the first place – it would become a worldless judgement. Affect 'is what sticks, or what sustains or preserves the connection between ideas, values, and objects': to be affected is 'to evaluate that thing. Evaluations are expressed in how bodies turn toward things' (Ahmed, 2009: 29, 31). At the same time, emotions can leave humans in a state that makes them vulnerable to prejudices and to jumping to conclusions. Indeed, as shown in countless studies, emotions are very easily manipulated (Thiele, 2006: 170).

To strengthen judgement therefore requires 'acknowledging, exploring, cultivating, and integrating affect' (Thiele, 2006: 199) without neglecting its imbrication with reason. It means to identify emotions not merely as a necessary, albeit unwanted, part of human life, but as an important pre-condition for good judgement.

Secondly, emotions can distort judgements and the perspectives they provide on a shared world. They require awareness of their potentially negative effects, rather than a naïve support of affect against rationalism. Arendt is often noted for her emphasis on the negative effects that publicly expressed emotions can have on politics. Particularly her book *On Revolution* provides a clear separation of a political sphere, with its abstract ideals of 'greatness', 'honour' and 'dignity', from sentiments, especially collective emotions. She rejected the corruption of solidarity by interpersonal, modern pity, with its incorporation of primarily social concerns, for example poverty (Arendt, 2006c: 88). Whereas compassion for Arendt provides the foundation for individual reaction to needs experienced in immediate encounters, pity offers a 'falsely idealistic, deliberately engineered emotion that reproduces itself further through the medium of public imagination' (Heins, 2007: 723). Collective emotions are problematic in so far as they group together individual misfortunes and relate these to abstract ideal groups – 'the poor' – that political action by default fails to respond to because of their vague character (Arendt, 2006c: 90). To acknowledge this danger is not to revert to rationalism as an attempt to repress and ignore emotions, which leaves democracy dangerously unprotected against their undemocratic expression (Mihai, 2014: 31). It is also not to argue that judgements of specific groups of people are more emotional – and therefore worse.

Thirdly, a concern with the affective and emotional elements to judgement must remain tied to the overarching project that arises from the pluralist dimension to judgement, in particular a concern with reality. I discussed in Chapter 2 how Arendt's political realism was often received critically; part of this reception goes back to claims of a lack of sensitivity to the emotional and affective dimensions to political action. As research on the role of emotions in Arendt's thought emphasises, this reading relies too much on a narrow, selective reading of her work (Degerman, 2019; Heins, 2007; Nelson, 2006). Arendt scholars dispute this reading: they emphasise for example that if 'we take [. . .] heartlessness and coldness as mere quirks of personality, we deprive ourselves of alternatives to intimacy and empathy' (Degerman, 2019: 158–159). Judgements attentive to emotions need to be part of a form of empathetic, intersubjective impartiality instead of a 'passionless objectivity' (Thiele, 2006: 186). This impartiality is not a form of sympathy, a coming 'face-to-face with the Other', but the project of coming 'face-to-face with reality in the presence of others' (Thiele, 2006: 88).

In summary, I have turned to a third project that extends Arendt's theory of judgement with regard to the non-conscious and affective dimensions to judgement. Scholars, informed by Arendt amongst others, address the limitations of both rational, deliberative and non-conscious, affective approaches to politics. They formulate a middle path that refuses to separate and distribute weight within the multi-layered processes that together make judgements on complicity possible. In so doing, judgement scholars open the space to develop a more suitable account of social conditioning that helps elucidate judgement as a pluralist practice.

The pre-discursive structuring of judgement

This section concludes my reconstruction of responses to Arendt's thought by engaging with two influential attempts to refine the conception of common and community sense as a key mechanism for making adequate reflective judgements.

Alessandro Ferrara (1999, 2008, 2014) supports a form of 'oriented reflective judgement' (2012: 40) guided by the 'force of what is as it should be or the force of the example' (2012: 2–3). The key question for him is how this force of the example, which he associates for instance with great works of art, can move beyond its cultural origins. In response, Ferrara combines a focus on exemplary validity with a thick conception of common sense grounded in authenticity. He describes authenticity as the enduring fusion of norms and facts that is directed towards the 'concrete universal' (Ferrara, 2008: 40) of human flourishing, whereby judgements are exemplary in so far as they expand and realise 'our' sense of what constitutes a flourishing life. The abolition of slavery for Ferrara constitutes such an exemplary judgement. Ferrara's work also proposes criteria by which to judge whether a person's life is flourishing: coherence, vitality, depth and maturity (Ferrara, 2008: 3, 32). These criteria find their expression in a shared and universally held sense of whether one's own life is stagnating or flourishing. Ferrara's contribution to debates on common sense and exemplarity fruitfully brings out the link between human flourishing and judgement, which I will draw out as well as I discuss an improved ethos of reality, but it also seems to reproduce the project of seeking standards of validity outside the public sphere that people must agree to. A commitment to a 'pre-social realm of shared intuitions' means that his pre-discursive structuring of judgement understates 'the problem of entrenched social division and deep difference' and thus undertheorises 'the antagonism and conflict that these may produce in political interaction' (McNay, 2019: 138).

Albena Azmanova responds to this problem. She focuses our attention on 'the encoding of structurally produced injustice into the phronetic – experience-based – structure of public reason and the way these codes are activated in the course of argumentation and judgement' (2012: 179). Azmanova takes from Arendt that political judgement is intersubjectively and pre-discursively patterned: the spectator's judgement is made in reference to a plurality of spectators who give meaning to events. This plurality of perspectives shapes judgement independently of the spectators' actual communication of their judgements. The middle ground that Arendt provides between particular and universal, in the form of the intersubjective general, is thus inherently structured by social practices. However, Arendt's account is ill equipped to fully lay bare this social coding of judgement, because she is primarily concerned with giving the appearance of particulars meaning. As a consequence, her conception of reflective judgement neglects the structures of privilege and disadvantage that influence, without determining, the appearance of any particular (Azmanova, 2012: 147). Azmanova concludes that political judgement should instead be concerned with exactly those phenomena that capture these patterns, for example of power or systematic injustice, rather than what Arendt focuses on – the unprecedented.

Azmanova calls the distinctions that form a community sense and frame judgement the 'paradigms of articulation and signification' (2012: 161), or 'matrix of relevance' (2012: 157). The matrix of relevance has a horizontal and a vertical dimension. By 'horizontal signification', Azmanova means the way people make judgements in reference to a plurality of spectators and their separate perspectives, which give meaning to appearances. Vertically, reference points for judgement are ordered in hierarchies of significance, for example what is to be seen as an important issue according to the community's worldview. Azmanova draws attention to the social code that is embedded in both dimensions, in the meaning and significance given to points of reference prior to judgement. Judgement becomes a 'process of simultaneous cognitive and evaluative signification' (Azmanova, 2012: 161) which enables the contestation of norms and consensus building through the pre-discursive structuring of judgement in its horizontal and vertical dimensions.

A focus on the social patterns that shape judgement changes also our view on exemplarity and the example as a central tool that links judgement and common sense. Azmanova suggests that we concentrate on the distinctions that make an example comprehensible to members of a certain society. Examples embody and disclose a 'selective societal code of valorisation' (Azmanova, 2012: 176). We cannot reduce this code of exemplarity to the factual knowledge of the context and origin of an example, nor is it the mere product of moral assessments. As a case in point, we may have judged an issue by referring to the exemplary courage of Achilles. The success of turning the position we take up into a political judgement that is communicable to others and transcends our partial perspective on the world does not depend on excellent knowledge of the Trojan War, nor on the approval of Achilles' behaviour through moral deliberation. Instead, it is dependent on the meaningful and significant shared distinctions that are imbued with structural injustice.

Azmanova provides a more expansive conception of the pre-discursive matrix of relevance that underpins the practices of the plurality of judging spectators, by emphasising the social coding of the matrix. Whereas for Arendt, common sense is primarily agential, the result of judging spectators enlarging their perspectives through engagement with others, Azmanova conceives of structuring as primarily social. To uphold Arendt's project, judgement scholars must therefore find ways of attending to the social without denying human plurality and without falling prey to a heroic view of agency. A focus on social structuring, in turn, bears within it a problematic tendency visible in Azmanova's writing: her response to the primarily social structuring of judgement is overly agential. As Mihaela Mihai elaborates, Azmanova 'maintains a firm belief that the solution lies with the flexibility and instability of the matrix, which she sees as forever vulnerable to the power of discursive confrontations' (Mihai, 2016b: 35). To understand how we can avoid both tendencies, we need to delve even further into the second dimension to judgement – the interplay between structure and agency – than has been proposed by the various Arendt scholars discussed in this chapter.

Concluding thoughts

The purpose of this chapter has been to introduce the debate that followed on from Arendt's writings about reflective judgement. My analysis traces two phases to the debate and aligns this book with the second. The chapter has discussed four attempts at extending Arendt's theory within the second phase, with a view to preparing the ground for an engagement with the topic of social conditioning. From the perspective of the judge, Zerilli's work reveals that persuasion and radical imagination offer vital mechanisms that ensure judgement's world-building and freedom-affirming potential. The question remains how this potential is shaped by the relationship between judge and context. Secondly, the chapter has introduced different accounts of storytelling, a practice deeply interrelated with action and judgement. My discussion of Disch, Lara and Schiff captures different ways in which the pluralist potential can be used by telling stories that go visiting and rework accounts of the past, but also identifies situated human agency as key to a critical form of storytelling, and by extension, judgement. From the side of context, I consider, thirdly, the enthusiasm for studying the affective and non-conscious layers to judging. Drawing on Zerilli and Thiele, amongst others, I affirm that a suitable account of the pluralism of judgement must take note of these elements of judgement, which, in turn, require us to address how they are connected to the intersubjective practices of a pluralist politics. Finally, Azmanova and Ferrara provide important insights into common sense, one of the key concepts in Arendt's thought. They highlight the need to address the social patterning of common sense, which we need to account for if we wish to put forward a non-rationalist framework of judgement.

Beyond the invaluable insights into judgement that the debate provides, it also clearly states that any adequate account of political/reflective judgement must tell us more about the interrelationship between judge and context that constitutes judgement. How are persuasion, imagination, the unconscious, the affective, stories and common sense patterned to enable and constrain the pluralist potential in judgement? The debate on political judgement therefore makes it clear that I will only be able to address the problem of how humans can engage better with an unjust and violent world, particularly when faced with their own, deeply rooted entanglement in injustice and violence, once I have delved more deeply into the issue of social conditioning, the core of debates on 'structure–agency'. It is to this issue that I turn next.

Notes

1. This first phase includes the works of Ronald Beiner (1982, 1983; Beiner and Nedelsky, 2001), Seyla Benhabib (1988, 1990), Richard Bernstein (1986), Jürgen Habermas (1977) and Peter Steinberger (1990).
2. This phase offers a wide scholarship in defence of Arendt's account of judgement, which includes the work of Leora Bilsky (1996), Annelies Degryse (2011), David Marshall (2010), Waltraud Meints (2014), Remi Peeters (2009a, 2009b), Jonathan Schwartz (2016), and Linda Zerilli (2005b, 2012).
3. This category contains scholarship more or less explicitly influenced by Arendt's theory, which does not necessarily seek to respond to the first phase. Beyond numerous articles, it includes the work of Albena Azmanova (2012), Alessandro Ferrara (1999, 2012, 2014), Bronwyn Leebaw (2011), Leslie Thiele (2006), Jonathan Schwartz (2016), Maša Mrovlje (2018) and Linda Zerilli (2016a).
4. For recent discussions of Arendt's theory of judgement, see Landemore et al. (2018) and Steinberger (2018).
5. McNay largely formulates the contribution of social conditioning in negative terms, 'tempering' the potentiality identified in radical imagination. I characterise this kind of approach to the interplay between structure, agency and plurality as reductive and pertaining to a problematic framework which Margaret Archer terms 'duality', to be discussed in Chapter 4.
6. Arendt provides an important starting point for feminist narratives, despite her difficult relationship with feminism. For an overview of feminist scholarship on storytelling see Stone-Mediatore (2016).
7. The classic treatment of political judgement and the emergent insights from psychology seldom build one comprehensive theory of judgement. The political-philosophy engagement with psychological literature, for example Judith Shklar's (1990: 27) adoption of psychological insights into judgement in the context of injustice, as yet remains too sporadic. The psychological literature has retained a positivist focus, that is, a concern with observable or measurable behaviour, which cannot capture the complexity of judgement discussed in this book.

8. Research has explored how human beings make judgements by focusing on, for example, verbatim instead of gist information, relying on hot cognition (subconscious emotional reaction to information) and responding to affective cues (Clore and Huntsinger, 2007; Corbin et al., 2015; Cornwell et al., 2015; Hibbing et al., 2014).
9. Care ethics (Gilligan, 1982) provides a corrective to rationalism, adding to the dispassionate moral judgement of rationalist theories of justice a feeling of care for others, emerging from the private sphere, which provides important additional knowledge for the right action. In philosophy, Nussbaum continues to be central for highlighting the crucial role emotions may play in politics (Nussbaum, 2013). A fear of relativism means that she reintroduces rationalist tendencies into her affective theory (cf. Krause, 2008: 59ff.). Emotions 'thus appear conveniently amenable to political reforms' (Degerman, 2019: 169). Krause (2008) also explores in detail the Humean, sentimentalist contribution on emotions.

CHAPTER FOUR

Social conditioning and analytical dualism

The first part of this book argued that to improve our judgements on complicity, we (especially those of us benefiting disproportionately from pervasive injustice and violence) must cultivate an ethos of reality attentive to the human condition of plurality. Chapter 3 discussed the need to combine the focus on human plurality with a consideration of the link between a community of judges and their context. Specifically, it introduced different ways in which judgements are socially conditioned, which can constrain but also prove a vital potential for making good judgements, for example the way unconscious processes facilitate routine decision making. This chapter turns to Margaret Archer's contribution to the debate on structure and agency to delve more deeply into the potential in social conditioning.[1]

A discussion of Archer's thought is particularly valuable for my argument as her elaboration of the distinct powers of human agency alongside social structures explicitly builds on, and moves beyond, Arendt's thought. Archer sought 'to put forward a model that is recognisably human; one that retains Arendt's notion of the "Human Condition" as entailing a reflexive "Life of the mind"' (Archer, 2016: 138). Her theoretical framework aims to capture the core human experience of feeling both free and enchained, or, in other words, that we shape society and society shapes us (Archer, 2000: 307). Archer terms this 'authentic' feeling the 'vexatious fact of society and its human constitution' (Archer, 1995: 2). We can think of her understanding of social conditioning along similar lines to Arendt's treatment of the human condition of plurality: while essential to who and what we are at this point in time, we can lose a sense of and capacity to feel both free and enchained and this can have a devastating impact on our ability to engage with reality. For instance, someone who is consistently denied basic rights within society can lose the ability to shape the world around them, while those in positions of privilege may come to expect that there are no limits to what they are able to do. Archer focuses on tendencies in social theory to conflate the distinct causal powers of structure and agency, which leads to an overreliance on one or the other to explain social (trans)formations.

The first section of this chapter explores the practical implication in relation to the complicity scholarship. The second part summarises how Archer suggests we should cultivate a stance, or ethos, of reality that accounts for the vexatious fact. Her argument comes in the form of a theoretical contribution to the structure–agency debate, but this should not obscure the fact that for Archer the theoretical points are linked to human experiences and tendencies towards conflating structure and agency in everyday life.

Responsiveness and duality

I have previously shown that efforts to tackle the threefold problem of judging complicity (how to identify, attribute and acknowledge complicity) come with two diverging conceptions of judgement. These conceptions, in turn, are embedded in radically diverging visions of the relationship between structure and agency. The dominant position on complicity relies on moral judgements that are supported by methodological individualism. Individualism reduces structures to the actions of the collective of actors and everything social to the individual, allowing a narrow focus on the thoughts and motivations of a social actor. The person judging complicity can focus on their actions and consider whether these meet the standards of blameworthiness and culpability. Archer criticised this vision of society as upward conflation (Archer, 2003; McAnulla, 2002, 2006). Its counterpart is structuralism, or downward conflation, which reduces the individual to Durkheim's 'indeterminate matter' (Durkheim, 2014: 87), whose thoughts and emotions are held collectively. Put together, these positions reduce either agency or structure to an epiphenomenon, instead of accounting for their interplay (Archer, 1995: 65). The critical approaches to complicity focused on in this book avoid these forms of conflation by suggesting the interpenetration of structure and agency. Within debates on structure–agency, this third option has become associated with amongst others Anthony Giddens' structuration theory (1984) and Pierre Bourdieu's habitus (1990). Iris Marion

Young's *Responsibility for Justice* (2011) draws on both to criticise a framework of judgement narrowly focused on blame and guilt: the dominant position does not account sufficiently for the way that our actions and judgements are the product of social processes and help reproduce injustice without ever having to actively seek unjust outcomes. As an example, Young describes how middle-class people tend to have similar preferences when it comes to housing, especially a safe and quiet neighbourhood, that unintentionally reproduce prejudices about marginalised groups including ethnic minorities and poorer people (2011: 62). Young suggests the need for a reflective form of judgement that accounts both for our contributions to unjust social processes and for the largely structural nature of injustice and violence. The ethics of responsiveness expands on the interpenetration of structure and agency to fruitfully capture the impact of structural injustice on the responsiveness of the privileged. It suggests that judgements on complicity must account for human situatedness and dispositions to disavow any responsibility for injustice.

I want to suggest that the ethics' important insights into how to overcome these constraints on responsiveness, in their current form, come with drawbacks. To capture these shortcomings, I deploy Archer's critique of duality, with some abstraction from its original context. Duality emphasises the inseparability between structure and agency, which are imagined as two complementary sides of a coin and require a focus on the structured character of action (Archer, 1995: 93). As Archer put it in relation to 'Graham', a person she interviewed for her research on reflexivity, for proponents of a duality

> there never comes a point at which it is possible to disentangle Graham's personal caution (a subjective property of a person) from the characteristics of his context (objective properties of society). [. . .] 'Graham' has now become so inextricably intertwined with his social background and foreground that it is no longer clear *who* is 'standing back'. Therefore, it becomes impossible that Graham can deliberate upon his circumstances as subject to object, because these are now inseparable for 'Graham' (Archer, 2003: 12, original emphasis).

The duality produces an 'ontological complicity' between structure and agency in the form of an 'intentionality without intention, and a practical mastery of the world's regularities which allows one to anticipate the future without even needing to posit it as such' (Bourdieu, 1990: 11–12). The consequence for addressing complicity, in Archer's

(2014b: 26) reading, is that complicity scholars can never attribute responsibility separate from structure. This is clearly not a problem for the responsiveness approach, and I therefore focus on the following, distinct problem: that the emphasis on inseparability leads to an oscillation between '(a) the hyperactivity of agency, whose corollary is the innate volatility of society, and (b) the rigid coherence of structural properties associated [...] with the essential recursiveness of social life' (Archer, 1982: 459). What I want to emphasise is that a primary focus on the way that unjust structures shape responsive agency can come at the cost of considering the contribution of structures to positive transformation and human agency to injustice. In other words, I argue that the conceptions of responsiveness bear within them an impulse to seek refuge in a break-through crisis or other ways of circumventing, rather than accounting for, the imbrication of structure and agency and its complex influence on responsibility. I will now discuss the tendency in relation to each of the proponents first introduced in Chapter 1, starting with Jade Schiff's *Burdens of Political Responsibility* (2014).

Schiff provides a sophisticated account of how the privileged could potentially become more responsive following critical moments, such as the 2008 financial crisis. The account highlights the role narratives can play that engage with the contingency of unjust processes and the burdens of everyday human existence. Duality comes into play when Schiff suggests that situated humans rely primarily on an unconsciously held late modern, capitalist habitus to navigate everyday life. 'Habitus' is a term adopted from Bourdieu and, in brief terms, implies that agency is shaped by, and dispositioned towards, a person's context in such a way that they can buy things unreflectively with little concern for the moral and ethical implications (Schiff, 2014: 27). The aim therefore must be to disrupt this habitus through crisis and an appropriate story which will hopefully stimulate receptiveness to other people's suffering (cf. Schiff, 2014: 15). Archer and her colleagues (Archer, 2010; Porpora, 2015) have continuously challenged this reliance on extraordinary crisis for reflective responses to emerge. They suggest that it risks neglecting the potential of the continuous repositioning that constitutes everyday life in a complex social system and overestimating the contribution of single moments of crisis. Schiff is sensitive to the improvisatory capacities of habitus to bridge the gap between expected and actual effects of action, which both limits the impact of moments of disruption and indicates that habitus can/will still play a role in responding to complicity. Stories on crisis, as discussed in Chapter 1, are also not meant to disembed people from their context, but to use the links between past, present and future creatively to showcase the contingency of unjust processes and practices – that things could and should be different. Lastly, crisis is for Schiff experienced differently by different people, which means that complex combinations of responsiveness and denial may occur. The commitment to a largely unreflective engagement with a late modern, capitalist context nonetheless leaves unanswered the question of where the responsive agency originates. The lack of conscious (moral) agency in everyday life means that responsiveness scholars seem to presuppose responsive agency that only emerges at the moment of significant structural incoherency.[2] The outcome of Schiff's argument is a vision of a responsive person who relies heavily on autonomous agential capacities, for example for receptivity and ironic storytelling, and this issue is not resolved by emphasising the contingency of such agential responses and their embeddedness in the numerous demands life puts on us. In short, my point is less to discredit the power of extraordinary events and subsequent moments of resistance to systemic injustice, but to embed them in an appropriate description that accommodates the various dimensions to reality that, in continuous interplay, produce injustice and its transformation.

Barbara Applebaum's *Being White, Being Good* (2010) considers the challenges for white pedagogy of acknowledging systemic racism. It proposes to address the problem of responsiveness by developing a practice of vigilance, critique, humility and uncertainty as part of an ethic of non-violence that resists the closure of norms and identity formation processes. Such a practice could undoubtedly prove important in tackling systemic racism. Applebaum reproduces the duality in relying too heavily on the hyperactivity of agency to challenge ignorance and denial. Even if we assume a reflective, continuous engagement with violence, it remains unclear how a vigilant person can resolve these omnipresent limitations to human agency by themselves. My criticism here is not directed against the refined conception of human capacities for critique, or the argument in favour of an openness to listen to the voices of the marginalised; nor do I suggest that poststructuralism ignores the need for structural transformation. The problem is that this approach privileges vigilance because it assumes the duality between an inherent incapacity to grasp complicity and the need to acknowledge this complicity. The duality both implies the impossibility of being responsive and entrenches the view that improved acknowledgement is the only way forward. Of course, theorists adhering to the responsibility-in-complicity account, on which Applebaum implicitly draws, have stressed that it does not provide a sufficient condition for resolving injustice, only a pre-condition. Furthermore, this is not to suggest that there is a one-size-fits-all, and final, 'solution' to situated agency's complicity in systemic injustice. Nonetheless, to avoid the duality, proponents of the ethics must combine the emphasis on increased vigilance with an image of social change that considers a range of sources for tackling structural transformation. I turn to two such sources in the following: disruptive politics and collective care for a world.

Clarissa Hayward (2017) rejects the emphasis on the capacity of privileged people to cultivate responsiveness and instead focuses on disruptive politics by the seemingly powerless as a potent tool that can help disrupt the epistemic, white ignorance of the privileged. The approach retains the duality in so far as disruptive politics remains the source of a 'tipping point' (Hayward, 2017: 406) that helps move people from a disposition of ignorance and passive acceptance of the unjust status quo to motivated resistance. Hayward holds on to an approach to responsive agency and the unjust system in which the privileged are either incapable/unwilling to respond to injustice or motivated to do so. Yet, Hayward's approach does not only encounter the problems I identified with Schiff's argument about crisis. The scepticism about humans' capacity to judge their complicity leads Hayward to favour strategies that change the privileged masses' unconscious dispositions, which kept them passive supporters of the status quo. Hayward suggests a change 'at the level of habit' which 'does not require regular conscious thought and decision on the part of the relevant agent' but can be 'formed and maintained by a favourable incentive structure' (Hayward, 2017: 407). Her argument is therefore open to the challenges against affect theorists, who explore the visceral dimensions to politics, discussed in Chapter 3. I embraced the importance of the affective and non-conscious dimensions to human agency but insisted that this move is hostile to the political practices that are irreducible to visceral reactions to a social context. Judgement and action may not enable a person to realise their white ignorance, a point Hayward astutely makes. Yet politics can help us avoid a narrow focus on the binary 'privileged–exploited' that engenders our disavowal and heightens ignorance, by turning our focus on to the wellbeing of the world that humans together make their home. This conclusion arises out of the work of Ella Myers, the fourth and final contributor to the ethics I wish to evaluate.

Myers's *Worldly Ethics* (2013; cf. Myers, 2008) highlights the impact of injustice not only on a dominated Other, as with post-structuralist theorising, but on the ability to act together. Informed by Hannah Arendt, Myers points to the impact injustice has on the world-in-between people and proposes the cultivation of a democratic ethos as a care for the world that refines Arendt's notion of *amor mundi*. Especially valuable for the present discussion is Myers's recognition that the common world is 'a conditioned and conditioning habitat' and that humans are 'of the world and not just in it' (2013: 91). Drawing on Bruno Latour and Jane Bennett, Myers emphasises that a worldly thing is always shorthand for the larger interplay of things and humans at various levels. Care for the world entails an interplay between human agency and other sources of power (Myers, 2013: 101–102). Myers's contribution is marred by the relative brevity of its discussion of the interplay of structure and agency. Instead, *Worldly Ethics* largely falls back on the image of a person, or a group of people, encountering an unjust world that should be responded to through collective action. 'Care for the world' remains too unidirectional a concept, reducible to 'collaborative world-centred projects' (Myers, 2013: 143) and the task of specifying 'features of worldly conditions as the appropriate object' (Myers, 2013: 144) of our care.

Each of the approaches introduced in Chapter 1 thus offers an invaluable contribution to capturing the problem of responsiveness and how to resolve it. The benefits are undermined by the fact that each scholar remains wedded to the duality of unconsciously reproduced unjust structures and responsive agency – articulated in diverse ways and to different degrees. The consequence is that these critical conceptions of complicity bear within them an impulse to seek refuge in a break-through crisis or other ways of circumventing, rather than accounting for, the imbrication of structure and agency and its complex influence on responsibility. The following turns to Archer and her insight into how we can avoid these conflating tendencies by upholding a simultaneous focus on structure and agency in our ethos of reality.

Analytical dualism as an alternative approach to social conditioning

This section maps out three central features of Archer's analytical dualism with a focus on the benefits for the present investigation. First, I elaborate Archer's commitment to a temporal and analytical distinction between structure, culture and agency. The second section deepens the distinction and shows how Archer upholds and combines an object- and a subject-focus. In the concluding section, I introduce Archer's work on reflexivity as internal conversation, which she identifies as a key mediation process between structures and agency.

Archer's morphogenetic approach

Archer's alternative model of social transformation focuses on a temporal and analytical distinction between structure and agency, which she terms analytical dualism. The aim is to move beyond simplistic empiricist notions of allocating causality to one or the other (Archer, 1995: 69). To give an illustrative example, the ethnic prejudices that continue to have a negative impact on the success of job applications in the UK in general are neither the sole consequences of racist HR divisions nor the mere product of a colonialist past. Structure and agency are for Archer also not aspects of the same thing, that is, the more agential or structural part of a singular phenomenon or mechanism; we should instead conceive them as having distinct powers and properties. We need to separate structure and agency in order

> (a) to identify the emergent structure(s), (b) to differentiate between their causal powers and the intervening influences of people due to their quite different causal powers as human beings, and, (c) to explain any outcome at all, which in an open system always entails an interplay between the two (Archer 1995: 70).[3]

The separation allows Archer to distinguish between subjective and objective causal contributions as part of one process of social interaction. Structural and cultural properties, with their powers to constrain, enable and motivate, objectively shape the situations that agents encounter involuntarily. Humans, in turn, subjectively define their concerns and through their reflexive deliberations produce courses of action, by subjectively determining their practical projects vis-à-vis their objective circumstances (Archer, 2003: 135).

In other words, the approach relies on a layered ontology, where every social outcome is the consequence of an interplay between the irreducible properties and powers of structure, culture and agency. Key to this model is that structures pre-date the action that reproduces and changes them, which enables the analytical separating out of the causal contributions and properties of structure and agency along a temporal horizon – before, during and after a particular action (Archer, 1995: 15). Of course, empirically, such a distinction is much more difficult to make.

Archer offers four propositions that help map out the key elements of structural–agential interplay. Firstly, she states that because dualism insists on a temporal distinction between structures and agency, there must be internal and necessary relations between and within social structures that exist prior to present action. They are the consequences of past processes of social conditioning. Take, for example, the teacher–pupil or the privileged–disadvantaged relation. The position of teacher (privileged) makes sense only in connection to the social position of pupil (disadvantaged), and the relationship between these two positions as part of the educational (economic) system has relatively enduring characteristics that shape action and agency in the present. The transformation of structures takes time and includes existing structures showing temporary resistance to transformative action. Structures encourage action that contributes to their continued existence; change is constrained by vested interests which shape the costs and benefits of different actions (Archer, 1995: 206). Vested interests are not causal social forces in the empiricist sense of causality. People can reflect on these interests and, to be effective, they require a certain level of social acceptance (Archer, 1995: 205). However, a person's neglect of the constraints and conditions that come with social positions and the structural context may lead to further limitations on future actions (Archer, 1995: 208). Successful transformation of structures is likely to result not only in a change of structures, but also in a change in these vested interests and the creation of new social possibilities and constraints. These intermittent changes highlight that other analytical dualisms complement the general dualism of structure and agency, including that between actor and social position. To address complexity, we therefore need to learn to habitually consider the structures that exist prior to our thought and actions and how the pre-existing relations between social positions shape our responses to the social context.

As the second proposition that helps map out the key elements of structural–agential interplay, Archer proposes that structures exert causal influences on social interaction, what social theorists term social conditioning: social practices are always processes of restructuration (1995: 140). Restructuration means that as humans attempt to shape their context, they too are shaped. Thirdly, Archer claims that causal relationships between groups and individuals exist at the level of social interaction. We are part of various collectives, from the family to political parties and nation states, and these come with bonds and obligations but are also dependent on our reproduction of these bonds and obligations. Fourthly, social interaction elaborates social structures by modifying the internal and necessary structural relationships and (a) if morphogenesis occurs, developing new ones or (b) if morphostasis continues, reproducing these existing relationships (Archer, 1995: 168–169). The three phases of this 'morphogenetic' approach to society are therefore conditioning, interaction and elaboration or reproduction. We can reuse the model in connection with culture. For Archer, structural emergent properties, social and physical, are to some extent distinct from cultural ones by virtue of their dependence on material resources (1995: 175). I follow Archer in concentrating on the structure–agency problematic, turning to the distinct role of culture where necessary. In a cultural model of transformation, 'cultural system' replaces 'social structure' and 'socio-cultural interaction' replaces 'social interaction' (Archer, 1995: 169). A society remains morphostatic at the macro level if one of the two spheres, culture or structures, experiences large-scale changes, while the other sphere reproduces the pre-existing order – making such claims at the empirical level is again going to be difficult. Under these circumstances, society remains continuous as the changes in culture or structures are simply absorbed: new structures retain the same meaning as the previous material formations, or new ideas and concepts build on the old structures. To give an example, the emergence of environmental concerns does not lead to society-wide changes unless the ideas about a healthy planet come with transformations to the capitalist framework of profit maximisation underpinning modern societies.

Analytical dualism and the morphogenetic approach capture central elements of what I term the second dimension of the ethos of reality, that is, the embeddedness of our engagement with an unjust and violent world in complex processes of social conditioning and transformation. Judgement and complicity scholars seek to understand social conditioning as the source of (and obstacle to) the critical potential of judgements on complicity. Archer tells us that this potential emerges from the subjective contributions of agency in interplay with the objective contributions of structures. Social conditioning always presupposes the existence of relatively enduring social structures, and any social process entails three phases: conditioning, interaction and elaboration or reproduction. We can improve our ethos of reality by becoming more sensitive to the way that culture, social structures such as class or gender and capitalism or the nation state, and individual agency come together to collectively reproduce and change the institutions, processes and practices within society.

Developing a suitable focus on structures

I now delve deeper into analytical dualism and how Archer maintains simultaneously a focus on human agents who shape the world – what Marx described as people 'making their own history' – and the conditions that constrain and enable their capacity to do so – 'but not as they please' (Marx, 2008: 15). I begin with the latter part, the conditions, and note that Archer's analytical dualism is deeply intertwined with the philosophy of social science known as critical realism (CR), which offers critical insights into the independence of social reality from our perception of it. As a philosophy of social science, its argumentation offers a sophisticated conception of a suitable account of structure, from which we can also draw practical conclusions beyond its original context.[4] After all, analytical language and rigour aside, CR does not make a categorical distinction between scientific and non-scientific engagement with reality.

Critical realism, in full 'transcendental realism and critical naturalism', is a variation of scientific realism, particularly concerned with social scientific practices. CR opposes philosophies that adhere to empirical realism, which limits knowledge to what can be experienced. As an alternative, Roy Bhaskar offers transcendental realism, which he defines as follows:

> For transcendental realism, the objects of knowledge [. . .] are neither phenomena (empiricism) nor human constructs imposed upon the phenomena (idealism), but real structures which endure and operate independently of our knowledge, our experience and the conditions which allow us access to them (Bhaskar, 2013: 25).

Transcendental realism, or ontological realism, entails a belief in a mind-independent world, which consists of intransitive objects whose continued existence remains independent from human activity, for example sound. These objects act on the transitive world, including 'the antecedently established facts and theories, paradigms and models, methods and techniques of inquiry available to a particular scientific school or worker' (Bhaskar, 2013: 21), through generative mechanisms. What critical realists mean by mechanisms is best understood by giving some examples: gravity, the structure of an atom, the mechanics of a clock or human rationality. Each captures a causal structure that we attribute to an object or phenomenon to explain how it works. Generative mechanisms can be thought of as the 'way of acting of a thing' (Bhaskar, 2013: 51) (its force), rather than the necessary, general or universal causal connection between specific events (if-then) (Porpora, 2015: 46, 49–50). Key to CR's ontological realism is that reality is stratified into the empirical, the actual and the real (Bhaskar, 2013: 56). Generative mechanisms are part of the intransitive realm of the real, which means that we cannot measure or experience them directly. These mechanisms are constantly active with their own independent powers. As they interact and influence each other, their powers may or may not be actualised and lead to specific effects. The intake of alcohol, for example, is likely to impede the capacity of humans to think rationally (whatever we mean by that). Critical realists refer to the likelihood of a generative mechanism causing a particular effect as a tendency: drinking alcoholic beverages tends to cause 'irrational' behaviour. The empirical layer to reality offers what we experience and measure as observables, that is, a person being drunk. Research into social phenomena must consider all three realms, the real, the actual and the empirical. To maintain the multi-layered character of reality, CR turns to theories of emergence: characteristic of emergent properties for critical realists is that they are unilaterally dependent, taxonomically irreducible and causally irreducible and efficacious (Bhaskar, 2012: 12). This means, in simple terms, that society as an emergent stratum is dependent on the existence of both structures and human agents, but it also has properties and powers irreducible to the specific properties and powers of structures and human agency.

Of course, the current investigation does not seek to map out what social research ought to be like, nor is it concerned with philosophy of (social) science. Nonetheless, the turn to ontological realism gives us a sense of how one can in principle – and at a high level of abstraction that nonetheless captures something essential about human existence – maintain a focus on an independent object irreducible to our knowledge of it, and helps take the world seriously as a causally efficacious object that contributes to our wellbeing. In what follows, I will routinely refer to the importance of accounting for a multi-layered reality, and one key thing I have in mind is the role played by emergence, and by the separability of the empirical, the actual and the real, in how we approach a social context not of our choosing. Accepting that objects are not simply what we make of them (that they do not bend to our judgements upon them) does not mean, however, that they can be the source of unmediated 'objectivity'.

Alongside an insistence on ontological realism, critical realists like Archer embrace epistemological relativism. This form of realism accepts that any conceptualisation of the world is relative to our regional practices at a specific time. Epistemological relativism includes the language we use to describe phenomena, the debates we are participating in and therefore the knowledge we can use to make our claims and observations. Through its commitment to epistemological relativism, CR guards against overstretching predictive claims, as it emphasises the limits of scientific social study and its political character. Critical realists furthermore support methodological pluralism, because they accept that objects of study are multifaceted, dynamic, socially constructed and often unobservable, and they must be identified in their complexity (Kurki, 2010: 139).

CR combines its views on ontology and epistemology with an account of social transformation that seeks to provide a careful attribution of power to agents and avoid individualism/voluntarism or holism/structuralism (Joseph and Wight, 2010: 51). In particular, critical realists point to the fact that humans' emergent power of mind, as irreducible to matter, creates a society that in comparison to the natural world is to a much larger extent an open system. Social scientists cannot make largely open systems subject to laboratory closure (Lawson, 1998: 149). Key to this openness is that people have a capacity for intentionality, and they can reflect critically on their performance, with significant causal implications. Although social structures set limits to human action, they do not pre-determine them. In other words, socialisation describes an achievement rather than an unconscious mechanical process, in which skills, competencies and habits reproduce or transform society (Bhaskar, 1998b: 216).

A commitment to epistemological relativism does not mean that CR reduces the search for knowledge to relativism. Archer and her colleagues commit to the possibility of rational justification (or judgemental rationality). Despite epistemological relativism, according to CR, some theories are always rationally better than others. We can make judgements because the objects of our theories are not reducible to these theories and therefore resist (to some extent) the postulation of innumerable different theories about them. This resistance of reality to our theorisation about it enables the differentiation between good and bad theories (Bhaskar, 1998a: xi). Truth is therefore to some extent tied to practical adequacy and specific contexts, as CR emphasises that knowledge must 'generate expectations about the world' that 'are actually realized' and 'intersubjectively intelligible and acceptable' (Sayer, 1992: 69). To give an example that brings all the points made together, global warming is unobservable in so far as humans can only experience climate change through its effects. Global warming may be the result of one or more generative mechanisms interacting, and for CR it exists independently of us acknowledging it happening. As other effects may interact, global warming could also not be actualised nor be experienced by specific people. However, as is widely accepted, the denial of global warming in leading industrialised countries, or the focus on only specific easily visible effects of global warming, has significant repercussions for any attempt to respond to it, showing the importance of accounting for the multiple layers of reality. CR therefore emphasises the need to consider whether one account of global warming describes reality more adequately than another – which remains independent from any scepticism towards humans' capacity for knowledge and judgement.

In sum, a commitment to ontological realism for CR incorporates the belief that a theory should not only portray a transitive object of knowledge, embedded in specific historical and regional practices, but also refer to an intransitive object of knowledge. Any 'adequate philosophy of science must be capable of [. . .] sustaining both (1) the social character of science and (2) the independence from science of the objects of scientific thought' (Bhaskar, 2013: 24). The 'holy trinity' – ontological realism, epistemological relativism, judgmental rationality – provides the starting point for an appropriate engagement with social ontology, and by extension the issue of social conditioning. What I hope to have made clear, and what

I take from this brief discussion of the key commitments of CR, is that we, scientist and layperson alike, can separate out the contributions of the objective dimension to reality, without losing the connection to a subjectively constituted world. As realism, CR demands attention to a stratified reality with unobservable entities that shape our action in unobservable ways, but critical realists also insist tirelessly on the contingency of judgements and their embeddedness in collective practices of giving meaning to a world.

Archer on being human

Archer complements the focus on ontological realism by spelling out the distinctive qualities of human agency. In line with Arendt's concern with the threat to human plurality, Archer addresses tendencies in society and scholarship to 'evacuate' agency and accredit its powers to 'disembodied texts, the abstract interplay of signs, and the vacuity of eternally deferred meanings' (2000: 315). Her project is the 're-emergence of humanity, meaning that due acknowledgement is given to the properties and powers of real people forged in the real world' (Archer, 2000: 306). At the same time, her realism is explicitly non-anthropocentric. This is because of the underlying critical realist insistence that we need to separate out 'what is' from 'how humans perceive it' and that humans share their embodied engagement with the world with other animals. Archer therefore adds to the object-focus a subject-focus without falling for an 'impossible' subjectivism, that is, the belief that all that matters is what matters to a person (2000: 23; cf. Chernilo, 2017: 197). I will now introduce two important conceptual distinctions that frame Archer's argument on human agency. The first distinguishes between the human being as person, as social agent and as social actor, while the second distinguishes between humans' engagements with the natural, practical and social (or specifically discursive) orders of reality.

Archer offers a stratified view of being human whereby the formation and differentiation of personhood is fundamental to humans' way of being in the world before the acquisition of language (2000: 122). Human beings are persons in so far as they have a self-perceived identity – a sense of self – based on a continuous consciousness (Archer, 1995: 282).[5] The sense of self is best understood as self-awareness, that 'it is the *same* self who has interests upon which constraints and enablements impinge *and* that how they react today will affect what interests they will have tomorrow' (Archer, 1995: 282, original emphasis). A person develops this sense of self through the early use of bodily powers, which leads them to differentiate between their body and the environment, and which they keep throughout their lives (Archer, 2000: 125–126). The capacity for self-awareness and critical self-reflection, the fact that we are 'evaluative beings', makes us a source of social innovation (what Arendt called natality): 'human beings have the unique potential to conceive of new social forms. Because of this, society can never be held to shape them entirely' (Archer, 1995: 289).

A person's sense of self emerges from their engagement with the natural, as opposed to practical and social, order of reality.[6] The orders of reality are interrelated, but they also pose different, and often conflicting, challenges and potentials for human agency. Furthermore, in everyday life these orders are often difficult to separate, but this should not lead to, for example, the conclusion that other orders are reducible to the social. Instead, each order comes with distinct forms of knowledge – embodied knowledge that helps us secure our physical wellbeing; practical knowledge that allows us to master objects; and discursive knowledge which can produce a sense of self-worth in the social order – and brings with it distinct concerns and affective cues that lead to different clusters of emotions, which provide commentaries upon our concerns (Archer, 2000: 195, 203). For instance, in the natural order, we experience first-order emotions such as physical pleasure and pain – emerging from the body–environment relation – viscerally (Archer, 2000: 199). Concerns together with emotions enable a prioritisation of what we care about and thus constitute the prism through which individuals interpret their life (Chalari, 2009: 151).[7]

Through the distinctions, Archer challenges the dominance of an approach in sociology that defends the primacy of language and the social order for the development of human agency (2000: 121). At the same time, she embraces an emphasis on human relationality and sociability, as visible in her next distinction, between actors and agents. Human beings are also agents, who are part of a collective with certain aims and privileges, prior to becoming actors. We are agents by virtue of our position in society, for example our 'working-class' background amongst other social distinctions. Agents, as groups or collectives, have properties irreducible to individual people; agency is a relational property of people (Archer, 1995: 274).

This means that although humans have a relatively independent sense of self, personhood is always already embedded in a context that shapes the logic of future action. The social actor, in contrast, emerges out of a person's active pursuit of goals in society; an actor – always singular – is irreducible to agency – always collectively held – and irreducible to the person (Archer, 1995: 280). Socialisation entails that humans become aware of the distinction between self and others, and between the social and the non-social, and that they use performative and memory capacities to learn how to take part in social practices (Archer, 2000: 126).

In summary, to respond to complicity we need a greater awareness of the people who engage in social transformation and reproduction. Following Archer, such awareness must focus on our distinct personhood, as a crucial source of social innovation and of the 'it-seems-to-me'. We must also consider our engagement with different orders of reality, the concerns and interests that come with them, and the collective identities that we are part of and that we continuously reshape through our action. A focus on the distinct properties and mechanisms of structure and agency thus amounts to a commitment to a mind-independent, stratified reality alongside a concern with an embodied, self-aware subject that emerges out of a varied engagement with the world.

THE MEDIATION BETWEEN STRUCTURE AND AGENCY THROUGH REFLEXIVITY

As the final piece of Archer's dualism, I turn to her work on reflexivity.[8] The concept of reflexivity has become popular in recent years as an external phenomenon attributed to social systems rather than individuals (Archer, 2008: 2).[9] In contrast, Archer considers reflexivity as an internal phenomenon (constituted by an internal conversation) that mediates between structure and agency. She claims that reflexivity possesses genuine interiority, and is ontologically subjective and causally efficacious. It is exactly these irreducible, distinctive personal properties of reflexivity that make it an important mechanism of mediation required for an 'adequate account of social conditioning' (Archer, 2003: 16).

Reflexivity is a personal emergent property, which gives people authorship over their own social projects and makes them active agents (Archer, 2003: 34, 94). Internal conversation is the talk all people 'have with themselves, within their own heads, usually silently and usually from an early age' (Archer, 2007: 2). It provides a prism through which to negotiate between the internal and the external context, and between the personal and the social. Over time, the reflexive practice produces a modus vivendi that responds to the varied concerns that arise from the three orders of reality. This modus vivendi frames how a person perceives a context. Archer terms the failure to formulate such a prism, through which to evaluate the various demands that our context puts on us, 'fractured reflexivity' (2003: 164). The notion of fractured reflexivity overlaps with the notion of thoughtlessness in that both lead to an inability to act and judge by engaging with one's context. In Archer's terms, for fractured reflexives the sequence – concerns, projects and practices – becomes distorted and leaves the person in a state of passivity and emotional distress.[10]

The focus on the internal mediation between structure and agency through reflexivity has led to a debate about the relationship between habitus as Bourdieu conceived it and Archer's reflexivity. Some suggest the two projects complement each other in specific ways (Adams, 2003, 2006, 2007; Caetano, 2015; Chandler, 2013; Elder-Vass, 2007, 2010; Farrugia, 2013; Fleetwood, 2008; Mouzelis, 2008; Mutch, 2004; Sayer, 2009; Sweetman, 2003; Vogler, 2016; Wimalasena and Marks, 2019). Archer, however, rejects the hybridisation of the two key mechanisms for social conditioning at the ontological, theoretical and empirical levels. Critics of her position suggest that she reduces habitus to routine, obscures the creative potential of the non-cognitive and more generally provides a problematic preference for activity over passivity (Burkitt, 2016). Archer underplays the role of structures by describing them as only affecting the projects human beings reflect upon, but not the reflection itself and how socialisation can also happen internally (Caetano, 2015: 66), and overemphasises the private nature of reflexivity (Burkitt, 2012: 464). Due to these clear lines drawn on both sides, I think of habitus and reflexivity, as Archer and Bourdieu conceive of them, as different tools that help capture distinct elements of the social conditioning process with a greater emphasis on the structural and agential contribution to the mediation process. At the same time, I want to show that Archer continues the emphasis in previous sections on avoiding an impossible objectivism and subjectivism by foregrounding the situated character of reflexivity. This comes out in her empirical research into patterns to reflexivity.

Archer provides comprehensive empirical research into reflexivity through internal conversation using two series of explorative interviews, conducted in Coventry and at her department at the University of Warwick (Archer, 2003, 2007, 2012) – recent research in the post-colonial context of Sri Lanka has also indicated the wider applicability of these modes beyond the Western context (Wimalasena, 2017, 2022). This research has enabled her to identify three main modes of reflexivity, alongside what she categorises as underdeveloped and fractured reflexivity (Archer, 2012: 250). The three modes are communicative reflexivity (CoR), autonomous reflexivity (AuR) and meta-reflexivity (MeR) (Archer, 2003: 165). The research indicated that these modes of reflexivity are distributed unevenly across society and that most participants had one distinctive dominant mode, either communicative, autonomous or meta-, with a small group possessing two dominant modes of reflexivity (Archer, 2007: 94). I introduce their key characteristics briefly, before elaborating further on the relevance of these insights for the argument put forward in this book.

Communicative reflexives (CoRs) externalise elements of their internal conversation through discussion and the solving of problems interpersonally, as they mistrust their private deliberation (Archer, 2003: 167). They adopt a 'thought and talk' reflexive approach that relies on contextual continuity, surrounding themselves with an extended circle of trusted friends and often a large family that defy modern atomising tendencies. CoRs consequently show 'smooth dovetailing of concerns' (Archer, 2003: 169) by prioritising family and friends over other concerns and other potential sources of happiness. Communicative reflexives seek to maintain their social horizon, once identified. They therefore tend to be apolitical as they believe that they have already established their desired micro-cosmos (Archer, 2003: 184). Dominant CoRs constituted 21 per cent of the Coventry sample of interviewees (Archer, 2007: 27). In her sample of students from the sociology department at Warwick University, Archer identified CoRs to be the smallest dominant group of reflexivity with 13 per cent, shrinking in their final year to 9 per cent (2012: 128). This can be explained by the group's tendency not to recruit and the development of students' reflexivity into other modes throughout their studies.

Autonomous reflexives (AuRs), in contrast, are decisive and self-assured and see their deliberative process as self-sufficient, partly out of suspicion of alternative positions. AuRs are willing to include others' expertise on their own terms (Archer, 2003: 210). Similar to CoRs, they are good at dovetailing their concerns but are individualists and search for contextual discontinuity and 'supra-contextual knowledge' (Archer, 2003: 251). The AuRs have articulate social concerns and yet lack relational goods as they were 'parented by *two individuals rather than by a couple*' (Archer, 2012: 168, original emphasis). Their reflexive approach is instead instrumental, and task-oriented. In contrast to the other groups, AuRs are uncritical of employment in corporate enterprises or governmental bureaucracy but see it as a means to an end; they incorporate ethical concerns into their personal agendas (Archer, 2012: 188). They therefore represent for Archer the Third Way/Lib–Lab position in politics (2012: 205).

Meta-reflexives (MeRs) – who constituted 20 per cent of the Coventry sample and 39 per cent of the sociology student sample – use their reflexive deliberation to interrogate their sense of self (Archer, 2003: 255). They are critical of the possibility of effective action in society and problematise the social order instead of normalising or internalising it. MeRs' reflexive approach is therefore value-oriented. They receive relational goods, especially familial stability, support for university entry and financial help (Archer, 2012: 245), but their MeR develops as they encounter mixed messages concerning normative claims about the social order, leaving them to find their own position from an early age. Meta-reflexives had to disengage from their natal context first, to be able to re-engage with the social order on their own terms and concerns. MeRs are particularly adamant about the importance of education as a source of finding their own identity (Archer, 2012: 246). Disenchanted with politics because of the similarity between parties (and what they perceive as a general failure of governance), they emphasise voluntarism and charity, and at the global level, support social movements such as Fridays for Future.

Drawing on this brief overview, one might conclude that we all need to cultivate meta-reflexivity as the suitable pre-condition for reflective forms of judgement about complicity. In contrast, autonomous reflexives' instrumentalism seems particularly detrimental to responsiveness and responsibility. There is certainly something to this observation and Archer, like Arendt, recognises these tendencies. As I elaborate further in the following section, Archer underlines the increase in reflexivity and meta-reflexives in our times. Both theorists thus make connections between politics, morality and thinking that raise worries about 'intellectualism' (cf. Walsh, 2017). However, Archer also adds significant caveats to her claims on reflexivity. Reflexivity is only one, albeit important, property of human agency. The dominant mode of reflexivity that a person exhibits is not statically linked to socio-occupational backgrounds or stable from birth onwards. In addition, none of the participants in the interviews scored 0 on any of the modes, which shows that they only varied in the degrees of possessing each mode of reflexivity. Indeed, Archer (2010) highlights that the demands on reflexivity vary according to the order of reality, with the social sphere the least habituated, and that humans use different modes of reflexivity depending on the context. This complicates any conclusions that we might wish to draw from this explorative research. Instead of hypothesising further about the 'suitability' of different modes of reflexivity for making judgements about complicity, I conclude that Archer's research affirms key points of Arendt's underdeveloped account of thinking. She shares a concern with fractured reflexivity and its effects on humans and society, and she affirms, and adds concreteness to, the heterogeneity of the person, emerging out of the patterned internal conversation, that underscores Arendt's commitment to a thick conception of plurality.

In articulating an account of reflexivity, Archer also moves beyond Arendt's insights in important ways. Arendt turns to Socrates for a sense of everyday thinking and thus privileges an ideal form of thought (Arendt, 2003: 167–168). This leads judgement scholars to turn to Bourdieu's notion of habitus as a counterweight. Archer's sociological approach, in contrast, upholds her dualism by tying thought to a 'functional general theory of society' (Walsh, 2017: 171), where each mode plays a different economic, social and political role that shapes the trajectory of society and is shaped by it. Archer argues not only that humans think differently, but also that these variations have larger, micro- and macro-scale, implications for society. The modes of reflexivity produce distinct stances towards opportunities for social mobility and these reflexive stances '*constitute* the macro–micro link' (Archer, 2003: 343, original emphasis), because they provide one of the most basic means of orientation of subjects to society. In the case of CoRs, their modus vivendi is continuous with the subject's original context and tends towards social immobility. They tend towards contextual continuity and are willing to sacrifice social opportunities to maintain their natal context. AuRs tend towards contextual discontinuity and react strategically towards social mobility. They reveal a self-disciplinary stance towards social tasks (Archer, 2007: 190). Lastly, MeRs tend towards contextual incongruity and exhibit subversive stances towards social mobility. They are characterised by volatility, both through recurrent contextual incongruity and a tendency to frequently requalify, leading to a voluntarily chosen sideways mobility and a gravitation towards work in the third sector, for example education, social care and charity work (Archer, 2007: 252). They react to tasks in a self-transcendent and questioning manner (Archer, 2007: 316). Together these patterns shape how responsiveness is interpreted and adopted and we must learn to attend to these differences in thinking through complicity and how we respond to it. They are not simply a burden to our capacity to judge and act, but essential to our capacity to engage with an unjust and violent world. Which is not to suggest that they cannot change, as Archer shows in relation to the late modern context.

The late modern context

Late modernity refers to the period from the 1980s onwards that began with the launch of the World Wide Web and the 'expansion of multi-national corporations and the deregulation of finance markets' (Archer, 2012: 4).[11] It is characterised by 'giving way to a morphogenesis that is increasingly unbound from its morphostatic fetters' (Archer, 2012: 4). To reiterate, morphostasis occurs in a society when the interaction of agency, structure and culture leads to an overall reproduction of the status quo. This state allows for morphogenesis in one sphere, for example the transformation and emergence of new cultural entities, whereas the overall formation is characterised by continuity. At a high level of abstraction, developed countries can be identified as having started off from morphostatic social formations. Societies were governed by negative feedback loops and a lack of alternatives in both the cultural and structural orders that together discouraged innovation. Modern formations are characterised by simultaneous morphostasis in one sphere and morphogenesis in another. The contextual discontinuity caused by urbanisation or industrialisation continued to enable habituation, due to the relative slowness of the overall changes in modern society.

The crucial question for critical realists is what the concrete generative mechanisms are that helped morphogenesis take off and become increasingly unbound in late modernity – but never fully – from the maintenance of the overall morphostatic framework of pre-modern and modern society. The synergetic cooperation between science and capitalist enterprises from the 1980s onwards provides a suitable example of a generative mechanism that helped transcend the cyclical motion of morphostatic society (Archer, 2014a: 12–13). This generative mechanism also emblematically captures critical realist efforts to show the potential for positive social transformation, contra the often negative portrayal of the move towards late modernity. Technology linked capitalist innovation and university research in a hitherto unknown manner. While this interplay between science and capitalism is open to exploitation by capitalist enterprises, it also provides the starting point for new alternative strategies, as deployed by techno-scientific 'diffusionists', for example the founders of Wikipedia.

Particularly valuable in Archer's conception of late modernity is her insight into how different modes of reflexivity respond to the late modern context – with significant implications for their social mobility and distribution in society. Archer identifies a new imperative of reflexivity, as 'increasingly all have to draw upon their socially dependent but nonetheless personal powers of reflexivity in order to define their course(s) of action in relation to the novelty of their circumstances' (2012: 1). Instead of a form of institutionalised individualism, the reflexive imperative is based on an increasing and accelerated double morphogenesis of both structure and culture, leading to almost constant social transformation (Archer, 2012: 41–42). The far-reaching implications of the reflexive imperative are particularly visible in attempts to protect oneself from change, which in late modernity becomes itself part of the process of reflexive deliberation, in full awareness of the increasing costs of such a choice (Archer, 2012: 305). To keep the current socio-economic and cultural context, a person can no longer rely on old shortcuts and instead has to constantly reflect upon the changes in society and attempt to stop or follow them. People therefore no longer reproduce the status quo unquestioningly over generations. Instead, it is constantly and consciously maintained, which leads to higher risks and costs.

These new circumstances are more beneficial for certain dominant modes of reflexivity, and, as a result, a decline or increase of different modes of reflexivity is likely. CoRs are particularly unprepared for these developments, with their aim for contextual continuity and dovetailing of opportunities, which leads to a decline in their numbers in society (Archer, 2012: 165). Change has simply become too widespread for intergenerational socialisation to work. The unstoppable decline in CoRs will leave space for an increase in AuRs, who benefit from their strategic attitude to the new options of social mobility available to them (Archer, 2012: 205). The contextual incongruity and extensive requirement to reflect deliberatively could eventually lead to a dominance of the morphogenetic social order by meta-reflexivity, alongside an increase in fractured reflexives. The increase in fractured reflexivity coincides with the decrease of CoRs, leaving fractured reflexives with a double negative burden: internal anxiety and disorientation without external, collective support, traditionally provided through CoRs' social solidarity (Archer, 2012: 190).

In summary, I discussed how Archer identifies a morphogenesis of both structure and culture, which results in widespread social transformation (2012: 4–5). Change has become too far-reaching to be responded to by intergenerational socialisation and, in consequence, a new imperative of reflexivity emerges and transforms the distribution of modes of reflexivity in society. These thoughts on late modernity suggest that the structural context has indeed changed significantly and has had a marked impact on agency. In judging complicity, it is important that we do not perceive agency as a static and continuous thing that exercises responsiveness and responsibility in a pre-set, appropriate way, but that we take into account how these transformations create new opportunities and challenges for tackling injustice and violence, from rising inequality to the move back to the mainstream of anti-Semitic sentiments.

Concluding thoughts

This chapter has focused on the issue of social conditioning to develop the second dimension of an ethos of reality. Mirroring the argumentative moves made in Chapter 2, I depart from the assumption that social conditioning is essential to our capacity to engage with reality, but that certain conflating tendencies in society and scholarship risk undermining this capacity. I discuss critically how the ethics of responsiveness utilises the emphasis on the interpenetration of structural injustice and responsive agency to highlight the limits to human responsiveness and to construct different ways these limits could be overcome. Utilising Archer's critique of central conflation and duality, with a degree of abstraction from its original context, I argue that this emphasis on interpenetration is important but in its current form risks oscillating between recursive structures, unconsciously reproduced, and responsive agency. Against these conflating tendencies, Archer suggests that we can improve our engagement with reality by accounting for the analytically and temporally distinct role of agency and structure in society. A critical realist, Archer defends both objectivism and subjectivism: the practice of attending to mind-independent objects that are stratified into observable and non-observable layers and the practice of attending to what it means to be human – a stratified agent with a sense of self, which is embodied, relational, emotional and capable of evaluation and innovation. The concluding section of the chapter turned to the key mediation process between agency and structure, reflexivity, as a subjective, causally efficacious and internal phenomenon. Through Archer, we gain paradigmatic empirical research that brings to light the stratified character of reflexivity from within which judgement develops. Archer's research into late modernity also reveals how varied human responses to different transformations in late modernity are. It reveals that the increased cultural and structural transformation put new weight on humans' capacity to think – and by extension to judge and act upon the world.

I take from Archer that this second dimension to an ethos of reality requires attentiveness to the dualism of structure–agency or, in short, objectivism, subjectivism and their mediation through reflexivity alongside the structural dispositions highlighted by the responsiveness approach. A focus on the distinct properties and mechanisms of structure and agency amounts to a commitment to a mind-independent, stratified reality alongside a concern with subjectivity that is embodied, emotional, relational, capable of social innovation and with a sense of self, emerging out of a varied engagement with a stratified world. The dualist approach enables a person to attend to the object and the subject of social reality, without denying their interrelation or the crucial role that a public sphere plays in identifying, attributing and acknowledging complicity.

Notes

1. Structure is an ambiguous concept. It can refer to anything from stable patterns of aggregate behaviour to systems of human relations amongst social positions (cf. Elder-Vass, 2010; Porpora, 1989). Typical examples

include class, gender, race, disability or more generally the capitalist system. Agency is a similarly opaque term. At the most general level, agency refers to a person's ability to act and respond to their social context – which includes a capacity for non-action and passivity.
2. In identifying this problematic duality between non-reflective everyday agency and critical responsiveness in moments of crisis, I do not wish to take sides in the debate over the interpretation of Bourdieu's habitus. Whether habitus is ultimately a much more creative and dynamic mechanism, as Loïc Wacquant (2016) highlights, or not, is not crucial for my investigation. Instead, I point out that responsiveness scholars provide a problematic framework, in part by drawing on Bourdieu's habitus, which oscillates between a rigid society largely unconsciously reproduced and a hyperactive agent that is able to – albeit always at risk of failure – experience suffering and act upon it. To avoid this oscillation, they first need to provide an account of the emergence of responsive agency, which also includes a clarification on the social conditioning of that agency.
3. Emergence entails that properties and powers of one stratum (structure and agency) are anterior to those of others (society), precisely because the latter emerge from the former over time. After the emergence, the powers and properties defining and distinguishing the strata have relative autonomy from one another and exert independent causal influences that are the subject of study of analytical dualism (Archer, 1995: 14). A (relatively) open system is characterised by producing outcomes that are not fully determined by the aggregation of its components.
4. Its contributions have to be weighed against its shortcomings. CR does not provide a theory of politics, and relies on at times vague core concepts or research criteria and limited insights into how to address judgement rationality and methodological pluralism (cf. Kurki, 2010: 144).
5. Archer relies on the Lockean formula of selfhood as body plus continuity in consciousness, but merely insists on a sufficient rather than a perfect continuity (2000: 137). The 'eidetic and the procedural [memories], supply a continual resort for defining our selfhood, above and beyond our bodily identity. They are thus the modern ways of specifying what a neo-Lockean means by the "continuity of consciousness", which is something distinct from perfect recall' (Archer, 2000: 152).
6. The similarities to Arendt's thought are clearly visible, starting with their distinction between the biological/natural, practical/fabricating and social/political spheres and activities. Of course, Arendt's emphasis on the role of speech and appearance goes beyond Archer's concerns; nonetheless, both share the concern with the failure in modern philosophy to give primacy to practice (Archer, 2000: 145; Arendt, 1998; Sindic, 2013).

7. Ian Burkitt suggests (2012: 463) that Archer limits emotions to individualised commentaries, which misses the role of relational emotions, that is, the way humans emotionally identify with others and how this affects their internal conversation. Reflexive dialogues entail feelings and emotions not just as 'attendants to reflexivity; they are the basis and motive of reflexive thought, [...] our thoughts are always coloured by emotion so that we never see the world in a neutral way' (Burkitt, 2012: 469).
8. Arendt pointed to the mental activities of thinking and willing as central places of contestation in post-foundational modernity, but her philosophical treatment of reflexivity remained underdeveloped. Archer shares this view on Arendt's account of thinking and challenges Arendt's suggestion that the inner dialogue resembles talking to a friend (Archer, 2007: 67). Archer's research in turn can be criticised for linking reflexivity too closely to its implication for action, neglecting the distinct role of thinking captured by Arendt and discussed in Chapter 2 (cf. Walsh, 2015). Archer distinguishes reflection as the 'action of a subject towards an object', for example reflecting on the merits of 'Brexit' or whether it is safe to cross a road, from the self-referential character of reflexivity in the form 'subject-object-subject' (Archer, 2009: 2), that is: what are the effects of 'Brexit' for me, or is this road safe for me to cross? Clearly, the boundary between these two categories is hazy. I refer to reflective judgement primarily to indicate a focus on representative thinking and the engagement with a plurality of perspectives.
9. The popularity of terminology such as reflexive sociology or reflexive modernity culminated in the extended reflexivity thesis in social theory, which identifies an increase in reflexivity – referring to a need and ability to shape one's own identity – in Western society over the last few decades (cf. Adams, 2006: 512). What this thesis entails may vary extensively. Giddens and Ulrich Beck, for example, identify the lack of social structure as a basic feature of late modernity, leading to heightened reflexivity (Beck and Beck-Gernsheim, 2002; Giddens, 1991). Archer and other critical realists in turn take issue with their claims of institutionalised individualism (Archer, 2012: 3).
10. Fractured reflexivity may cause drifting without developing an active agency, which can be resolved through changes in the context of reflexivity (Archer, 2012: 290). For example, impeded reflexives, a sub-group of fractured reflexives, can sometimes substitute their rejected natal background with new friend relations in order to exercise their preferred mode of reflexivity. Expressive subjects, another such sub-group, lack a personal identity formation process, which would help mediate external information and shape internal concerns and emotions; they, however, do not see this as a lack (Archer, 2012: 281).

11. Archer's theorisation on late modernity responds to the influential work on late modernity by Giddens, Beck, Zygmunt Baumann and Hartmut Rosa. The first three theorists have been highly influential by accounting for late modernity as liquid modernity (Bauman), risk society (Beck) and high or late modernity (Giddens) (Bauman, 2013; Beck et al., 1994; Giddens, 1991). A common association of these three thinkers highlights their shared transcendence of modern class analysis through a focus on late modern individualism (cf. Atkinson, 2008; Dawson, 2010). Rosa (2013) provides a comprehensive critical theory analysis of the move towards late modernity that identifies a change in the temporal structures of society at the heart of this last stage of modernisation. For a critique of their approaches from a critical realist perspective, see Archer (2014a).

CHAPTER FIVE

Responding to complicity through an improved ethos of reality

The previous chapters have shown that judgement is not merely a capacity to apply moral or legal standards to a particular case of potentially complicitous behaviour, in order to decide whether a person has acted in morally blameworthy or legally culpable ways. Judgement is a reflective and reflexive process and practice that we use (often with little deliberation) on specific cases to make sense of the times we live in. As Hannah Arendt (1981a: 193) underlined, judgements position us in relation to (and within) the common world and give it, and our understanding of the world, contours. This has two implications. Firstly, that when we judge that something is unjust, 'we thereby also judge that action should be taken against it', as Iris Marion Young (2011: 180) astutely notes. Our judgements about injustice reveal to us and others our moral stance and are therefore both a source of responsibility that we bear by virtue of contributing (often involuntarily) to unjust societies and the subject of criticisms for failing to respond to our complicity. Of course, as the ethics of responsiveness showed, this sense of responsibility is met with an equally strong urge to disavow responsibility in our judgements on complicity. The second implication is that our judgements on complicity are integral to, informed by and dependent on the individual and collective effort to come to understand reality within a community (however conceived). At the level of the person judging complicity, their judgements are part of an ethos of reality, the habitual stance and prism we develop that filters information and positions us towards the world to allow us to address it (more or less) adequately. The second point is central to this book and in this chapter, I outline the ethos of reality and its role in responding to complicity.

Key features of an ethos of reality

My formulation of an ethos of reality draws on Arendt's fragmentary realism, which I introduced in Chapter 2. Patricia Owens describes this realism as an 'ethic of reality' and as 'a form of "realism" in which attentiveness to reality itself and the cultivation of a character trait in which to face and enlarge one's sense of reality are ends in themselves with serious ethical implications' (Owens, 2008: 105). The shift in focus becomes clearer when we turn to a second scholar of Arendt's realism, Rei Terada (2008), who challenges suggestions that Arendt lacked an ethics to frame her response to the trial of Adolf Eichmann, and totalitarianism more generally. Rather, Terada emphasises, Arendt suggests that when they were most needed, morality and ethics proved to be nothing more than complex systems of customs and habits (Arendt, 2003: 50). They are therefore better captured using the Latin and Greek terms *mores* and *ethos*, that is, as something akin to social norms. From this, I draw three important conclusions.

At a general level, the concept of ethos or ethic of reality has an explicit ethical dimension in the sense that our engagement with reality and the status of the intersubjectively constituted reality are not just the backdrop of moral and ethical deliberations – especially in the form of an unfortunate constraint to our moral reasoning and willingness to tackle injustice that we must find ways to overcome. Our ability and willingness to face up to and come to understand reality should itself be the subject of ethical and moral considerations.

At the level of society, we cannot disentangle the moral standards we develop about what constitutes injustice and violence from a community's engagement with reality, which is not to suggest that they are reducible to dominant views held in a society at any one time. Instead, to tackle injustice and violence we must also work on our capacity to form an opinion and connect it to the wellbeing of the common world(s). Violence and injustice constitute one important way in which a common reality deteriorates but they require a particular way of thinking about them to capture the necessary focus on the wellbeing of a common world. Inequality and injustice direct our attention to the systematic disadvantaging of individual people, which is morally problematic; yet we must focus additionally on the long-term and devastating impact on their capacity to participate equally in the shaping of society, for instance by denying marginalised groups adequate representation in elections or legislative processes. Violence in the forms of the destruction of the planet, and of mass society, which for instance punishes extraordinary bodies (cf. Garland-Thomson, 2009), are morally questionable in themselves, but we must again consider their devastating impact on reality and our capacity to view it from different perspectives. This distinct ethical dimension is key to Arendt's at times problematic separation of the social from the political.

At the level of our individual stance, an ethos of reality is not a stable pre-given framework of principles but a moving, complex stance we develop individually and collectively towards the world that is always prone to failure. Our stance towards reality is unique to us as a person, although never truly individual or personal. It is also, crucially, open to improvement. This chapter focuses on this normative potential for improving our stance towards reality and on what it means to care for the wellbeing of the common world, rather than seeking to provide a systematic approach to how each of us develops an ethos of reality from childhood onwards. Nonetheless, before I explore this normative dimension further, here are some important markers that delineate my interpretation of what an ethos of reality necessarily entails.

Each of us has a particular ethos of reality, a multi-faceted stance towards the world that is the by-product of our everyday engagement with reality and with the relationship between our self and the world. This prism on reality patterns the way we respond to demands put on us by our context, whether we react positively, negatively, hopefully, out of fear, proactively or cautiously, or even if we do not recognise the demand in the first place. We might best think of an ethos of reality as combining elements of Margaret Archer's modus vivendi, which arises out of a person's attempts to respond appropriately to all three orders of reality (the natural, the practical and the social order), and Arendt's community sense, which is connected to the shared meanings and objects in a society. It may therefore not be one coherent thing, but several interlinked stances and prisms that are to varying degrees personal and social, and within and outside the body. The ethos emerges out of the way we approach others and their individual contributions to our society, the relationships between us and the need to act together, and the social and cultural structures and material objects that shape the way we make our way through the world.

Our ethos is positional, an expression of our position in relation to the world. Judging, as the activity that positions us in the world, plays an integral role for developing an ethos of reality, even as it simultaneously provides a key source for critical engagement with how we respond to reality. All stances towards reality are therefore to some extent reflexive, as past deliberations and judgements affect our position towards the future and we always converse internally even if that conversation bears little on the acts pursued and takes many different forms. The ethos is also relational (constituted by our relationship with others and the world), embodied (experienced and dependent on our body) and emotional (coloured by our feelings and what affects us through and through). It is structured by a person's context and habitus, but it is also distinctly individual, subjective and causally efficacious. It crystallises as we seek to complete the mundane tasks of our life, including eating or working, just as much as when we participate in political activities, including voting or the discussions we have about how society should tackle issues of common interest, for example social injustice. Some activities may, of course, be particularly relevant for the development of an ethos in that they directly concern someone's engagement with a shared reality and what a political community has in common. Yet, it will ultimately depend on the specific person, their background and the humans and non-humans around them, as to what has (had) the most influence on their individual way of being in the world.

Our ethos of reality is shaped by two facts of the human condition that are central to our establishment of a sense of reality. The first fact describes humans' experience of reality through the interplay of structures with human agency, the coming together of objective and subjective dimensions to reality. Archer terms this the 'vexatious' fact of social reality, as 'it is part and parcel of daily experience to feel both free and enchained, capable of shaping our own future and yet confronted by towering, seemingly impersonal, constraints' (Archer, 1995: 65). This fact is easily undermined by modern conflating[1] strategies to overemphasise structure, agency or their inseparability, which we encountered in the form of a duality of structure and agency and in methodological individualism. The challenge is therefore to accommodate and explain both: genuine experiences of agential and structural possibilities and constraints to making our way through the world. A suitable response to the vexatious fact of social reality must promote a possible objectivism and subjectivism, literally a subject- and object-focus. By this I mean that theorists and judges alike must account for a multi-layered, mind-independent reality that is shaped by unobservable mechanisms and a stratified agent that is embodied, relational, emotional, with a sense of self and the capacity to mediate the internal and external world through an internal conversation.

The second fact of the human condition is that humans – in plural – share a world which, as world-in-common, can give their lives meaning. Arendtian scholars term the normative implications that arise out of this second fact 'worldliness'. Worldliness is at risk if we reduce human plurality to a focus on individual or aggregate concerns. Attentiveness to the plural fact of human existence entails an awareness of both the distinctiveness and the sameness of human agency, and the existence of a common world that needs to be continuously rebuilt and protected. The common world is not the same as 'reality'; it refers to the objects, structures, culture and interactions that become common by viewing and judging them in relation to the plurality of distinct perspectives in a community. Commonness is both an ontological fact and an achievement, arising out of realising the potential in human plurality. The three features of Arendt's thicker notion of plurality – sameness, distinction and common world – are best thought of in relation to her metaphor of the common world as a table (Arendt, 1998: 108). A table both provides a physical connection between people who are sat around it and keeps them at a distance by providing a separation between them. Without that table, or generally any object or material that divides and connects, people sitting at a distance from each other would seem to some extent disconnected. In choosing to sit closer together to bridge the empty space between them, they would lose their ability to both share views and remain at a distance from each other. The common world as a table both holds humans together, ensuring that they remain connected through shared concerns and interests, and separates them sufficiently to protect their distinct standpoints from forced convergence, as visible, for Arendt, in mass society.

The metaphor of the table also reveals the intimate relationship between pluralism and dualism. To uphold plurality and the importance of a shared common world requires that other elements of society, physical, cultural and social structures and other people and non-humans, are given equal weight in our engagement with reality alongside our own judgements and actions. This is, of course, what individualism traditionally failed to do, due to its reduction of social explanation to the capacities of singular powerful agents. More precisely, to uphold plurality and the importance of a shared common world requires a serious engagement with the simultaneous separation and interplay of structure and agency. Put provocatively, on the one hand if we embrace Arendtian pluralism without a focus on the interplay of the distinct causal contributions of structure and agency, we risk falling for conflation and, if done systematically and routinely, conflationism. Conflationism obscures what pluralism entails, that is, not just a plurality of perspectives but a common world that arises out of confronting similar objects and events that shape interrelated interests and concerns. On the other hand, if we concentrate on the dualism of structure and agency, without analysis of what it means to have a world in common, we risk embracing reduction and reductionism. Reductionism obscures social conditioning as it fails to capture an important part of social reality: its collective constitution. It is by pointing to the necessity of avoiding both these pitfalls for an ethos of reality that this book contributes a fresh perspective to the literature.

This short summary of what I take to be core features of an ethos of reality shares affinities with the dispositional ethics of responsiveness. Both approaches reject conceptualising responsibility in terms of universal moral standards and focus our attention on the practice of situated human agency as the source of ethical behaviour. However, I want to shift the focus of complicity scholarship further away from the problem of why the privileged remain unresponsive to injustice, towards our ability to improve our ethos of reality and create a hospitable common world along the two dimensions of dualism and pluralism. It is important not to overstretch the differences between the approaches: many of the scholars I engage with, from Hayward to Young, are keenly aware of the importance of improving public engagement with reality for tackling injustice. Other scholars who draw on Young's seminal book on responsibility and complicity, notably José Medina (2013), similarly discuss how injustice and violence undermine collective opinion formation processes. In response, Medina calls for an epistemic resistance that constantly interrogates the operations of the social imagination and imaginary in the form of white ignorance, that is, a racialised form of not-knowing as knowing (Medina, 2013: 259). I am sympathetic to such a call – also considering how easy it is to end up with exclusionary conceptions of reality and politics, as I highlighted in relation to Arendt in Chapter 2. This book sets out the need for an improved ethos of reality to guide (and benefit from) responses to complicity in the mode of, for instance, epistemic resistance.

Judging complicity as part of an improved ethos of reality

Up to this point I have sought to delineate in broad strokes what an ethos of reality entails. I now sketch the role that an improved ethos of reality could play in responding to complicity. To get a sense of the shift in judgement on complicity this book is proposing, let me turn briefly to an illustrative example – complicity in the use of plastic in the food and drink industry. At the most basic level, the problem is as follows: every year, large amounts of plastic, for example in the form of bottles, are not recycled and end up in the ocean, causing the death of animals, which either get entangled in the plastic or digest it. Plastic pollution encompasses macro-, micro- and nanoplastic debris and consists in the 'intrusion or invasion by plastic materials (that is, polymeric systems), either through direct introduction or degradation processes, of environments (to which they are not native) to negatively or undesirably impact such environments' (Iroegbu et al., 2021: 19344). In light of this problem, how should we, for example as consumers, identify, attribute and acknowledge complicity?

Here is a brief summary of the different possible responses discussed thus far. If we subscribe to the legal-moral philosophical way of pinning down what we mean by complicity, we are likely to focus on those that are clearly identifiable as contributing to wrongdoing. We identify a clear-cut wrong – the long-lasting effects of plastic on the environment – and specific, powerful actors that sustain it, for example the wilful action of consumers who should know better than to buy products that require plastic packaging. If instead we turn to the social connection model, our focus lies less on identifying culpability and instead on how we can act collectively to reduce the use of plastic. The onus is on us as ethical beings to use our, unevenly distributed, resources and join collective efforts to transform society. As supporters of the complicity-as-being approach, we focus on our immersion in a plastic-dependent economic system and affirm our connectedness with those directly affected by the plastic pollution, to find ways of reducing the use of plastic. We accept that plastic use is unavoidable but seek to limit our use in whichever way is possible. Finally, if influenced by the ethics of responsiveness, we acknowledge the ways power relations and unjust processes obscure our complicity and our ability to challenge complicity. We become concerned with finding ways of cultivating human receptivity to the damage caused by plastic that are sensitive to the dispositions preventing us from identifying alternatives to heavy plastic use.

These different responses are likely to be familiar to readers of this book, based on their own discussions about the use of plastic bottles and other similar issues. Indeed, the approaches within complicity scholarship have an important role to play in addressing injustice and complicity, from efforts to increase responsiveness to the desire to hold powerful corporations accountable in courts. The purpose of this book is not to deny the value of approaches that tackle injustice and violence directly, for instance by highlighting ways in which we can reuse plastic bags. After all, we are often confronted with information – the shocking images of animals dying because of plastic pollution brought to a global audience by the BBC documentary series *Blue Planet 2* come to mind – that should motivate us to act. In judging complicity, we nonetheless have to be aware of the limitations to responses directed at whatever we feel passionate about, or at the specific injustices that catch our attention. Immediate responses to suffering can be counterproductive to assuming responsibility because there is no necessary causal link between receptivity and positive social transformation. On the contrary, humans have finite resources, for example time and money, and the time we spend in trying to find products without plastic packaging is likely to affect our ability to care for other issues. Attentiveness to one problem is likely to be detrimental to tackling the numerous other injustices that we are implicated in. A concern with finding temporary solutions may come at the cost of formulating enduring, far-reaching solutions to systemic injustice. Furthermore, the reactions are often a means by which the privileged maintain their ethical appearance of being good people, without showing any real willingness to make necessary changes to their lifestyle. Put differently, while the approaches identified above have an important role to play in tackling injustice, our capacity to identify adequate responses to injustice rests on the quality of our ethos of reality and the common world. I therefore suggest that judgements on complicity, as a capacity and practice that by its very essence contributes to our engagement with reality, should embed a concern with how to tackle instances of injustice within a concern for how to improve one's ethos of reality and the common world.

To develop this point, I initially build on the important insights in Ella Myers's worldly ethics, which I discussed in Chapters 1 and 4. Myers (2013) argues that alongside a focus on improving our self and alleviating the suffering of others we need to develop a care for the worldly conditions that produce injustice and violence and that shape how we engage with it. Myers distinguishes between caring about and caring for something. We encountered the former, caring about, in relation to Young's insight that when we judge something to be unjust we reveal that things should be different and that we, as ethical beings, should care about transforming the injustice. The care for the world Myers has in mind is stronger. We care for something by both holding it in high regard and feeling a deep emotional commitment to it that leads us to actively tend to its wellbeing as best we can (Myers, 2013: 87). It therefore entails both an orientation towards and attempts to change the world. In my discussion of judging complicity, I focus more on the former without denying the importance of the latter, as the ethos of reality and the wellbeing of the common world are inseparable.

The subject or author of this care for Myers is not an individual self but an 'association of selves' who may work together as a group or who compete against each other in public. The object of worldly care is the things that at any point in time are viewed in public as important matters up for debate, for instance the housing crisis, pandemics, poverty, corruption, controversies in TV shows and so on (Myers, 2013: 86).[2] Different people and groups have these worldly things in common, in the sense that they accept their importance even as they may disagree on their definition or content. Worldly things are also always both material and immaterial and constituted out of a constantly changing constellation of objects and perspectives that we often refer to using widely understood shorthand terms such as 'poverty' or 'plastic waste'. Lastly, Myers emphasises that care for the world is not any action focused on important issues. Instead, action should ideally pursue both procedural and substantive ends – only together do they help create a common world that balances our similarities and differences and facilitates future action and judgement (Myers, 2013: 133). Procedurally, the focus lies on 'sustaining democratic practices that enable the world to emerge as an in-between' (Myers, 2013: 126). Care for worldly things takes the issue of plastic waste as a motivation to join others in protest and collective discussion, in voting for parties that promise to challenge the overreliance on plastic in affluent societies – and criticising those that do not, and in participating in and exploring new practices of democracy that may help develop a fuller expression of plurality. Substantively, a world can only be in common if all humans and non-humans have the basic means needed to live and thrive in the world and call it home – what disability advocate Jacobus tenBroek (1966) called the right to live in the world. The focus is therefore on creating worldly conditions that help groups whose very existence is threatened. In so far as the injustice or violence we focus on concerns those groups, the approach aligns with the responses to complicity highlighted above. It is therefore up to the person judging their complicity how they combine the responses to help reduce the threat of plastic waste on the habitat and environment of different people and animals. However, for Myers the focus always has to be on the world as world-in-common rather than just a desire to rectify an injustice or alleviate the suffering of others.

Myers emphasises the 'pivotal role' played by the common world as a 'third term' alongside the self and the Other (Myers, 2013: 98). This general focus on the contribution of plurality was central to my discussion of Arendt in Chapter 2. I discussed Arendt's concept of *amor mundi* and her emphasis on the 'joy and the gratification that arise out of being in company with our peers' (Arendt, 2006a: 250), out of acting and speaking with and to others, out of shaping the world together, and out of refining our understanding by presenting our viewpoint and learning from others who are both similar and different to us. To love the world is to fiercely protect our ability to remain connected and share similarities with others to such an extent that we can transform the world together, yet distant enough that we can disagree on how to do so without losing our common reality as the basis for judgement and action. It means a deep commitment to the power of plurality to change our world, ideally for the better, and a willingness to think about what plurality entails, how it has changed across time and space, and whether the way we experience it today is problematic or beneficial. Representatively, Arendt highlighted that plurality helps us tackle a violent past but also traced the way modernity has reduced plurality to largely private, consumption-orientated instrumental relations. It finally means a vigilance against the ways that one's conception of plurality and the expression of plurality in society are exclusionary. Plurality itself thus becomes the object of our worldly care, as Myers notes, but plurality is also always the subject of social formation and transformation, a force in and of itself. Tackling plastic waste can be the focus of such worldly care but finding (technical) solutions to it cannot be the sole focus of our judgements and actions. These are practices in world making and world revelation that come with responsibilities to look after the world which our actions and judgements inherit, bring into being and leave behind for future generations.

From a care for pluralism, I turn to dualism and Archer's brief discussion (2014b) of potential responses to complicity in market harm to distant others. The topic throws up an important and particularly challenging dimension to the impact of plastic waste. While there is increasing recognition of the pervasiveness of the problem of plastic in the environment, as a result of studies suggesting that plastic has colonised all corners of the planet, two problems limit responses. Firstly, the impact is relatively slow when contrasted with the speed of everyday life. This problem has been captured by Rob Nixon's (2011) research into slow violence and how to address it. Secondly, the impact of modern strategies of exploitation and expropriation to meet the demands of consumerism in affluent societies is predominantly felt by distant others outside the centres of heightened consumption. The impact on the environment, with the collapse of ecosystems, is least felt by those living in cities in the most temperate parts of the world although this distance is increasingly hard to maintain as the climate catastrophe worsens. Archer initially attributes a shared responsibility to those with the greatest freedom and potential for influencing society but ultimately warns against reliance on powerful good people. Such an approach ignores the multiple layers of social reality. It endorses the 'very individualism that is at the heart of the crisis' and rests 'on the old fallacy that good people make for a good society, which denies emergent structures any role in shaping societal outcomes' (Archer, 2014b: 34). An approach to tackling market harms to distant others must instead focus on both the context and the actors, in short on dualism. Archer asks that we consider how structures like the capitalist market condition action by restricting some avenues of future action, while enabling others, and providing benefits and harms for specific action. Capitalist structures produce practices that frame – without determining – any care for distant others. Vested interests, opportunity costs and the situational logic of action go far to explain the lack of help given to distant ecosystems and people whose livelihood is endangered by plastic pollution. Proximate privileging over the distant Other may beset those seeking to change systemic injustice, as well as those ignoring complicity. While we may be unhappy with structures that engender plastic waste, care for the world means that we embrace the fact that our knowledge and action are socially conditioned and learn more about how these structures shape us as individuals and collectives rather than seeking to deny or distort their impact.

To attend to dualism, Archer combines the focus on structures with a deep commitment to human agency, in this case expressed through her consideration of the fact that we have different internal conversations that shape how we engage with society at the micro and macro level. A person's way of thinking is the outcome of the continuous interplay between personal concerns and social contexts. While we use different modes of reflexivity depending on the circumstances, humans for Archer hold a dominant mode – communicative, autonomous, meta- or fractured reflexivity – which comes to bear on our ethical stances and moral outlook on society. In current Western late modern democracies, communicative reflexives' moral communitarianism and autonomous reflexives' libertarian stances provide opposing influences. The former hold on to collectivist values and seek to strengthen social integration, while the latter embrace economic productivity and adhere to individualism. The decline in communicative reflexivity as a dominant mode suggests that we can no longer rely as a society on traditional responses to suffering. We might therefore turn in hope to the changes in the way young autonomous reflexives think about capitalism, for example 'responsible enterprise'. The question remains to what extent 'sandpapering away the rougher edges of the profit motive' (Archer, 2014b: 46) provides a key source of responding to complicity. Of particular interest for responses to complicity is instead the likely future dominance of meta-reflexives in society.

Meta-reflexives reject the ethical stances of autonomous and communicative reflexives, but their contribution to social transformation has not yet reached its full potential (Archer, 2014b: 38). Their reflexive stance towards society combines with changes occurring as we move towards a morphogenic society, specifically the increased synergy between generative mechanisms in the cultural and structural sphere. Both social structures and the corresponding cultures become subject to heightened transformation, which increases the variety of social formations and opportunities available in a society. These conditions demand a modus vivendi that is unstable, repositioning and changing according to the developments in culture and of structures.[3] We may therefore turn to late modernity's globalisation and the increase in meta-reflexivity as the hoped-for potential for positive social transformation. Young meta-reflexives have the potential to embrace new variations of social formations and break with the logic of competition and zero-sum market dynamics. They reveal that there are alternatives to the paradigm of profit maximisation, even if this impetus expresses itself, as yet, primarily in the third sector and is easily co-opted by market and state. Archer also cautions that responsiveness to harm caused against distant others remains of little concern to the privileged irrespective of their mode of reflexivity. Moral responsibility for the poorest in the market seems 'to be confined to the most proximate and most visible poor where offering a "better deal" can, with suitable media exposure, even become a new form of market competition' (Archer, 2014b: 49–50).[4]

Archer's theoretical discussion shows – at an analytical level and in relation to the important problem of how to judge harm to distant others – how we can attend to dualism by affirming the contribution of both human agency and structures to injustice and its transformation. Her approach may sound abstract, but as highlighted in Chapter 4, for Archer dualism and her recuperation of human agency are endeavours to express our experience of the vexatious fact. Care for the world therefore invites us to explore further what feeling both free and enchained entails. Social theory can help us understand its dimension further, but we mustn't forget the link to an innate experience that, for Archer, is undermined by social tendencies towards conflation.

Now, one of the intuitive responses to this need to care for dualism and pluralism might be to try to address as much of, and avoid as much reduction of, the subjective, objective and intersubjective dimensions to our everyday life as possible. Such an effort cannot succeed and too often comes with claims to increased objectivity and validity. As the ethics of responsiveness shows, reductions of different dimensions to reality are an innate part of human situatedness in complex social contexts not of our own choosing and of the ethical burden of our capacity to judge and act upon the world (and all the responsibilities and complicity that come with it). Drawing on ever-increasing knowledge within society about different dimensions to reality can be beneficial in reducing our tendency to fall for reductionism, but as a maxim, to introduce as much knowledge as possible can similarly prove counterproductive, by paralysing judgement. As Mathias Thaler (2011) points out, judgement is often faced with a difficult balancing act between the need for decisions and results and the need to incorporate the wider views in a divided society. Judging politically, humans should instead ask themselves what the costs of reducing reality in its dualism and pluralism are and, indeed, whether we can even make claims about the costs considering the unexpected consequences that judgement and action inevitably hold. An improved ethos of reality, in my view, does not propose 'attentiveness to a multi-layered reality' as a general standard of judgement, but first of all an increased awareness of the heavy price we incur as human beings when we fail to account for the vexatious – society shapes us, and we shape society – and worldly – humans come to terms with the world together – character of being human. Such awareness accepts that humans continuously emphasise some aspects of reality over others in their everyday practices of judging. Indeed, the need to judge and reflect on the world arises in the first place to articulate what is important and of interest to us, in the hope that this reduction of a reality that we can never fully understand may make our lives sufficiently meaningful and enable us to make our way through the world. The cultivation of a (routinised) ethos of reality similarly helps us to simplify the world we encounter, in an effort to grasp complex developments without dedicating all of our time to them. To avoid judging altogether, and acting on these judgements, would therefore be dangerous. Yet, ignoring the impact of plastic may not only be problematic because it disadvantages some and privileges others and negatively impacts the environment. Instead, in seeking to mould, and thus reduce, the world to our preferred vision of it, reductionism of reality has proven exceptionally dangerous to the possibility of meaningful human existence. Key to responding to ethico-political problems is therefore an effort to disentangle the necessary and inevitable ways in which we simplify our understanding (and the actual character) of reality, and the pernicious reductions that impoverish the common world. In making judgements on plastic waste, we need a deep commitment to decreasing impoverishing and increasing flourishing conditions of the common world and to looking at the contributions of structure, agency and plurality to each of these states.

A world in common is impoverished when large parts of a community are increasingly unable or unwilling to recognise the vexatious and worldly character of reality, or, worse still, where these facts have indeed become increasingly implausible. This sense or state leads to what Arendt described as an 'irritating incompatibility between the actual power of modern man [sic] [. . .] and the impotence of modern men [sic] to live in, and understand the sense of, a world which their strength has established' (1973: viii), and it can take different forms along one or more of the three dimensions to human existence. In terms of plurality, the irritating incompatibility manifests itself in our inability or unwillingness to speak to each other, to meet each other in our differences and communalities. The problem is not the lack of a shared framework of standards and values that could help adjudicate between different claims on reality, or an unwillingness of the 'left' and the 'right' to compromise. Instead, the sections of the population in conflict are no longer able or willing to think representatively from different viewpoints – a pre-condition of a shared world – which leads to an 'us versus them' mentality that facilitates injustice and oppression on a mass scale. Society becomes increasingly permeated by a sense of existential crisis in which the survival of a particular group within it – consumers in affluent societies reliant on plastic to maintain their steady stream of untainted consumer products – is only possible or plausible at the cost of others – usually oppressed minorities and distant others with the least power to influence society. Structurally, the irritating incompatibility leads to an inability or unwillingness to protect the worldly conditions on which we depend (for instance in relation to climate change and the destruction of the planet) as well as a sense in which physical, cultural and social structures are becoming or have become hostile to large parts of society who struggle to survive in the midst of droughts and heatwaves and ever more competitive and exploitative working conditions. Lastly, in terms of human agency, an impoverished common world leads to an over- or underestimation of the powers and properties of structure, agency or plurality, and the desire to claim these powers to one's own advantage or to deny them altogether. The impoverished common world is the product of systematic and systemic reductions of structure, agency and plurality and threatens the potential in the worldly and vexatious character of society to shape the world for the better.

In response, we need to cultivate an ethos that is sensitive to how the powers and mechanisms of structure, agency and plurality negatively impact on a multi-layered reality and affect the capacity to share a world. We can ask a number of guiding questions, such as: how are we, as agents capable of emotionality, reflexivity and social innovation, contributing to and denying our complicity in plastic waste? What are the reductive stories that I tell to justify my complicity? What are the social norms and institutions that force us to become complicit? To what extent are they beyond our reach for the purpose of transformation? How do we respond to them? And, what are the contributions of others – my friends and family, my employers, co-workers and various socio-economic and political organisations – and how have we together failed to create a world in which 'the burdens of living together' are 'distributed more evenly' (Schiff, 2014: 9)? How we ask and respond to these questions is ultimately a matter of receptivity, the conditions that shape and produce our actions and judgements, and our distinct ethos of reality as elaborated in great detail by the responsiveness approach. However, only in learning to ask these kinds of questions along all three dimensions can we avoid the reductionism that facilitates oppression and injustice.[5] They help us attend to limited and distorted forms of interaction or collective action that engender our complicity in plastic waste.

Thus, we might highlight how plastic pollution is accompanied by reductive strategies and narratives that undermine our capacity to act and judge politically. The use of plastic waste combines with various mechanisms that prevent more forceful discussion about how we as a (global) community can reduce plastic waste at a regional, national or international level. Instead, the problem is largely left to political regulation at nation state level, individual responses or social movements, all of which have an important role to play but are only microcosmic expressions of the kind of potential a concerted effort could bring to tackling the multiple issues surrounding climate change (plurality). The resolution passed in March 2022 at the United Nations Environment Assembly in Nairobi to adopt a treaty on ending plastic pollution is a positive step forward but does not change this problem. The questions also help us focus on the structures and culture that engender plastic waste. These include, for example, a consumerism that relies on one-time use of plastic containers and an 'environmental crisis industry' that generates a range of minor 'apparent solutions to the predicament that promise to assuage' our concerns with the environmental impact of our consumerism and 'help us feel that we are helping to ameliorate the problem' (Smith and Brisman, 2021: 290) (structure). Finally, they make us sensitive to the ways our individual capacities as human beings facilitate this problem, for example the denial that our reliance on plastic bags and packaging can have a significant role to play in damaging the environment (agency). The point here is less to come up with a comprehensive analysis, but to learn to judge and experience the world along all three components.

We also need to gain a greater awareness of the way that the reductionism along these three components affects the world in common. In the case chosen, this seems straightforward: plastic in the ocean creates a deeply hostile environment, not least by damaging the global food chain, with, as yet, unforeseeable negative consequences for humans, and displacing water with numerous knock-on effects including increased risk of flooding (Iroegbu et al., 2021: 19345). Yet, further questions can be raised, including: is plastic waste a key way in which the common world is impoverished? Are there other mechanisms and powers that we obscure by focusing on plastic? We can ultimately answer these kinds of questions only as part of a political community that judges what makes their lives meaningful and what endangers their continued common existence. Judgements can help by framing action in ways that are attentive to the importance of the common world and its multi-layered character.

Alongside attentiveness to the ways structure, agency and human plurality can impoverish the world, we need to learn to identify the specific aspects of our social context that (could) enable a flourishing, hospitable common world. A world in common is flourishing when large parts of a community are increasingly able or willing to embrace the vexatious and worldly character of reality and to face up to reality and change it for the better. We may ask, what are the structures, the powers of agency and the manifestations of human plurality that together shape a better world? How have we managed to keep these three contributions in sight, as a key way in which a common world can be improved? A suitable focus on plurality is visible in numerous collaborative efforts to counter injustice including attempts to build floating structures that remove plastic from the oceans such as the Ocean Cleanup project (Sterenborg et al., 2019). The objective is not so much to encourage people to invest more in these foundations, but to draw on and learn from positive examples of acting in concert. Each of us should ask ourselves, how do we interact with others, particularly those most distant or vulnerable in society, and what positive effect on the world as a common reality does this interaction have?

We also need to find a more responsive approach to the way that the world shapes us, or risk falling back on individuals acting upon the world. Tracking the negative effect of human activities on nature, for example by calculating the cost of one tonne of carbon emissions for the environment or the annual plastic waste produced by an average citizen, is an important step towards a more appropriate engagement with the world. However, the approach remains entangled in an attitude towards nature that sees it primarily as an instrument and resource – to be exploited in a more sustainable manner – unless we simultaneously acknowledge the role that materiality and social and cultural structures play in shaping our context. The various projects dedicated to identifying nature-based solutions to injustice are an example of this: the fact that larger plastic particles float on water is key to current efforts to clean up the ocean using buoyant systems (Sterenborg et al., 2019: 1). An appropriate judgement accommodates this role of structures alongside the potential in human plurality and avoids reducing the positive examples of responding to climate change to solidarity and collective responses.

But it requires more than the embrace of the potential in natural and social structures. It is about recognising a world that is stratified, in which relatively enduring relations and ideas shape humans and the social positions they inhabit in society through and through. We need to develop an awareness of the history of the emergence of different material and ideational conditions of how we act. This is again less about learning the history of generative mechanisms, although this may prove helpful, for example 'Where did the paradigm of profit maximisation come from?', 'What kind of alternatives existed in the past?', 'Why is it so pervasive and long-lasting?'. Instead, it is by learning how such mechanisms shape a world we recognise as flourishing that we can respond to our complicity in injustice. To attend to the network of relations between social positions with its norms and practices and its physical and material elements means to clearly separate out our capacity for embodied receptivity towards the world from the potential for social transformation in the world.

Finally, we also need to attend to how humans make their way through the world by relying on reflexivity, embodiment, a sense of themselves and creativity/natality.[6] My discussion of Archer's insights on complicity in market harms helped capture how we can recognise potential subjective contributions to social transformation without falling for individualism or reducing these agential powers and mechanisms to broader narratives of 'the social'. The reconstruction of a turn to the emotional and unconscious layers within judgement and imagination in Chapter 3 similarly added insights into how a different relationship with human agency can facilitate a more suitable way of living together. In relation to the Cleanup Project we might therefore ask what its researchers and supporters bring in passion and dedication to the realisation of the project, alongside the potential of structure and plurality.

A suitable account and practice of judging complicity situates our response to plastic waste in a multi-layered context. Social injustice is not transformed by one decision or judgement alone, and the cultivation of an ethos of reality is an open-ended process that continues throughout our lives and cannot be completed easily or quickly. In some ways, therefore, I am being much more demanding than the responsiveness approach, which seemingly offers us a (conditional) 'way out' through increased receptivity and moments of rupture. We might therefore be worried that my approach encourages denial of responsibility. Any response to complicity may seem daunting or unlikely, particularly in light of the various mechanisms of human disavowal. Humans grapple with injustice largely in relation to everyday activities that already make (some of) us feel conflicted and which catch us between a desire to flee our responsibility, a shameful recognition of our complicity and the seemingly insurmountable demands of late modern economies.

The broad scale of this project is also an opportunity: we are able to help create a better common world, because the vexatious and worldly character is something we grapple with every day, even when it seems so easy to ignore the suffering of others. Those seemingly most adapt at circumventing any responsibility for suffering still pursue some form of reflection on their engagement with reality, which is therefore always open to improvement. The weight of responsibility is also divided more evenly. The advantage of the framework is that it allows for both the transformation and the reproduction of oppression to come from various sources, often in unexpected ways; it strengthens the role of responsive agency – the potential of a love of the world that actively faces up to the multi-layered, shared character of reality – without thereby neglecting structures. Structures and plurality contribute to invoking positive social transformation. States, non-governmental organisations, and changes in the legal, moral, political and social context of action have a role to play in tackling complicity, alongside self-improvement, and the purpose of an improved ethos is precisely to recognise their combined contribution (and the limits to our ability to recognise it). Finally, the continuous process of cultivating an ethos also means that it is less about getting each and every situation right and more about developing a long-term stance that is more adept at caring for a multi-layered reality and supports a public sphere that enables such worldly caring. This care will look different for each person and must therefore always be thought of contextually.

In sum, central to our ability to judge complicity is an ethos of reality. The ethos provides a prism on the world and ideally ensures that taking up collective responsibility, acknowledging human foldedness and cultivating responsiveness towards suffering tackle the root causes of injustice and contribute to social transformation. To this end, judgements must be orientated towards the wellbeing of the common world, the space constituted by evaluating shared appearances, through which we can give life meaning. This book has highlighted that this necessarily entails an equal focus on the objective, subjective and intersubjective mechanisms and powers that together constitute the common world. Of course, what concretely an ethos of reality actually looks like is fully dependent on the person, their modus vivendi, social position, context and common sense. For this reason, I turn to an exemplary judgement in the next chapter that expresses this world-disclosing capacity in important ways and helps breathe life into the theoretical observations.

Notes

1. Archer (2000: 5) prefers the term 'conflation' to 'reduction', because it helps capture the central conflation of structure–agency, which strictly speaking does not reduce structure to agency or vice versa but denies both distinct causal powers. I will rely on the more common term

'reduction' to capture the general impulse of reducing the main elements, structure, agency and plurality. The terminology may require further differentiation to clarify the distinct quality of the kind of theoretical conflation Archer attributes to Bourdieu and Giddens and the pervasive, violent reductionisms emanating from the Romanian dictatorship, to be discussed in Chapter 6.
2. Myers emphasises that we first have to make something a worldly thing, that is politicise it by making an object appear in public and developing a sufficiently general sense within the population that it should be a matter of action and debate. The impact of plastic on wildlife, for instance, only became a topic of concern in recent decades. It is often the task of a care for worldly things to politicise the object in the first place.
3. The move from large-scale ethical and moral frameworks to an ethics of responsiveness illustrates the changing circumstances; this modus most closely resembles the one developed by meta-reflexivity.
4. Critics might suggest that this account relies similarly on an account of structural crisis that overemphasises, at times, the potential of reflexive agency. Hartmut Rosa (2017) in particular argues that Archer's emphasis on the morphogenesis of late modernity obscures the underlying morphostasis of capitalist societies, where the need for transformation becomes the precondition for modern morphostasis. However, even if the potential may be more limited than Archer imagines, the crucial point is that she identifies a way of turning to break-through moments without relying on their ability to change the relationship between structure and agency.
5. The emphasis on asking questions should not lead to the assumption that I am presupposing extensive moral deliberation. Instead, what I have in mind is a practice in which embodied and reflexive dimensions to human agency take part and through which we learn to position ourselves towards a stratified reality and attend to its vexatious and worldly character. This may at times require explicitly asking these kinds of questions, but often it is a matter of routinisation.
6. To give an example, Archer insists that a focus on reflexive deliberation allows her an improved view on social transformation, where 'personal subjectivity filters how agents respond to the same objective circumstances'. This enables us 'to explain the *universal absence of similar responses in situations that are objectively similar*' (Archer, 2009: 10, original emphasis).

CHAPTER SIX

Resisting complicity through an ethos of reality in practice

This final chapter adds concreteness to the argument developed in the book, by focusing on the writings and interviews of Nobel laureate Herta Müller. The Romanian-German writer gained world-wide attention in 2009, following the publication of her novel *Atemschaukel* (*The Hunger Angel*) about the deportations of Romanian-Germans to Soviet labour camps, and the award of the Nobel Prize for Literature.[1] Müller's reflections on the various ways of becoming entangled in pervasive oppression during Romania's national-communist dictatorship and her attempts to resist certain acts of complicity reveal what a cultivation of an improved ethos of reality, as a distinct ethico-political project, might look like. Before I explain her work's suitability for my purposes, let me briefly outline how my theoretical elaborations can guide us in studying her judgements on complicity.

As we look at someone's judgements on their complicity in injustice and violence, we ought to consider how they respond to systemic forms of reductionism of reality that impoverish the common world. Furthermore, we ought to look at the weight the person puts on creating a world in which humans can meaningfully come to terms with a multi-layered, shared reality. While this process can take many forms, it should be attentive to three interrelated components to human existence that together enable the formation of a flourishing common world: (a) the role of humans, as embodied, reflexive agents that produce causally irreducible contributions to society; (b) the relationships between people, based on humans' ability and need to act together; and (c) the social and cultural structures that contribute to what it means to be human. The crux of my improved ethos of reality is that a judgement attentive to these components and their impact on the common world should ideally be able to affirm the complexity of social reality while, at the same time, telling right from wrong, beautiful from ugly in relation to a specific event or context. My response to complicity is embedded in the belief that an acknowledgement of the stratified character of reality does not come at the cost of concreteness and a capacity for judgement. It is in making judgements informed by an ethos of reality, in general capable of this balance, that we can take a significant step towards addressing complicity adequately.

Müller offers a suitable case for the study of an improved ethos of reality, because (a) she engages in a difficult context that brings to the fore the kind of dehumanising strategies that judgements on complicity should respond to, and (b) her use of autofiction means that writing is both instrumental to her ethos of reality and a source for us to study the ethos, as her written self-reflections help crystallise its key elements. I draw on Müller's essays and interviews, especially *Der König verneigt sich und tötet* ('The King Bows and Kills') (2008) and *Mein Vaterland ist ein Apfelkern* ('My Fatherland Is an Apple Seed') (2014), written following her flight to Germany and situated at the intersection between literary work and theoretical reflection on repression. My focus on the writer, rather than primarily on the content and form of literature, does not follow conventional ways of using literary work to clarify moral or political philosophy (Hämäläinen, 2016). Müller helpfully argues that we rely on writers for insights not because they stand above society, but because their writing makes manifest their own agency (Müller and Liiceanu, 2011). Going back to my discussion in Chapter 2 about how Hannah Arendt democratised the spectator, we might say that Müller's writing does not seek the detachment of the thoughtful intellectual, because the actor and spectator are innately connected: the 'spectator sits in every actor' (Arendt, 1981a: 262). Furthermore, Müller offers a sophisticated approach to an ethos of reality that can serve as the starting point for thinking about our own ethos of reality and is also uniquely particular to her biography and the problems she faced. Müller captures the central aspects of my ethos of reality schematically, while, at the same time, exercising judgement in a way that is unique to her context. In my discussion of Müller, I therefore hope to find the right balance between particularity and abstraction for the sake of clarifying what an improved ethos of reality entails.

Herta Müller's life in Ceauescu's Romania

Müller's life trajectory plays an important role in her writing, as its motivation, as its source material and as a framing device. I therefore begin with a summary of key contexts and episodes.[2]

Müller was born in 1953 in Nitzkydorf (Romanian: Nițchidorf), a Banat-Swabian village in south-western Romania. She belongs to an ethnic German minority that had moved to eastern Europe over the previous few centuries as part of the colonising efforts by the Habsburg empire (Drace Francis, 2013). During the Second World War, members of the minority fought, alongside the Romanian army, on the side of Nazi Germany. After the war, many Germans in the Banat region were deported to labour camps, as disproportionate punishment for the war damage caused to the Soviet Union. Romania, initially an ally of Germany, switched sides just before the end of the war and maintained accordingly a victorious, 'innocent' position. To this end, scapegoating the German minority became a powerful means to negate the country's dark past. Müller's own family captures many facets of the historic developments: Her father Iosif Müller had joined the Waffen-SS during the Second World War, aged seventeen; the impact of national-socialist sympathies on Iosif's life would prove significant for his daughter's later rejection of totalitarianism of any kind. Her grandfather, formerly a well-off grocer of colonial goods and corn, had his properties nationalised by the communist regime. He had also been a prisoner of war following the First World War, and the shock of losing his status and livelihood only added to his already traumatised state. Finally, her mother Katharina had been deported at the age of nineteen to a labour camp in Ukraine, where she was retained for five years only to return as a broken woman.

This challenging context sets the scene for Müller's resistance through a distinct form of judgement in two ways. Firstly, her resistant agency is shaped by her experiences as a child living in a community with an unresolved, traumatic and shameful past; the inability and unwillingness to come to terms with the past expressed itself in various forms, including a general embrace of silence. This has implications for the role Müller attributes to communication through writing. The writer's first major book, *Niederungen* (*Nadirs*), portrayed the oppressive environment of her native village. Katharina's experience, together with that of other villagers and Müller's close friend and poet Oskar Pastior, resonate in Müller's more recent book, *Atemschaukel*. The novel binds together various stories of the Soviet labour camps to a fictionalised recounting of the German minority's camp experience. Müller's work is, secondly, framed by her experiences as a German-Romanian persecuted by the communist secret police. To fully understand why she became a target, let me first add to the background context. Between 1965 and 1989, Romania was ruled by Nicolae Ceaușescu and the infamous secret police Securitate, which relied on a widespread network of collaborators and informants (Mihai, 2016a: 151ff.). Under Ceaușescu's rule Romania proved unique in terms of the cult of personality, the repression of all opposition and pervasive control of all aspects of everyday life (Haines, 2013: 94). The general population responded to the difficult circumstances through social opportunism and political apathy (Müller and Liiceanu, 2011). Both entail an unwillingness or inability to respond to the plight of others and a desire to separate the supposed normalcy of everyday life from the implication in the suffering of others that one was encouraged to forget and pretend not to experience (Feitlowitz: 2011). Müller started to feel the full effects of the repressive state following her move to Temeswar (Romanian: Timișoara) at the age of fifteen, a city 30 kilometres from her native village.

Through the move to the city, Müller left behind an agricultural society with little patience for intellectual curiosity. In the city, she engaged with Romanian culture and language, which she had previously been taught only as a foreign language. She also met and became friends with members of the Aktionsgruppe Banat, a group of ethnic German left-wing writers who had a significant literary influence on her (Haines and Marven, 2013: 2). First attempts in prose and poetry emerged in 1969. In 1982, a heavily censored *Niederungen* was published. Müller's writing came at a considerable cost to her and her family. Yet the Nobel laureate also profited from an unsystematic and inconsistent approach towards minority literature and culture during the dictatorship, which enabled her to kick-start her literary career in the first place (cf. Eke, 2017: 8). The secret police terrorised the Aktionsgruppe, wary of its political position, and approached Müller to convince her to become an informant on Timișoara's artistic scene and the Aktionsgruppe's activities. She rejected the offer. Her refusal to collaborate did not prevent the group from eventually falling apart and, in retaliation at her refusal to become complicit, Müller was fired from her job as a translator in a machinery factory, where she had started working before the secret police approached her.

Müller's 1980s were marked by repression, including interrogation, death threats and house searches, but also growing literary success in the West. The success came with resentment and harsh criticism from her ethnic group and the dictatorship, who were displeased by her bleak depictions of her childhood and life in the Banat-Swabian village. However, it also provided some initial protection and the opportunity to travel to Germany. As she discovered upon reading her Securitate file, the secret police used this unusual freedom as a means to discredit Müller in the West as a Romanian spy: only someone collaborating with the government, so they thought, would be given such privileges to travel and criticise the dictatorship freely. Following her third departure, however, the Securitate revoked Müller's privileges. The secret police acknowledged that they had underestimated her literary impact in the West and the terror increased once more. Finally, Müller gave up and requested an exit permit. In 1987, after one-and-a-half years of anguished waiting, and close to insanity, Müller fled to Berlin together with her then husband Richard Wagner. The dictatorship collapsed in 1989 and Müller became part of the struggle to deal with this violent past that continues to overshadow the country's transition towards democracy. The increasing distance from the totalitarian experiences also seems to have marked a final shift in Müller's writing; today she focuses especially on producing collages, alongside a series of interviews that provide explanatory investigation into her writing style.

The impoverished common world

With the basic trajectory of Müller's life in place, I now trace the problem that she responded to. My discussion gives us a first insight into Müller's cultivation of an improved ethos of reality: her evaluation of the systematic reductionism of being human and a common world during the Romanian dictatorship that endangered humans' capacity to come to terms with reality and engendered complicity in oppression.

Key to Müller's resistance informed by a distinct ethos of reality is her analysis of how dictatorships impact on personhood and lead to paralysing loneliness and fear. She emphasises that, above all, her native village and Romania more generally were ruled by the fear that the individual 'I' could succeed over the institutionalised 'We' (Haines and Littler, 1998: 17, 22–23). The Romanian state, Müller claims, 'defined itself solely through repression. It had no other programmatic content than the control of its population' (Müller and Lentz, 2010: 15, my translation). The unpredictability of human beings was seen as a primary threat to this logic of control and the secret police targeted the individual qua individual. Under such extreme circumstances, the destruction of the person becomes inevitable and normal, a by-product of either the process of compliance with the regime's vision of society or the persecution experienced in response to acts of resistance (Müller and Klammer, 2014: 100, 123–124). Müller encountered the extent of the compliance as a kindergarten teacher. She reports that her pupils, ideologically conditioned from an early age, wished to stand like soldiers in a circle and sing an anthem that required no mental awareness (Müller, 2008: 187–188). Müller initially attempted to change these circumstances by teaching a different song, especially to young ones who might still be subjectively less constrained. The efforts failed and Müller quit her job after two weeks.

The destruction of personhood brings with it the end of a meaningful political existence as it obliterates the in-between of plurality known as common world. Müller captures this destruction of worldliness through the metaphor of the island, which the writer appropriates from the concept of *Inselglück* (island happiness) (Müller, 2008: 195ff.). Western countries' tourism advertisements have used a notion of island happiness to represent finding peace and tranquillity on a faraway tropical island. In contrast, Romania became an island, because the regime brutally prevented any attempts at escaping the country. The Banat Germans, too, lived isolated as if on an island, branded by the Romanians as Nazis and kept apart by their own twisted sense of cultural and ethnic superiority. Further examples include the island of the ruling elite, afraid of the masses and of losing their privileges, and the islands of the collaborators and spies, at risk of being found out. Lastly, the island metaphor refers to the isolation in the heads of those separated by systematic terror and fear. As the country divided into myriads of islands, politics in Romania turned into shallow public engagement. In sum, as succinctly concluded by

Norbert Otto Eke in relation to Müller's novel *Herztier* (*The Land of Green Plums*), Ceaușescu's dictatorship

> completely destroyed *Eigensinn*, individuality, and humanity: the dream of individual happiness *within society*, the dream of self-determination and self-assertion *in opposition to society*, the dream of friendship and sincerity as an alternative to a society gripped by fear emotionally frozen and downright loveless (Eke, 2013: 106, original emphasis).

The consequence of living under regimes that seek to destroy the singularity and plurality of being human is loneliness. Its effects are of particular importance for Müller's work. Müller experienced three contexts of (totalitarian) loneliness, first, the context of growing up in the Banat-Swabian village, then through her persecution by the Securitate, and finally, indirectly, the Soviet labour camps, the experience of which she learned about vicariously through her mother's and Oscar Pastior's narratives. Each comes with different combinations of fear and loneliness that prove highly destructive to personhood. I focus on the two that Müller experienced directly.

Loneliness became the defining characteristic of Müller's early life (Müller, 2008: 13). Her father's SS past, the trauma of the labour and prison camp weighing on her mother and grandfather, and the confiscation of her grandfather's livelihood and status, combined with the Romanian communist narrative about ethnic Germans, prevented her family from reckoning with their past. In fear of punishment, Müller's relatives, and the German minority more generally, turned highly opportunistic and politically ignorant (Müller and Klammer, 2014: 37). Keeping secrets and avoiding conversation became an acceptable way of life. An emphasis on solitude and a functional approach to thinking also linked well with the cyclical character of rural farm life, while reading and independent thought, so central to Müller's resistance, were seen sceptically.[3]

At the centre of this loneliness in the village was what Müller describes as '*Dorfangst*' ('village fear') (Müller, 2008: 61) – the built-in fear that arose from the various traumas which were not publicly addressed. Later, in the city, she encountered the planned fear created by the secret police in the fight against individuality (Müller and Klammer, 2014: 123). This fear arose from the penetration of the private sphere through repeated interrogations and the searching of her flat, but also the general ubiquity of threat: anyone who looked too closely could become a target, almost everything was forbidden (Müller, 2008: 62). A second loneliness thus emerged following the failed attempts by the secret police to recruit Müller and through the ensuing harassment (Müller and Klammer, 2014: 62).

The destruction of individuality and the production of fear and loneliness give rise to what Müller calls an 'alien gaze' (Müller, 2008: 163ff.).[4] The alien gaze refers to someone's inability to confidently and automatically engage with a surrounding that should be familiar to them (Müller and Klammer, 2014: 178–179). One of the central strategies employed by the secret police to achieve this deterioration of familiarity – of trust in the objects and people around us – was house searches. This penetration of one's privacy achieved its full effect by leaving the searched location seemingly untouched, while at the same time carefully changing small features, which, notwithstanding their unimportance, proved highly effective in destroying a person's relation to the world: 'nothing seemed certain any longer, whether it is this, or that, or something completely different. With time only inane things existed with important shadows' (Müller, 2008: 163, my translation). The quote gives us some sense of how the alien gaze affected Müller as she struggled to maintain her way of being in the world, undermined by the doubt sown by the secret police. The annihilation of confidence in one's perception of the world aggravates loneliness and fear. Together, they deny independent, critical thought, and leave behind a human being without the means to assure and confirm their perception on the world, in all its partiality. As a consequence, the person is continuously at risk of losing all confidence in adequately capturing and reacting to the world. Using the language established in Chapter 5, the context potentially prevents any cultivation of a suitable ethos of reality. Müller therefore concludes that to come to terms with possessing the alien gaze and to find a way to live with it as one becomes wary of oneself is an art (Müller, 2008: 180, 183).

Müller's ethos of reality – living in the detail

I now engage with Müller's self-reflective essays to consider her response to this reductionism. The section reveals that Müller continued to make judgements on complicity that sustained her unwillingness to collaborate with the dictatorship. These judgements are embedded in a unique ethos encapsulated by the motto she borrows from Eugène Ionesco and repeats in *Hunger und Seide* ('Hunger and Silk'): 'Let's live, but they don't let us live. So, let's live in the detail' (Müller, 2016: 61, my translation). This life in the detail has a twofold significance for Müller, both as a basic survival strategy and in its extension through her aesthetic-political resistance in her essays and novels. I first provide a discussion of how this motto frames her immediate response to loneliness, fear and the alien gaze. In elaborating her initial survival strategy, I highlight how Müller focuses on the dualist and pluralist dimension to being human. I complete this picture of Müller's judgement in the final section, where I show how she extends her ethos of reality – to live in the detail – through writing as 'invented perception'. In Arendtian terms, Müller's judgement begins to create 'the *space* in which the objects of judgement, the actor and actions themselves, can appear, and thus alter our sense of what belongs in the common world' (Zerilli, 2005b: 179, original emphasis).

By 'living in the detail', Müller acknowledges the necessity to live without the kind of plots and narratives that usually give someone's life meaning. Overcome by fear, her full attention had to be on an adequate response to the immediate moment, and that moment alone (Müller and Lentz, 2010: 37–38). Living from day to day, in the present, was essential, without concrete plans for the future. Faced with the dictatorship's distortion of social reality, Müller's resistance depended on the accuracy of her perception by focusing on the detail of specific objects and events.[5] Resistance thus expressed itself in the holding on to small things that ensured immediate survival. This accuracy sustains the basic survival strategy by providing the means to monitor continuously the aims and mechanisms of the apparatus of terror.

To defend herself she opened her own surveillance office. The observance of simple things and objects, their precise monitoring, Müller discovered, could give her a sense of control and provide some immediate protection against the anti-human strategies of the totalising regime (Müller and Lentz, 2010: 24, 33). Of course, as stated in relation to the alien gaze, such hyper-vigilance comes with its own costs and dangers, constantly putting a person on edge, which leads Müller to writing as its necessary extension. Yet, life in the detail emerges for Müller also as a larger point about judging reality:

> Who cannot live with the detail, who prohibits and despises it, becomes blind. A thousand details provide something, but not a thread of life, not an overall agreement, no utopia. Details are not to be put in a chain, transformed into a clear-cut logic of the world' (Müller, 2016: 61, my translation).

As the quote reveals, Müller holds on to the particular as juxtaposed to a superficial whole, which she often seems to associate with ideological oppression. Out of the immediate survival thus emerges a normative project – an improved ethos of reality dedicated to recuperating and protecting the common world. The rest of the chapter explores the different dimensions to her ethos of reality in more detail.

Resistant agency

Of particular interest for this book is that Müller displays an acute awareness of the importance of highlighting how structure, agency and plurality together constitute reality, *and* the tendency to distort their interplay. A 'life in the detail', or in my terms an 'ethos of reality', fails as a normative project that seeks to build and protect a common world, unless it is attentive to how the three components shape our capacity to judge and make our way through the world. For the sake of clarity, I address structure, agency and plurality separately, starting with human agency. In each step, I show how Müller reveals the deep ways in which the regime curtails and distorts the causal powers of a component, and also how she nonetheless holds on to the continued importance and potential of structure, agency and plurality for resisting reductionism.

Throughout this book, I have highlighted the centrality of what it means to be human contra modern dehumanising tendencies in society and sciences. Chapter 5 summarised that in order to cultivate a suitable stance towards reality, an improved ethos of reality, a person should be attentive to their distinct, emergent causal properties as a human. These include a capacity for reflexive engagement with the world; a sense of self, which builds on an emotional, embodied and relational existence; and a commitment to the unceasing potential in humans for social innovation. To fail to practise a stance towards reality informed by these characteristics may result in judgements and actions that systematically aggravate dehumanisation. In particular, judgement that lacks orientation towards the components of human existence risks a disconnection from the plight of others and one's involvement in their suffering. Müller's response centres on what she terms her 'individualism' (Haines and Littler, 1998: 19), through which she captures central features of human agency.

Attentive to the destructive force of totalitarianism on personhood, Müller holds on to the belief in people as a source of innovation:

'I wanted to address the unpredictable that inhabits each person, whether in me or in the powerful' (Müller, 2008: 57–58, my translation). Elsewhere, she adds that 'every person is a unique individual in the world and has a unique relationship with that world. And everything each one of us does we do differently, because we have no other option' (Müller and Liiceanu, 2011). Müller acknowledges that this individuality brought with it a failure to follow the implicit rules of the village, which would have made her life easier. As a child, Müller was unable to prevent the '*Irrlauf im Kopf*' ('rush in the head') (Müller, 2008: 16), and to avoid looking too closely and to raise unwanted questions (Müller, 2008: 101, 200), all manifestations of her unpredictability.[6] She struggled with uniformity, enforced in a predominantly Catholic region with the doctrine of an all-knowing God (Müller and Klammer, 2014: 20). Müller sought normality and yet foreclosed the possibility of assimilation through her independent, critical thought. Individuality also finds its expression in Müller's work through a sustained engagement with different ways of thinking.[7] Through her move from a village to the city, Müller learned to appreciate the continuum between silence and speaking, thought and non-thinking. At one extreme of the continuum, the members of her village, especially her grandmother, shied away from expressing their thoughts freely. Their communication remained closely connected to silence. In their narrative and fragmented character, their conversations also resembled more internal dialogues thought out aloud rather than external speech (Müller and Klammer, 2014: 19). In the city, Müller encountered the other extreme, abundant speech that seemed to lack prior thought or that actively sought to prevent it (Müller, 2008: 100–101). Finally, Müller herself could not escape the 'rush in the head', a double-edged term that captures a capacity for unpredictability and a form of restless challenging of reality.

Müller's work highlights patterns of thought familiar from Margaret Archer's theorising on modes of reflexivity. Müller's 'rush in the head' resembles a contrary meta-reflexivity, characterised by a critical stance towards society and the natal background, in a context of predominantly communicative, and even fractured, reflexive communities. Communicative reflexive practices played an important role in maintaining the coherence and homogeneous character of the 'ethnic island' and its supposed superiority and separateness from the larger ethnic group. Müller's meta-reflexivity also stands in stark contrast to her depiction of the people representing the oppressive orders who, in their almost caricatured portrayal, reveal typical autonomous reflexive concerns of instrumentality and social mobility.

The unpredictability and critical thought that marked Müller's early individualism came to the fore in her later life primarily in opposition to the secret police. They enabled a form of integrity that culminated in the decisive moment of declining the offer of collaboration. Müller summarises her refusal to collaborate as her willingness to lose anything but herself (Müller and Klammer, 2014: 65). To sign the Securitate pledge would have meant being a person '*gegen mich selbst*' (Müller, 2008: 83), against oneself.[8] This moral resolution arose in part from her engagement with her father's dark past. Müller was seventeen at the time the Securitate approached her, and her father had been enthusiastic about Hitler at a similar age. Müller therefore argued that she could not be critical of his acts and simultaneously collaborate with a different totalitarian system (Müller and Klammer, 2014: 37). The writer, however, rejects the idea that integrity is dependent on one's parentage and origin. With her individuality framed, as it undoubtedly is, by the unique context she grew up in, Müller states that no one can be forced to become something against themselves (Müller and Klammer, 2014: 40). Her resistance may therefore also entail a certain naïveté about the complex ways in which humans can become complicit, showing that an ethos of reality is always prone to failure and imperfection.

As a positive example of resistant agency irrespective of the context and background, Müller relies routinely on her close friend Jenny. Jenny was part of the socio-economic and political elite, which protected her from some of the dangers of living under a dictatorship. That said, her outspoken nature offered an uncompromising, robust approach to the anti-individualist strategies of the regime (Müller and Klammer, 2014: 147). Müller's integrity was also informed by the costs of collaboration and spying. The seemingly easy life of collaborators and spies is marred, claimed the Nobel laureate, by effectively having to live a double life. The situation is worsened further by the fear of being found out and the constant danger of being dropped by, and thus becoming the target of, the secret police (Müller and Klammer, 2014: 102). The attacks by the Securitate therefore created a reverse effect, emboldening Müller to defend her individuality – her right to be a source of innovation and to keep the 'rush in the head' going. She even seems to relish the secret police's frustrations and irritations that her strong inner moral commitments to truths and reality caused (Müller, 2008: 65).

In sum, the Nobel laureate paints a picture of a resistant agent, shaped by her unique autobiography and struggling with the demands of living under a dictatorship. She reveals an awareness of differences between humans, their unique modes of thinking and acting upon the world, and maintains the need for agency as source of innovation and integrity against oppression.

Objects and structures

The second dimension to 'life in the detail' entails Müller's engagement with material objects and the structures of society, notably gender, sexuality and language. This dimension does not simply provide a staging device to give judgement a particular tint. Nor are structures (and culture) and materiality merely an obstacle to being human, to be overcome. Ordinary objects are integral to human agency and structures.[9] Social and cultural structures provide the relatively enduring relations and ideas that shape humans and the social positions they inhabit in society. Their generative mechanisms are unobservable and their effects often invisible due to the interplay of many structures and agents in a multi-layered social reality, in which structures and agency equally provide emergent causal contributions. Structures like language, gender and sexuality, and objects play an active role in shaping resistance. Müller's writing establishes this function, as she seeks to capture their positive and negative contributions to social formations.

Müller emphasises the role material objects play in her encounter with reality. She provides a 'surreal but deeply materialist aesthetic' (Haines, 2013: 104). Objects are an extension of who we are and provide separate influences on our behaviour. Sensitive to this fact, Müller observes that humans define themselves through specific objects, including their clothing, and that in doing so they also express and display their character (Müller and Lentz, 2010: 25–26; cf. Müller, 2008: 17). Body and objects are interlinked, and the internal and external worlds of humans extend into each other. In her own writing, the multi-functional role of objects for human agency emerges in various ways. Müller takes mundane objects, a nut or nail scissors, and objects captured by using compound terms, such as a 'wood melon',[10] from their context and gives them multiple meanings to invoke in language a multi-layered reality. A nightgown that features in a German train advertisement, for example, links Müller back to a series of experiences during Romania's dictatorship that she remembers as connected to similar nightgowns. Objects and locations thus gain an important narrative function and are attributed an independent causal role (Müller, 2008: 121–122). They do not merely offer a passive backdrop but play an essential part in the story (Johannsen, 2013). As illustrated painfully by the secret police moving and repositioning objects in a flat to suggest their presence and instil fear, this interplay between materiality and agency, subjectivity and objectivity can have positive and negative implications.

Physical objects, together with agency and human interaction, constitute social structures – the network of relationships amongst social positions that frame human agency – which play a key role in how agency resists reductionism. To understand Müller's objectivism more fully, I focus on how she deals with the social function of gender, sexuality and language in Romania. Together, they reveal how structures both enable and constrain a person resisting a dictatorship. More specifically, as I focus on Müller's interviews and essays, I consider the role she attributes to structures, which in turn gives us a sense of how they framed her own response to persecution.

Müller challenges the totalitarian misuse of sexuality and gender that led to a highly poisonous system of gender relationships. She attributes the emphasis on gender and sexuality in her work to the fact that, during the dictatorship, all areas of the citizen's life were colonised, including the sexual. The erotic is both a site of oppression and a useful, necessary release valve for all the fears and anxieties: under the dictatorship, relationships and desires gained a more intense, immediate, and yet particularly vulnerable character (Müller and Klammer, 2014: 108). Müller is especially interested in how distorted structures of gender and sexuality impact on human relationships: 'I see humans, how they seem to act freely and not knowing that they do so under certain constraints, that they are part of a mechanism, that they act with the freedom of marionettes. I try to depict this mechanism' (cited in Eke, 1991: 12, my translation).

In her considerations of how structures such as gender and sexuality define and inform resistance to the totalitarian state, Müller describes various forms of oppression, from rape to sexual harassment as part of political interrogations. The cases are framed by her critique of the regime's inhumane reproductive health policies, part of a pro-nationalist population strategy banning contraceptives and abortions: 'the state monitored the most private aspects of people's lives, intimacy was owned by the state. Nasty methods were used to enforce check-ups on women, as they for example needed attestation by a gynaecologist to access treatment by a dentist' (Müller and Klammer, 2014: 107, my translation).

Müller highlights the interpersonal reproduction of domination. Although she makes a point of depicting both men and women as victims and perpetrators, they differ in that women's power remains derivative and secondary to men's and Müller often describes their power as a response to male violence (Bauer, 2013).[11] Women are caught in two hierarchical power relations, a patriarchal and a totalitarian. Both men and women are in a sense the victims and enactors of their asymmetrical interdependence, but it is men who are in a position to systematically exploit their dominance over women. Müller's story is therefore also one of (distorted) patriarchal structures in the contexts of her village and Romania more generally. Rural and city life followed a strict division of labour, men occupying positions said to require force or authority, a system only gradually transformed by the introduction of machines (Müller and Klammer, 2014: 58).[12]

Attentive to the gender dynamics of her time, Müller's ethos of reality seeks to open up a space in which resistance is possible – in full awareness that any resistance must successfully negotiate the system of gender domination, as she herself tries to. Her female characters are deeply shaped by the sexual violence they experience every day. They also continuously find ways of taking control of their bodies and sexuality, often seeking to participate in the exchange economy in ways that enable them to protect themselves from the threats of living under a dictatorship. Yet, whatever strategy the protagonists involved in sexual domination employ, Müller always articulates the looming negative consequences and the heightened vulnerability that come with it, defying any desire for a break-through moment.[13]

Language provided another structure of central importance in the relationship between Romania's citizens and between citizens and the totalitarian state. Müller's considerations on language as a tool of oppression and resistance are framed by her distinct position to her mother tongue, German, and to Romanian. I will address the gap caused by her movement between the two languages as part of the discussion of her writing approach in the final section. For now, my analysis focuses on how Müller approaches the political character of language and resists a simplistic connection between one's language and homeliness. Language, for Müller, means initially the German she learned in Nitzkydorf. An Austrian variation of German, the rural dialect is said to have 'slowed down' as if encapsulating an agricultural life at the periphery of the Habsburg empire (Müller and Lentz, 2010: 41). Later on, she encounters Romanian, as a more lyrical language rooted in its folkloric tradition.

Both languages became political instruments, and Müller surmises that all dictatorships instrumentalise language (Müller, 2008: 37). The first oppressive regime she encountered consisted in the Banat village's regime of conformity. Müller recreates the linguistic working of this dictatorship through the use of the proverb 'The devil is seated in the mirror' for the title of one of her novels. The devil in the mirror is meant to warn against vices including vanity, but Müller reads it as a means to discourage critical self-evaluation and impose an unreflective, collectively imposed identity. This proverb, representative of numerous phrases taught to children by their family to curb individuality, characterises how language was used as a form of indoctrination: 'One puts something into people's heads through a harmless phrase, which later gets stuck and takes effect in various situations. That is how you control people' (Haines and Littler, 1998: 17, my translation).

Language is for Müller innately political as it is tied to the relationships and interactions between people. Because of the danger of political misuse, Müller is especially disconcerted by the fact that German writers confronted her with the notion that 'language is homeland' (Müller, 2008: 33). She notes the problematic origin of this term – its use by emigrants fleeing from a totalitarian Germany – and the xenophobic character of those nationalists in Germany and Romania who continue to rely on the term 'homeland'. Her scepticism also links back to her general focus on a life in the detail as response to a context where home/homeliness has become foreign and a place of insecurity. Contra this naïve relationship with language, Müller encourages a critical engagement with language that considers in each case what meaning is conveyed and whether the action that language motivates is legitimate or unacceptable, good or bad (Müller, 2008: 46–47). And, while language, like gender dynamics, may at first seem to offer little in resistance, Müller finds new ways in which it moves from being a tool of interrogation and terror to providing a tool for resistance. These gain their full force in relation to her approach to writing.

Plurality through friendship

The pluralist dimension to being human refers to the fact that humans share a world in common which they can only make hospitable together. Furthermore, pluralism captures the fact that, as each person has a partial perspective on the world, they have to rely on others to make suitable judgements and come to terms with reality. In Müller's work plurality is framed by her insight that retaining moral integrity in the private sphere necessitated public failure (Müller and Klammer, 2014: 40). Put differently, to be successful under a totalitarian regime probably requires compromises and a show of support for the regime, both of which leave a person in a difficult moral situation. Plurality under Ceaușescu's rule proved highly constrained and distorted, undermined by a state-produced 'ugly' equality in all areas, from architecture and fashion to the party language (Müller and Klammer, 2014: 73, 76).

In Müller's childhood, plurality is primarily visible in the form of an acceptance of one's common identity, which in the German minority was presupposed rather than being formed in the process of acting together. The oppressive silence of the village created a state of loneliness further heightened by Müller's realisation that her own 'abnormality' had to be hidden from others (Müller and Klammer, 2014: 17–18).[11] The Aktionsgruppe Banat therefore proved crucial for Müller; in it she discovered something akin to a pluralist public sphere, in which views could be shared and strategies developed against the secret police. While such forms of togetherness and friendship can be looked at as ersatz pluralism, it too is marred by encroachment of the alien gaze. Müller later discovered that the secret police had bugged their rooms and used the information gathered clandestinely against the group. Her writing and its increasing success in Germany opened another public sphere to Müller, but again, the pluralist dimension to being human was undermined by the Securitate's extensive strategy of publicly defaming her (Müller and Klammer, 2014: 168–169). If we accept, as Müller does, that to be human is to meaningfully share a world together, the question therefore remains: what could friendship offer under these extreme circumstances?

Positively, friendship may have offered a means to cope with the planned fear produced by the secret police (Müller and Klammer, 2014: 114). Emblematic in this respect is Müller's fellow worker and friend Jenny who, despite being part of the Romanian political elite, remained supportive. Müller had been terrorised to force her to quit: she was removed from her office and rumours were spread about her being a collaborator. The friend nonetheless chose to sit with Müller during lunch and share a private friendship (Müller and Klammer, 2014: 150ff.). This support and confirmation by another person was of utmost importance to Müller during this difficult period. Jenny is, however, also a reminder that friendship is always potentially a source of fragility. Jenny became susceptible to the secret police's manipulation strategies following a diagnosis of terminal cancer. Desperate to see her friend, she agreed to spy on Müller, who by then had emigrated and settled in Berlin. Because of the importance of their friendship, this betrayal hit Müller particularly hard. It proved a traumatic event that Müller has tried to come to terms with throughout her work, not least as Jenny offered her a friendship outside the targeted artistic circles and therefore some distance and 'normality' – Jenny and Müller enjoyed conversations about non-political topics (Müller and Klammer, 2014: 148). Thus, friendship for Müller can at best enable one to avoid facing the terror alone and can help one cope with the planned fear of the secret police. For this function, the relationships are close and tight knit, as visible in her relations with the Aktionsgruppe Banat. Friends help share and temporarily ignore the fear (Müller and Klammer, 2014: 113–114). They cannot prevent or hinder the destruction of the individual as each is targeted separately and affected by terror and fear differently. This friendship becomes 'double-edged', as both a vital source of support and exposure to each other's fears and anxiety (Mihai, 2022: 164–165). Worse still, the Securitate acknowledged the friends from Müller's literary and cultural circles as a 'we'-group of resistance and set out to exploit the weaknesses of a collective. Additionally, people sought to avoid engaging and being seen with potential targets of the secret police, in fear of becoming targets themselves. Jenny and other people who ignored this separation between those deemed subversive and the *nomenklatura* were at great risk. This meant that friendship was restricted to those who were already targets of the secret police (Müller and Klammer, 2014: 112). In sharing their fear there is also a sense of being overexposed to each other. In so far as this limited measure of worldliness, instantiated through friendship, offered only scant protection, the totalitarian devastation achieved its full potential.

Friendship as source of plurality found its low point in Müller's life with the death of two friends. She was forced to find a different medium to express her life in the detail: 'I searched for words for the fear we had in common. I wanted to show what friendship looks like when it is no longer self-evident that one will survive' (Müller, 2008: 62, my translation). Another world-building form of judgement was needed, and Müller relied on writing to supplement a life in the detail.

Writing in defence of an ethos of reality

At stake for Müller and the regime under which she lived until 1987 was nothing less than control over the human ability to independently judge and come to terms with reality. To counteract the dehumanising reductionisms of the Romanian dictatorship, Müller proposed 'living in the detail'. It starts off with the basic survival strategy of maintaining one's sense of self from one moment to another – to simply hold on and avoid giving up – and requires attentiveness to the three components that together constitute the common world: agency, structure and plurality. Their function is curbed by the totalitarian experience and the encroachment of the alien gaze. Müller therefore mounts her strongest defence against persecution: a form of writing that she terms 'invented perception'. This writing seeks to strengthen a sense of reality, by insisting on the complexity of social processes. It opens space in the description of the world for all three components of human existence to play their part. The success of writing in Müller's case depends on whether it allows her to build, maintain and protect a common world denied by the state, as the source for concrete judgements that take the dualism and pluralism of human existence into account. It does not depend on the reproduction of the potential of structures, agency and plurality by other means. The purpose of invented perception is not to replace the deformed interplay of structure, agency and plurality with writing and its unique ability to recreate reality, but to both show the deformation and reveal their continued potential as sources of social transformation and resistance.

Müller's judgement through writing is dedicated to the production of what she terms 'erfundene Wahrnehmung' (Müller, 1991: 38), invented perception. This form of realisation is a variation of what I term affirming a multi-layered, shared reality, and entails the use of autofiction, surrealism and the gap between Romanian and German. It is the inversion of percepticide, the motivated separation from reality, because invented perception seeks to rebuild our sense of reality. To understand what Müller means by this form of realisation, we first need to consider the particular role she attributes to everyday realities that motivate invention. From this consideration emerges once more the central motto of her response to the dictatorship, 'life in the detail'. Building on these insights I analyse the three strategies of autofiction, surrealism and the valorisation of the gap between languages as her means to exploit the motto without falling for reductive narratives.

The continuous harassment in the factory and the death of Müller's father brought back the village experience and led her to search for some alternative hold in writing.[15] The need to write was therefore instinctive, part of the immediate survival strategy by living in the detail. Müller was compelled to put forward something protected from the regime's vigilant eyes by entering a quasi-fictional terrain (Müller, 2008: 18). Admittedly, writing may seem, at first, an unlikely solution when faced with the demands for a defence against fear and terror. To write is not to resolve the challenges to daily life under a dictatorship. If anything, writing ensures a deeper immersion in an environment of terror, as it often comes with a cultivation of a particular sensibility for the way the world is. Müller is certainly no exception to this problem for writers.[16]

Müller's extension of 'life in the detail' through writing is further faced with the difficulty of how to depict life under the Romanian dictatorship without creating a pedagogic, ideological book 'with reverse sign' (Haines and Littler, 1998: 18, my translation). Müller seeks to avoid any connections between her writing and socialist realism, that is, the compulsory style of glorified depiction of communist values cultivated by the communist regime, which provides a highly reductive narrative of reality. This form of realism contributed significantly to Müller's desire for the fictional and literary, and its capacity to create a space for reality to be complicated (Haines and Littler, 1998: 18). Painfully aware of these tensions that arise from the connection between writing and a 'life in the detail', Müller nonetheless insists that writing, over time, provides some certainty, some internal stability that can be used to oppose the pervasive fear (Müller and Klammer, 2014: 42; Müller and Lentz, 2010: 7, 15). To write is to hopefully gain access to the many things that have been silenced, distorted and perverted, to reveal the truths about everyday reality by expressing them in the simplistic beauty, and precision, of a written sentence (Müller and Klammer, 2014: 77). Her first attempts, including the novel *Niederungen*, enabled reflection on what had been silenced in her home village (Müller and Klammer, 2014: 81).

The different meanings – rather than functions – of writing interlink for Müller through her concern with individuality: the quality of a text is defined by its ability to create a 'rush in the head' that undermines silence and ideology and produces new understanding and meaning both in Müller and in her readers (Müller, 2008: 23–24). Its beauty depends on whether it reveals a multi-layered reality, and how it purposely avoids protecting humans from the truth by provoking a wild, independent thought beyond dogmatic presuppositions. Invented perception lacks direct reality and yet, crucially, enables a new, different perspective on reality (Müller and Lentz, 2010: 39). And, although writing remains an individual and silent activity, Müller further uses it as a platform for discussions with her audience, publishing essays and providing numerous interviews in German and Romanian. In seeking to strengthen the 'it-seems-to-me', to create a more hospitable common world, and in interacting with others to do so, Müller's writing constitutes an exemplary judgement that helps sustain a suitable ethos of reality.

There are numerous literary devices that Müller deploys to achieve this invented perception in her writings, starting with the focus on autofiction. Müller builds her understanding of autofiction on the writings of Georges Arthur Goldschmidt (Haines and Littler, 1998: 14). By autofiction Müller means that her work relies on a first-person narrator resembling Müller and that it constructs stories by relying on true occurrences. The choice of autofiction is a consequence of living under a state that forces the individual to engage with the question of how to live as a person under a totalitarian regime, and that turns the aesthetic into a space of political contestation. Müller uses her real experiences as a background, which is then extensively rewritten into fiction that shares similarities with reality, without directly reproducing any particular fact or event. Her fictionalised reality is hence juxtaposed with the contorted reality experienced, and achieves its credibility because of the latter – the experience of numerous actual interrogations enables the invention of a fictional situation of interrogation (Haines and Littler, 1998: 15, 18).

Müller frames autofiction with what commentator Paola Bozzi identifies as 'surfiction' – the critical encounter with the 'fictional' nature of reality (Bozzi, 2013). By this she means that surfiction rejects any clear-cut divide between reality and fiction where the latter is merely an 'unreal' abstraction of the former. Surfiction combined with autofiction thus becomes a form of realist surrealism or surreal realism. Indeed, Müller understands surrealism not as an alternative to reality, but rather as a deeper version of reality, as she seeks to capture the surrealism *inside* reality. In her Leipzig poetry lecture following the award of the Nobel Prize in 2009, Müller accordingly stated that for her

> reality is something far further-reaching than others might suggest. How far does reality reach, and where and when does surrealism begin? It certainly does not start outside the real and not underneath it. The surreal is always inside reality; [many may] believe that surrealism goes above or deep beneath reality. I simply go inside, to find the surreal (Müller and Lentz, 2010: 35–36, my translation).

Autofiction thus offers the first means by which Müller recreates the multi-layered character of reality as the source of a hospitable common world that enables her to judge and come to terms with this difficult context.

Müller's invented perception, or surreal realism, gains in strength through her reliance on fragmented narratives. Discontinuity is for Müller not the opposite of reality: we might perceive reality as continuous and embedded in simple stories with clear directions and with a beginning and an end, but in reality, as Müller emphasises, objects and events around us remain scattered and their connections complex (Haines and Littler, 1998: 18). Yet the prevalence of fragmentation in her work does not mean that the Nobel laureate denies the narrative dimension to reality altogether. Both continuity and discontinuity are part of a multi-layered reality in which some things are connected, and numerous things happen at the same time.

Other literary devices exploring the nexus between realism and surrealism include a particular attentiveness to the role of dreams and to how children, in taking things (too) literally, often reveal a surrealism that can make manifest something concrete that would otherwise be hidden (Haines and Littler, 1998: 18; Müller and Klammer, 2014: 21). Furthermore, Müller relies on repetitive use of numerous metaphors, including objects such as the nut in *Herztier* or the king in *Der König verneigt sich und tötet*. These metaphors are increasingly estranged from their original context and given numerous levels of meaning that help reproduce a sense of complexity and ambiguity to reality. Mathias

Thaler (2018) helpfully terms this kind of estrangement estrangement *for* the world, which can be differentiated from estrangement *from* the world. The metaphors are, however, also returned to their original contexts and resolved, which helps Müller maintain the connection between reality, especially materiality, and fiction in her writing (Haines and Littler, 1998: 18). All of these devices serve to create, build and protect a common world as part of which Müller is able to make concrete judgements about her context that affirm the multi-layered character of reality, contra the state narratives.

Lastly, Müller's production of invented perception gains in strength through her use of the gap between her mother tongue, German, and the second language she learned in her youth, Romanian. As Brigid Haines argues, 'Müller's texts create an Arendtian newness out of a reconfiguration of the gaps between languages and words' (2013: 102). Typical example is the pheasant, from her novel *Der Mensch ist ein großer Fasan auf der Welt* (*The Passport*) (2015c), an animal that for Germans epitomises arrogance and for Romanians being a loser. The gap is in part a result of Müller's lack of affection for her mother tongue, which she associates with her stifling community in the natal village. German, at best, provides her with a useful familiarity (Müller, 2008: 32). Romanian lacks this familiarity and Müller rarely writes in Romanian. However, by having to learn the language abruptly upon her arrival in the city aged fifteen, and struggling to do so, it is also a language Müller learned much more consciously. This gave her time to appreciate the gap between German and Romanian, the way things have different meanings in the two languages (Müller, 2008: 31).

Romanian takes part in all her German writings, and both languages encounter each other with every newly learned word (Müller, 2008: 32; Müller and Klammer, 2014: 84, 86). The language offers a particularly potent contribution here because it diverges significantly from Germanic languages. Müller claims that Romanian has also remained closer to its folklore roots which offer it protection from the totalitarian inversion of language (Müller and Klammer, 2014: 87–88). This Romanian, Müller argues,

> is in its sensuality and in its way of looking at the world, completely different, and I was always much closer to this different way of looking at the world. Structurally, this language's images, the metaphors, the idioms and the folklore, have always suited me better' (Haines and Littler, 1998: 15, my translation).

These differences enable Müller to make new poetic connections between words and extend her surreal realist conception (Müller and Klammer, 2014: 49).[17]

At the same time, language is a structure deeply embedded in the oppressive mechanisms of the dictatorship and Müller exploits language as a tool for writing in order to simultaneously highlight the multi-faceted role of language. The gap helps create a situated position sufficiently distanced to help interrogate the structural underpinnings of her culture and to simultaneously impose one's own individuality – as Müller exploits the gap to give new meaning to words. The gap also forces upon the reader a choice between meanings and thus creates, once more, a 'rush in the head'. Disembedded from the familiarity of one's own language, Müller's playing with words sustains multiple layers of meaning to a reality and also, crucially, an echo of the plurality of perspectives on shared objects that should be available to humans as they seek to come to terms with reality.

Concluding thoughts

Müller offers an insight into what judgement framed by an improved ethos of reality in practice might look like by focusing our attention on the difficult context of Romania between 1965 and 1989. Her ethos is encapsulated by the motto 'to live in the detail' and centres on a strategy of upholding the complexity of reality. She attends to how the ethnic German minority and the Romanian dictatorship sought to destroy both personhood and a world in common. This I have identified as the first objective of an improved ethos of reality: to explore the pernicious reductionisms of a multi-layered reality that impoverish the common world. Müller also affirms the need to create and protect a common world independent from the distorting strategies deployed by the secret police. Writing offers an appropriate judgement and maintains the ethos of reality by combining an everyday survival strategy of life in the detail with the abstraction and estrangement of surrealism. Deploying different devices, including autofiction and the gap between languages, Müller's work can thus be read as illustrative of the framework I develop in this book: the affirmation of a multi-layered, shared reality through which critical evaluation of events is made possible without falling for a problematic strategy of reductionism. As I indicated above during my discussion of a suitable toolkit for studying judgement, such an improved ethos can only be achieved through an engagement with its three components: structure, agency and plurality. My discussion of Müller's reflection on gender, sexuality, language, materiality, reflexivity and friendship has illustrated that Müller is sufficiently attentive to both the dualist and the pluralist dimensions of human existence. This makes Müller exemplary of the kind of ethos of reality I wish to put forward as suitable, good judgement.

Notes

1. Müller had started gaining international acclaim in the 1980s with the publication of a series of collected short stories, *Niederungen (Nadirs)* ([1984] 2011). The series was followed by the novel *Der Mensch ist ein großer Fasan auf der Welt (The Passport)* ([1986] 2015), dealing with her childhood in the Romanian countryside under dictatorship, and the novel *Herztier (The Land of Green Plums)* ([1994] 2007), which retells the effect of state terror on a circle of writers who shared a friendship.
2. For alternative biographical summaries, see Eke (2017); Haines (1998).
3. The village's isolation reflected its existence on the outskirts of the Austrian empire, far away from any major capital. Uninterrupted until the two world wars and the labour camp deportations, the villagers held tightly to their centuries-old traditions. Being stuck in a glorified and romanticised past enabled them to hold on to a belief in their superiority over the other ethnic groups, which was increasingly undermined by the political developments of the twentieth century (Müller and Lentz, 2010: 19, 23).
4. To possess the alien gaze does not mean that one is foreign to a place. Nor does it refer to the detachment of an intellectual from the events occurring around them. Both these common conceptions of alien (in German '*fremd*', 'foreign') gaze have been attributed to Müller's writing, which she, however, vehemently rejects. For such a reading misses the crucial point that the alien gaze arises out of a familiar environment and its trusted objects losing their familiarity (Müller, 2008: 179).
5. Bearing in mind that the Romanian dictatorship seemed capable of formulating regulations for any purpose it deemed necessary, Müller was initially puzzled by the secret police's decision to come up with trumped-up charges of prostitution and black market trading against her (Müller and Klammer, 2014: 193). This strategy, however, was not chosen arbitrarily. The invention of facts allowed the secret police complete control over what was to be considered as the legitimate narrative of reality, while retaining a thin connection to the real world – after all, prostitution and black markets were prohibited.

6. Accordingly, in her interviews, Müller recounts that she was aware that no one could know that, as she spent considerable time alone in the fields herding her family's cattle, she would eat flowers in order to become part of the surrounding nature or that she married flowers with each other – games that might indicate the child's 'abnormality' (Müller and Klammer, 2014: 14). Müller understood the drastic consequences of revealing her abnormality and the deviation of her behaviour and thoughts.
7. We can read Müller's writing, especially the novel *The Appointment* (2001), as a journey into the mind of the main protagonist that helps illustrate what happens to a mind under state persecution (cf. Boase-Beier, 2014). Her emphasis on reflexive agency furthermore must be read as part of a commitment to account for a situated, embodied human. Müller emphasises that thinking is tied together with feeling and goes beyond words (Müller and Klammer, 2014: 82, 141). Müller thought and felt loneliness and fear even though she could not adequately express them. The thirst to capture these experiences in speech ultimately animated her writing (Müller, 2008: 19).
8. Again, Müller recognises the limits of self-awareness during a heightened state of fear. Her vigilance during the period of intense persecution fostered a thirst for giving up the fight, not by assimilation but by the oblivion promised by insanity (Müller, 2008: 180). The writer was also for some time plagued by thoughts of suicide, which she, however, claims to have overcome because her suicide would have meant the ultimate triumph of the secret police: she realised that she would have done 'their dirty work for them' (Müller and Lentz, 2010: 29, my translation). Müller suddenly 'wanted to live, became addicted to life, exactly because she wasn't deemed worthy of it' (Müller and Lentz, 2010: 30, my translation).
9. The emphasis on material objects arises out of the objectivism introduced in Chapter 4. Contra anthropocentric models that focus primarily on intentionality and language, the critical realist framework highlights how structures consist in the relations between human and non-human material parts and their interaction and interrelation. For a discussion of the relationship between social structures and ordinary objects in critical realism and its importance for debates on social ontology, see Elder-Vass (2017).
10. Through the metaphor 'wood melon', Müller captures a failed transformation of an agricultural society into an industrial economy, as envisaged by communist social engineers: the farmers in the processing plants produce valueless wooden melons instead of harvesting fruit.
11. Possibly the most prominent example of male sexual victimhood in connection to Müller is her friend Oskar Pastior, who turned informant to evade reprisals for his homosexuality.

12. A farmer's wife, Müller notes in an interview, seems to have little independence in such a patriarchal context and yet her individuality and sense of self emerge out of practising a pragmatic self-confidence, out of always being seemingly able to respond appropriately to life (Müller, 1998: 19). Müller, however, remains sceptical of this pragmatism, and her scepticism is informed by the (political) disconnect that came with it in her ethnic group, as captured by her mother: traumatised by the labour camp and struggling with her husband's alcoholism, she practised an obsession with cleaning as a means to escape the everyday problems.
13. This is representatively visible in the case of Lola in *Herztier*, who defies the exchange system by engaging in numerous sexual activities before becoming pregnant and committing suicide.
14. Highly limited forms of solidarity emerged only between the deported who brought back from the labour camps a common, short hairstyle and teeth prostheses – external manifestations of the suffering caused by the terrible conditions in the camps, and the former soldiers who would drunkenly sing their national socialist songs together.
15. Brigid Haines reads Müller in connection with Arendt. She concludes that it is 'gestures, objects, and the free life of words that, for Müller, lend some temporary stability to Arendt's subject in crisis' (Haines, 2013: 104).
16. The complicated relationship between writing and a need to resist by living in the detail is heightened further through Müller's rejection of any means–ends thinking about literature. She emphasises that writing would be unlikely to fulfil the demands put upon it (Müller and Lentz, 2010: 8).
17. As elaborated above, Müller is aware of the ambiguous character of language as a source of resistance. Language remains a potent tool favoured by the dictatorship for its distorting state narratives. These narratives consist of a language that in its use of stock phrases could be reassembled in various combinations without any need for reflection. Müller's use of language also cannot be separated in style and content from the fear and loneliness she experienced (Müller and Lentz, 2010: 14).

CONCLUSION

A new approach to judging complicity

My interrogation into judging complicity started with the observation that recent public debate, informed by social movements including Black Lives Matter and #MeToo, has increasingly made it impossible for the privileged to deny their complicity in systemic injustice and oppression. I also argued that the continued, widespread failure to affirm complicity should serve as a catalyst for a sustained engagement with how we judge and respond to it. This book contributes to the project by providing a refined theoretical toolkit centred on debates about judgement, complicity and social conditioning. By way of conclusion, I provide a summary of the contribution this book has sought to make, a discussion of lessons and limitations, and a postulation of potential trajectories for further research.

This book puts forward three key findings. First, in response to the question 'How can human beings judge their complicity in injustice and oppression?', I argue that we must focus on our collective engagement with reality as an irreducible and paramount problem of political theory. Chapter 2 retraces Hannah Arendt's thought and highlights the relationship she identified between a person's ability to make judgements, their sense of reality, and the public opinion formation process. Put simply, judgements depend on, but also gain their strength from, the ability to come together as a community and to look at issues from different perspectives. The interdependence between judgement and the public sphere gains in importance following the modern erosion of historical standards of judgement such as customs and traditions that facilitated, to some extent, easy judgements. The erosion opened the door to the twentieth century's totalitarianism, but the break in tradition also provides a unique opportunity to re-embed the process of giving meaning to reality within the public interaction of citizens, away from the coercive, external force of traditional sources of authority.

Central to Arendt's argument that connects judgement, politics and reality is a particular conception of plurality, by which I mean the implications she drew from the fact that humans can only make the world hospitable together. Arendt identified three key elements of the human condition: plurality, the distinction and sameness of human beings, and the existence of a common world. This notion of plurality stands opposed to a dominant view in society and political philosophy that perceives politics as reducible to means–ends thinking and focuses on issues of sovereignty, violence and domination. In its place, Arendt highlighted that politics provides one or more separate spaces that enable people to appeal to others without reliance on exhaustive moral frameworks and, in so doing, produces meaning. Pluralist politics at its best reveals what connects and separates people and ensures that new developments become issues of common interest and contestation. Heightened concerns about complicity are a good example of this. Judgement contributes to this political manifestation of plurality, by enabling people to take up a position towards public appearances. As part of a political, reflective process, judgement also benefits from the ability to bring together a plurality of spectators and actors; to incorporate a diversity of perspectives through representative thinking; and to elaborate the sense of community further by creating new stories and exemplars. Together these mechanisms enable a judging person to expand their sense of reality without ever reaching 'objectivity' or losing the connection to their partial, yet unique, perspective on the world.

The second finding of this book concerns the role that social conditioning plays, alongside human plurality, for refining judgements on complicity. Chapter 3 offers a summary of the debate that followed Arendt's theorisation on political judgement and identifies two phases with a variety of different responses. The second phase affirms the focus on human plurality but suggests it does not resolve the problem of how judgement can gain critical purchase – once freed from the clutches of supposedly pre-given, fixed principles. I consider several theorists who respond to this problem through a discussion of the related concepts of imagination, emotions, the unconscious, storytelling and the pre-discursive structuring of judgement.

Through their projects, the book gains invaluable insights on judgement and shows how Arendt scholars identify in situated agency the key to the critical potential in (political) judgement – without yet fully unpacking what this situated agency entails.

Chapter 4 extends the insights of judgement scholars by introducing Margaret Archer's contribution to debates on the relationship between structure and agency. Archer shares Arendt's concern with how humans (can) engage with reality in the context of modern dehumanising tendencies. Specifically, she identifies a tendency to conflate social structures and human agency, which fails to account for the vexatious fact of reality that people feel equally free and enchained in their actions. Archer proposes a morphogenetic approach to structure and agency as a solution, which accounts for the analytically and temporally separate powers and mechanisms of agency and structure that shape society together. I take from Archer that judgement benefits from attentiveness to the dualism of structure–agency or, in other words, objectivism, subjectivism and their mediation through reflexivity. A focus on the distinct properties and mechanisms of structure and agency amounts to a commitment to a mind-independent, stratified reality alongside a concern with personhood that is embodied, emotional, relational, capable of social innovation and with a sense of self, emerging out of a varied engagement with a stratified world. The dualist approach enables judgement scholars to attend to the object and subject of judgement, without denying their interrelation or the crucial role that a public sphere plays for judgements.

The third finding of this book is therefore that we should judge our responses to complicity by their ability to account for the dualism and pluralism to human existence. We can ask, does the judgement help create, build, maintain and protect a world that is multi-layered and held in common, through a suitable focus on the interplay of structure, agency and plurality? Of note is that judgements inform, and are part of, our habituated stance towards reality – what I call an ethos of reality. To improve our ethos of reality, we need to pursue two objectives, explored in Chapter 5. Firstly, the ethos should respond to the subjective, objective and intersubjective powers and mechanisms that impoverish the common world, notably the systematic reductionism of a multi-layered reality. Secondly, the ethos should identify and engender contributions by structure, agency and plurality that facilitate a more hospitable, flourishing common world as the prism through which we can make concrete judgements on complicity that affirm the multi-layered character of reality.

The importance of adhering to dualism and pluralism in judging complicity became evident in relation to the methodological individualism that continues to frame the dominant legal and moral philosophical perspective on complicity, but also in the critical responses that oppose it. The complicity-as-being approach and the work of Iris Marion Young have helped articulate a broader conception of complicity that leads to a collective responsibility and affirmation of human foldedness in contexts of systemic injustice and oppression. The most recent critical formulation, an ethics of responsiveness, highlights that (although both the complicity-as-being approach and Young acknowledge socially embedded human agency) they fail to account for the difficulties of cultivating responsiveness towards the marginalised, victimised, excluded and suffering. This is something that authors who build on these perspectives do and I am supportive of their attempts to expand the critical alternatives by engaging with the problem of receptivity. To refine their approach, I observe that their proposals for how the privileged can become more responsive to injustice rely too easily on the image of a duality. The duality opposes deeply rooted systemic injustice with receptive agency, which leads to a theorisation of responsiveness in separation from the structural contributions to transformation.

Chapter 6 takes up the challenge of mapping out what actual judgements of complicity, embedded in an ethos of reality, could look like. I draw on the reflections of Romanian Nobel laureate Herta Müller on the everyday challenges of resistance and complicity during the Romanian communist dictatorship. The writer's ethos of reality manifests itself in a resistant practice of 'living in the detail'. Living in the detail highlights the need to hold on to the complexity of reality and the concreteness of particulars contra a regime that distorted reality to oppress its citizens. At the same time, Müller's writing helps protect and strengthen reality through attentiveness to variations in agency, the contributions of objects, places and structures, and the friendships and exchanges that together create a hospitable common world, as well as to the ever-present possibility of their destruction. Literary devices including autofiction and surrealism serve to maintain the ambiguity and complexity of this reality, as they deny the closure and simplistic narratives offered by the dictatorship.

Leading on from the overview of this book's contribution, let me address some potential criticisms one might wish to raise against my argument. As a primarily theoretical project, the book would benefit from more empirical research, for example into reflective judgement and its connection to the identified changes to reflexivity in late modernity. In awareness of this limitation, I have refrained from stretching the extensive empirical research done by Archer beyond its original purpose. This restriction undoubtedly leaves an important gap to be filled by research into the relationship between political judgement and reflexivity, as well as into politics as Arendt understood it and the conditions of late modernity. For such a project to get off the ground, however, significant under-labouring is necessary. To this end, I have sought to provide an appropriate articulation of Arendt's and Archer's positions. For the purpose of an immanent critique of approaches to judging complicity, the theoretical insights prove crucial. A second challenge may focus on the (over)emphasis on the three dimensions of structure, agency and plurality, which risks obscuring other categories, for example, time and space, that could potentially help evaluate the limitations of how people take and theorise complicity. Critics might additionally point out that the separation of the three dimensions is insufficiently attentive to their interplay. Chapters 4 to 6 underline the value of a focus on the separate categories of structure, agency and plurality, even as I accept that we must also take account of other categories and their interpenetration. Such a focus provides a potent tool that lays bare the strengths and weaknesses of different theoretical and practical approaches to complicity. Theorists of complicity show an acute awareness of the challenge of structure–agency and the need to create a hospitable world together amidst pervasive violence and injustices. Without further refinement of the approach to social conditioning and judgement along the lines outlined in this book, however, the various positions in debates on complicity ultimately risk endangering their shared goal of facilitating positive social transformation through an improved account of complicity. Lastly, readers might challenge a turn to critical realism without a prior consideration of the realist position available in contemporary political theory. Arendt had a strained relationship with major political realists, notably Isaiah Berlin (Dubnov, 2017; Hiruta, 2014), and a comparison of their work may help further delineate Arendt's contribution to an improved ethos of reality. While I agree that political realists provide a means to distinguish Arendt's pluralist realism further, they lack a suitable approach to political judgement and recent realist criticisms of John Rawls do not provide a sustained attempt at putting forward a comprehensive alternative to Arendt's realism (Bourke and Geuss, 2009; Galston, 2010; cf. Vogler and Tillyris, 2021).

The discussion of potential limitations gives a sense of the many ways that the insights in this book warrant extension. On its own, the constantly changing interrelationship between structure, agency and plurality in late modernity demands further investigation and reimagination; one avenue could here be a turn to debates on trans- and posthumanism (cf. Chernilo, 2017). The following focuses briefly on an aspect to this project that I take to be particularly important and most open to further reflection in this book: the relational dimension of the common world. My hybridisation of Arendt's pluralism and Archer's dualism goes some way in refining our understanding of the three components that constitute the common world, structure, agency and plurality. If we fail to address adequately one of the three dimensions of human existence, we risk falling back into an overly structuralist or individualist conception of reality. However, 'worldliness' and 'common world' remain opaque terms whose full meaning has not been sufficiently unpacked in terms of plurality, beyond Arendt's insight that we can only make the world hospitable together and that our actions and judgements depend on and bring into being a common world or worlds. For this purpose, a cross-pollination of different theories of human relationality may prove fruitful.

As a potential avenue for further research, I tentatively suggest departing from this project by interrogating different approaches focused on capturing the irreducible qualities of plurality in relation to the concepts of worldliness and world-in-common. Within social theory, one could begin with Archer's theory of relational goods and evils, and social theorist Hartmut Rosa's work on resonance. Together with Pierpaolo Donati, Archer argues for a conception of relationality as 'we-ness' where the relation itself has emergent properties irreducible to the intentionality of the participants (Donati and Archer, 2015). People offer reflexive orientations towards the emergent relational goods, for example, trust or evils (distrust). In his recent monograph *Resonance: A Sociology of Our Relationship to the World* (2019), Rosa argues that critical theory must concern itself with the elementary issue of the state of human relationships with the world. His work looks at how people resonate with the world, as a suitable response to forms of alienation, which he defines as the dominance of non-resonating modes of being. This focus on foregrounding the independent, emergent properties of the relationship between self and world, and the resonances between world and humans, offers a gateway to broader reflections on human relationality within and beyond social and political theory. Readers may turn for instance to the important, yet diverse, contributions by indigenous thinkers who articulate a deeper conception of interdependence (cf. Lovern, 2021). With these theories, it is my intuition that it is our responsibility as academics to recuperate a stronger theoretical notion of plurality and relationality in order to create a hospitable world as the starting point for tackling injustices and oppression. For now, this book has shown that judging and responding to complicity should come with the cultivation of an ethos of reality attentive to the three dimensions to being human – structures, agency and plurality – that together constitute the common world.

Bibliography

Adams M (2003) The reflexive self and culture: a critique. *British Journal of Sociology* 54(2): 221–238.
Adams M (2006) Hybridizing habitus and reflexivity: towards an understanding of contemporary identity? *Sociology* 40(3): 511–528.
Adams M (2007) *Self and Social Change*. London: Sage.
Afxentiou A, Dunford R and Neu M (2016) *Exploring Complicity: Concept, Cases and Critique*. Lanham, MD: Rowman & Littlefield International.
Ahmed S (2009) Happy objects. In: Gregg M and Seigworth GJ (eds) *The Affect Theory Reader*. Durham, NC: Duke University Press, pp. 29–51.
Aksenova M (2016) *Complicity in International Criminal Law*. Oxford: Hart.
Applebaum B (2010) *Being White, Being Good: White Complicity, White Moral Responsibility, and Social Justice Pedagogy*. Lanham, MD: Lexington.
Archer MS (1982) Morphogenesis versus structuration: on combining structure and action. *British Journal of Sociology* 33(4): 455–483.
Archer MS (1995) *Realist Social Theory: The Morphogenetic Approach*. Cambridge: Cambridge University Press.
Archer MS (2000) *Being Human: The Problem of Agency*. Cambridge: Cambridge University Press.
Archer MS (2003) *Structure, Agency and the Internal Conversation*. Cambridge: Cambridge University Press.
Archer MS (2007) *Making Our Way through the World: Human Reflexivity and Social Mobility*. Cambridge: Cambridge University Press.
Archer M (2008) Continuing the internal conversation. *Theory: Newsletter of the Research Committee on Sociological Theory*, Spring/Summer, 2–3.
Archer MS (ed.) (2009) *Conversations about Reflexivity*. Abingdon: Routledge.
Archer MS (2010) Routine, reflexivity, and realism. *Sociological Theory* 28(3): 272–303.

Archer M (2012) *The Reflexive Imperative in Late Modernity*. Cambridge: Cambridge University Press.
Archer MS (2014a) *Late Modernity: Trajectories towards Morphogenic Society*. Cham, Switzerland: Springer.
Archer MS (2014b) Structural conditioning and personal reflexivity: sources of market complicity, critique, and change. In: Finn DK (ed.) *Distant Markets, Distant Harms: Economic Complicity and Christian Ethics*. Oxford: Oxford University Press, pp. 25–52.
Archer M (2016) *Structure, Culture and Agency: Selected Papers of Margaret Archer* (eds Brock T, Carrigan M and Scambler G). Abingdon: Routledge.
Arendt H (1959) Reflections on Little Rock. *Dissent*, Winter, 45–56.
Arendt H (1970) *Men in Dark Times*. New York: Harcourt, Brace & World.
Arendt H (1973) *The Origins of Totalitarianism*. New ed. New York: Harcourt Brace Jovanovich.
Arendt H (1981a) *The Life of the Mind*. Boston: Houghton Mifflin Harcourt.
Arendt H (1981b) *The Life of the Mind II*. Boston: Houghton Mifflin Harcourt.
Arendt H (1982) *Lectures on Kant's Political Philosophy* (ed. Beiner R). Chicago: University of Chicago Press.
Arendt H (1998) *The Human Condition*. 2nd ed. Chicago: University of Chicago Press.
Arendt H (2003) *Responsibility and Judgment*. New York: Schocken.
Arendt H (2005a) *Essays in Understanding, 1930–1954: Formation, Exile, and Totalitarianism* (ed. Kohn J). New York: Schocken.
Arendt H (2005b) *The Promise of Politics*. New York: Schocken.
Arendt H (2006a) *Between Past and Future: Eight Exercises in Political Thought*. New York: Penguin.
Arendt H (2006b) *Eichmann in Jerusalem: A Report on the Banality of Evil*. New York: Penguin.
Arendt H (2006c) *On Revolution*. New York: Penguin.
Atkinson W (2008) Not all that was solid has melted into air (or liquid): a critique of Bauman on individualization and class in liquid modernity. *Sociological Review* 56(1): 1–17.
Azmanova A (2012) *The Scandal of Reason: A Critical Theory of Political Judgement*. New York: Columbia University Press.
Baehr P (2007) Philosophy, sociology, and the intelligentsia: Hannah Arendt's encounter with Karl Mannheim and the sociology of knowledge. 人文及社會科學集刊/*Journal of Social Sciences and Philosophy* 19(3): 341–373.
Baehr P and Walsh P (eds) (2017) *The Anthem Companion to Hannah Arendt*. London: Anthem Press.

Bauer K (2013) Gender and the sexual politics of exchange in Herta Müller's prose. In: Haines B and Marven L (eds) *Herta Müller*. Oxford: Oxford University Press, pp. 154–171.
Bauman Z (2013) *Liquid Modernity*. Hoboken, NJ: John Wiley & Sons.
Beausoleil E (2014) The politics, science, and art of receptivity. *Ethics and Global Politics* 7(1): 19–40.
Beausoleil E (2017) Responsibility as responsiveness: enacting a dispositional ethics of encounter. *Political Theory* 45(3): 291–318.
Beausoleil E (2019) Listening to claims of structural injustice. *Angelaki* 24(4): 120–135.
Beck U and Beck-Gernsheim E (2002) *Individualization: Institutionalized Individualism and Its Social and Political Consequences*. London: Sage.
Beck U, Giddens A and Lash S (1994) *Reflexive Modernization: Politics, Tradition and Aesthetics in the Modern Social Order*. Stanford, CA: Stanford University Press.
Beiner R (1982) Interpretive essay. In: Arendt H *Lectures on Kant's Political Philosophy*. Chicago: University of Chicago Press, pp. 89–156.
Beiner R (1983) *Political Judgment*. London: Methuen.
Beiner R and Nedelsky J (eds) (2001) *Judgment, Imagination, and Politics: Themes from Kant and Arendt*. Lanham, MD: Rowman & Littlefield.
Benhabib S (1988) Judgment and the moral foundations of politics in Arendt's thought. *Political Theory* 16(1): 29–51.
Benhabib S (1990) Hannah Arendt and the redemptive power of narrative. *Social Research* 57(1): 167–196.
Benhabib S (2003) *The Reluctant Modernism of Hannah Arendt*. Lanham, MD: Rowman & Littlefield.
Bennett J (2009) *Vibrant Matter: A Political Ecology of Things*. Durham, NC: Duke University Press.
Bernstein RJ (1986) *Philosophical Profiles: Essays in a Pragmatic Mode*. Cambridge: Polity Press.
Bernstein RJ (2018) *Why Read Hannah Arendt Now?* Cambridge: Polity Press.
Bhaskar R (1998a) General introduction. In: Archer M, Bhaskar R, Collier A et al. (eds) *Critical Realism: Essential Readings*. London: Routledge, pp. ix–xxiv.
Bhaskar R (1998b) Societies. In: Archer M, Bhaskar R, Collier A et al. (eds) *Critical Realism: Essential Readings*. London: Routledge, pp. 206–257.
Bhaskar R (2012) Critical realism in resonance with Nordic ecophilosophy. In: Bhaskar R, Høyer KG and Næss P (eds) *Ecophilosophy in a World of Crisis: Critical Realism and the Nordic Contributions*. Abingdon: Routledge, pp. 9–24.

Bhaskar R (2013) *A Realist Theory of Science*. Abingdon: Routledge.
Bickford S (2011) Emotion talk and political judgment. *Journal of Politics* 73(4): 1025–1037.
Bilsky LY (1996) When actor and spectator meet in the courtroom: reflections on Hannah Arendt's concept of judgment. *History and Memory* 8(2): 137–173.
Birmingham P (2006) *Hannah Arendt and Human Rights: The Predicament of Common Responsibility*. Bloomington: Indiana University Press.
Boase-Beier J (2014) Translation and the representation of thought: the case of Herta Müller. *Language and Literature* 23(3): 213–226.
Borren M (2013) 'A sense of the world': Hannah Arendt's hermeneutic phenomenology of common sense. *International Journal of Philosophical Studies* 21(2): 225–255.
Bourdieu P (1990) *The Logic of Practice*. Stanford: Stanford University Press.
Bourke R and Geuss R (eds) (2009) *Political Judgement: Essays for John Dunn*. Cambridge: Cambridge University Press.
Bozzi P (2013) Facts, fiction, autofiction, and surfiction in Herta Müller's work. In: Brandt B and Glajar V (eds) *Herta Müller: Politics and Aesthetics*. Lincoln: University of Nebraska Press, pp. 109–129.
Burkitt I (2012) Emotional reflexivity: feeling, emotion and imagination in reflexive dialogues. *Sociology* 46(3): 458–472.
Burkitt I (2016) Relational agency: relational sociology, agency and interaction. *European Journal of Social Theory* 19(3): 322–339.
Caetano A (2015) Defining personal reflexivity: a critical reading of Archer's approach. *European Journal of Social Theory* 18(1): 60–75.
Canovan M (1992) *Hannah Arendt: A Reinterpretation of Her Political Thought*. Cambridge: Cambridge University Press.
Chalari A (2009) *Approaches to the Individual: The Relationship between Internal and External Conversation*. Basingstoke: Palgrave Macmillan.
Chandler B (2013) The subjectivity of habitus. *Journal for the Theory of Social Behaviour* 43(4): 469–491.
Chernilo D (2017) *Debating Humanity: Towards a Philosophical Sociology*. Cambridge: Cambridge University Press.
Chouliaraki L (2013) *The Ironic Spectator: Solidarity in the Age of Post-Humanitarianism*. Cambridge: Polity Press.
Ciurria M (2011) Complicity and criminal liability in Rwanda: a situationist critique. *Res Publica* 17(4): 411–419.
Clapham A (2003) Issues of complexity, complicity and complementarity: from the Nuremberg trials to the dawn of the new International Criminal Court. In: Sands P (ed.) *From Nuremberg to The Hague: The Future of International Criminal Justice*. Cambridge: Cambridge University Press, pp. 30–67.

Clore GL and Huntsinger JR (2007) How emotions inform judgment and regulate thought. *Trends in Cognitive Sciences* 11(9): 393–399.

Clough PT (2009) The affective turn: political economy, biomedia, and bodies. In: Gregg M and Seigworth GJ (eds) *The Affect Theory Reader*. Durham, NC: Duke University Press, pp. 206–225.

Clough PT and Halley J (2007) *The Affective Turn: Theorizing the Social*. Durham, NC: Duke University Press.

Coles R (2016) *Visionary Pragmatism: Radical and Ecological Democracy in Neoliberal Times*. Durham, NC: Duke University Press.

Connolly WE (2002) *Neuropolitics: Thinking, Culture, Speed*. Minneapolis: University of Minnesota Press.

Corbin JC, Reyna VF, Weldon RB et al. (2015) How reasoning, judgment, and decision making are colored by gist-based intuition: a fuzzy-trace theory approach. *Journal of Applied Research in Memory and Cognition* 4(4): 344–355.

Cornwell JFM, Bajger AT and Higgins ET (2015) Judging political hearts and minds: how political dynamics drive social judgments. *Personality and Social Psychology Bulletin* 41(8): 1053–1068.

Dawson M (2010) Bauman, Beck, Giddens and our understanding of politics in late modernity. *Journal of Power* 3(2): 189–207.

Degerman D (2019) Within the heart's darkness: the role of emotions in Arendt's political thought. *European Journal of Political Theory* 18(2): 153–173.

Degryse A (2011) *Sensus communis* as a foundation for men as political beings: Arendt's reading of Kant's *Critique of Judgment*. *Philosophy and Social Criticism* 37(3): 345–358.

Dépelteau F (ed.) (2018) *The Palgrave Handbook of Relational Sociology*. Cham, Switzerland: Palgrave Macmillan.

Derrida J (1989) *Of Spirit: Heidegger and the Question*. Chicago: University of Chicago Press.

Disch LJ (1993) More truth than fact: storytelling as critical understanding in the writings of Hannah Arendt. *Political Theory* 21(4): 665–694.

Disch LJ (1994) *Hannah Arendt and the Limits of Philosophy*. Ithaca, NY: Cornell University Press.

Donati P (2011) *Relational Sociology: A New Paradigm for the Social Sciences*. Abingdon: Routledge.

Donati P and Archer MS (2015) *The Relational Subject*. Cambridge: Cambridge University Press.

Drace-Francis A (2013) Beyond the Land of Green Plums: Romanian culture and language in Herta Müller's work. In: Haines B and Marven L (eds) *Herta Müller*. Oxford: Oxford University Press, pp. 32–48.

Dubnov AM (2017) Can parallels meet? Hannah Arendt and Isaiah Berlin on the Jewish post-emancipatory quest for political freedom. *Leo Baeck Institute Year Book* 62: 27–51.

Durkheim E (2014) *The Rules of Sociological Method: And Selected Texts on Sociology and Its Method* (ed. Lukes S). New York: Free Press.
Eke NO (ed.) (1991) *Die erfundene Wahrnehmung: Annäherung an Herta Müller*. Paderborn: Igel.
Eke NO (2013). '"Macht nichts, macht nichts, sagte ich mir, macht nichts": Herta Müller's Romanian novels'. In: Haines B and Marven L (eds) *Herta Müller*. Oxford: Oxford University Press, pp. 99–116.
Eke NO (2017) Biographische Skizze. In: Eke NO (ed.) *Herta Müller-Handbuch*. Stuttgart: JB Metzler, pp. 2–12.
Elder-Vass D (2007) Reconciling Archer and Bourdieu in an emergentist theory of action. *Sociological Theory* 25(4): 325–346.
Elder-Vass D (2010) *The Causal Power of Social Structures: Emergence, Structure and Agency*. Cambridge: Cambridge University Press.
Elder-Vass D (2017) Material parts in social structures. *Journal of Social Ontology* 3(1): 89–105.
Farrell M (2014) Critique, complicity and I. In: Schwöbel C (ed.) *Critical Approaches to International Criminal Law: An Introduction*. Abingdon: Routledge, pp. 96–113.
Farrugia D (2013) The reflexive subject: towards a theory of reflexivity as practical intelligibility. *Current Sociology* 61(3): 283–300.
Feitlowitz M (2011) *A Lexicon of Terror: Argentina and the Legacies of Torture*. Rev. ed. New York: Oxford University Press.
Ferrara A (1999) *Justice and Judgment: The Rise and the Prospect of the Judgment Model in Contemporary Political Philosophy*. London: Sage.
Ferrara A (2008) *The Force of the Example: Explorations in the Paradigm of Judgment*. New York: Columbia University Press.
Ferrara A (2014) *The Democratic Horizon: Hyperpluralism and the Renewal of Political Liberalism*. New York: Cambridge University Press.
Fine R (2008) Judgment and the reification of the faculties: a reconstructive reading of Arendt's *Life of the Mind*. *Philosophy and Social Criticism* 34(1–2): 157–176.
Fleetwood S (2008) Structure, institution, agency, habit, and reflexive deliberation. *Journal of Institutional Economics* 4(2): 183–203.
Galston WA (2010) Realism in political theory. *European Journal of Political Theory* 9(4): 385–411.
Gardner J (2007) Complicity and causality. *Criminal Law and Philosophy* 1(2): 127–141.
Garland-Thomson R (2009) *Staring: How We Look*. New York: Oxford University Press.
Giddens A (1984) *The Constitution of Society: Outline of the Theory of Structuration*. Berkeley: University of California Press.
Giddens A (1991) *Modernity and Self-Identity: Self and Society in the Late Modern Age*. Stanford, CA: Stanford University Press.

Gilligan C (1982) *In a Different Voice: Psychological Theory and Women's Development.* Cambridge, MA: Harvard University Press.
Gines KT (2014) *Hannah Arendt and the Negro Question.* Bloomington: Indiana University Press.
Gratton P and Sari Y (eds) (2020) *The Bloomsbury Companion to Arendt.* London: Bloomsbury Academic.
Grossberg L (2009) Affect's future: rediscovering the virtual in the actual. In: Gregg M and Seigworth GJ (eds) *The Affect Theory Reader.* Durham, NC: Duke University Press, pp. 309–338.
Gunnell JG (2007) Are we losing our minds? Cognitive science and the study of politics. *Political Theory* 35(6): 704–731.
Gunnell JG (2013) Unpacking emotional baggage in political inquiry. In: Vander Valk F (ed.) *Essays on Neuroscience and Political Theory: Thinking the Body Politic.* Abingdon: Routledge, pp. 91–116.
Habermas J (1977) Hannah Arendt's communications concept of power. *Social Research* 44(1): 3–24.
Haines B (1998) *Herta Müller.* Cardiff: University of Wales Press.
Haines B (2013) 'Die akute Einsamkeit des Menschen': Herta Müller's *Herztier.* In: Brandt B and Glajar V (eds) *Herta Müller: Politics and Aesthetics.* Lincoln: University of Nebraska Press, pp. 87–108.
Haines B and Littler M (1998) Gespräch mit Herta Müller. In: Haines B (ed.) *Herta Mueller.* Cardiff: University of Wales Press, pp. 14–24.
Haines B and Marven L (2013) Introduction. In: Haines B and Marven L (eds) *Herta Müller.* Oxford: Oxford University Press, pp. 1–16.
Hämäläinen N (2016) Sophie, Antigone, Elizabeth – rethinking ethics by reading literature. In: Hagberg GL (ed.) *Fictional Characters, Real Problems: The Search for Ethical Content in Literature.* Oxford: Oxford University Press, pp. 15–30.
Hayward CR (2017) Responsibility and ignorance: on dismantling structural injustice. *Journal of Politics* 79(2): 396–408.
Hayward CR (2020) Disruption: what is it good for? *Journal of Politics* 82(2): 448–459.
Hayward C and Lukes S (2008) Nobody to shoot? Power, structure, and agency: a dialogue. *Journal of Power* 1(1): 5–20.
Heins V (2007) Reasons of the heart: Weber and Arendt on emotion in politics. *European Legacy* 12(6): 715–728.
Herzog A (2000) Illuminating inheritance: Benjamin's influence on Arendt's political storytelling. *Philosophy and Social Criticism* 26(5): 1–27.
Hibbing JR, Smith KB and Alford JR (2014) Differences in negativity bias underlie variations in political ideology. *Behavioral and Brain Sciences* 37(3): 297–307.
Hiruta K (2014) The meaning and value of freedom: Berlin contra Arendt. *European Legacy* 19(7): 854–868.

Iroegbu AOC, Ray SS, Mbarane V et al. (2021) Plastic pollution: a perspective on matters arising: challenges and opportunities. *ACS Omega* 6(30): 19343–19355.

Jackson M (2015) *Complicity in International Law*. Oxford: Oxford University Press.

Johannsen A (2013) Osmoses: Müller's things, bodies, and spaces. In: Brandt B and Glajar V (eds) *Herta Müller: Politics and Aesthetics*. Lincoln: University of Nebraska Press, pp. 207–229.

Joseph J and Wight C (eds) (2010) *Scientific Realism and International Relations*. Basingstoke: Palgrave Macmillan.

Kadish SH (1985) Complicity, cause and blame: a study in the interpretation of doctrine. *California Law Review* 73(2): 323–410.

Kant I (2000) *Critique of the Power of Judgment* (ed. Guyer P). Cambridge: Cambridge University Press.

Klusmeyer DB (2011) Contesting Thucydides' legacy: comparing Hannah Arendt and Hans Morgenthau on imperialism, history and theory. *International History Review* 33(1): 1–25.

Kornprobst M (2011) The agent's logics of action: defining and mapping political judgement. *International Theory* 3(1): 70–104.

Kornprobst M (2014) From political judgements to public justifications (and vice versa): how communities generate reasons upon which to act. *European Journal of International Relations* 20(1): 192–216.

Krause SR (2008) *Civil Passions: Moral Sentiment and Democratic Deliberation*. Princeton, NJ: Princeton University Press.

Krimstein K (2018) *The Three Escapes of Hannah Arendt: A Tyranny of Truth*. London: Bloomsbury.

Kurki M (2010) Critical realism and the analysis of democratisation: does philosophy of science matter? In: Joseph J and Wight C (eds) *Scientific Realism and International Relations*. Basingstoke: Palgrave Macmillan, pp. 129–146.

Kutz C (2000) *Complicity: Ethics and Law for a Collective Age*. Cambridge: Cambridge University Press.

Kutz C (2007) Causeless complicity. *Criminal Law and Philosophy* 1(3): 289–305.

Kutz C (2011) The philosophical foundations of complicity law. In: Deigh J and Dolinko D (eds) *The Oxford Handbook of Philosophy of Criminal Law*. New York: Oxford University Press, pp. 147–166.

La Caze M (2010) The judgement of the statesperson. In: Celermajer D, Schaap A, Karalis PV et al. (eds) *Power, Judgment and Political Evil: In Conversation with Hannah Arendt*. Farnham: Ashgate, pp. 73–85.

Landemore H, Panagia D and Zerilli LMG (2018) Judging politically: symposium on Linda MG Zerilli's *A Democratic Theory of Judgment*, University of Chicago Press, 2016. *Political Theory* 46(4): 611–642.

Lara MP (1998) *Moral Textures: Feminist Narratives in the Public Sphere.* Berkeley: University of California Press.
Lara MP (2007) *Narrating Evil: A Postmetaphysical Theory of Reflective Judgment.* New York: Columbia University Press.
Lawson T (1998) Economic science without experimentation – abstraction. In: Archer M, Bhaskar R, Collier A et al. (eds) *Critical Realism: Essential Readings.* London: Routledge, pp. 144–186.
Leebaw BA (2011) *Judging State-Sponsored Violence, Imagining Political Change.* Cambridge: Cambridge University Press.
Lepora C and Goodin RE (2013) *On Complicity and Compromise.* Oxford: Oxford University Press.
Leys R (2011) The turn to affect: a critique. *Critical Inquiry* 37(3): 434–472.
Liljeström M (2016) Affect. In: Disch L and Hawkesworth M (eds) *The Oxford Handbook of Feminist Theory.* New York: Oxford University Press, pp. 19–38.
Livingston A (2012) Avoiding deliberative democracy? Micropolitics, manipulation, and the public sphere. *Philosophy and Rhetoric* 45(3): 269–294.
Loacker B and Muhr SL (2009) How can I become a responsible subject? Towards a practice-based ethics of responsiveness. *Journal of Business Ethics* 90(2): 265–277.
Lovern LL (2021) Indigenous concepts of difference: an alternative to Western disability labelling. *Disability Studies Quarterly* 41(4).
McAnulla S (2002) Structure and agency. In: Marsh D and Stoker G (eds) *Theory and Methods in Political Science.* 2nd ed. Basingstoke: Palgrave Macmillan, pp. 271–291.
McAnulla S (2006) Challenging the new interpretivist approach: towards a critical realist alternative. *British Politics* 1(1): 113–138.
McGeer V and Pettit P (2009) Sticky judgment and the role of rhetoric. In: Bourke R and Geuss R (eds) *Political Judgement: Essays for John Dunn.* Cambridge: Cambridge University Press, pp. 47–72.
McNay L (2014) *The Misguided Search for the Political: Social Weightlessness in Radical Democratic Theory.* Cambridge: Polity Press.
McNay L (2019) The politics of exemplarity: Ferrara on the disclosure of new political worlds. *Philosophy and Social Criticism* 45(2): 127–145.
Marshall DL (2010) The origin and character of Hannah Arendt's theory of judgment. *Political Theory* 38(3): 367–393.
Marx K (2008) *The 18th Brumaire of Louis Bonaparte.* Rockyville, MD: Wildside Press.
Massumi B (2015) *Politics of Affect.* Cambridge: Polity Press.
Medina J (2013) *The Epistemology of Resistance: Gender and Racial Oppression, Epistemic Injustice, and Resistant Imaginations.* New York: Oxford University Press.

Meints W (2014) *Partei ergreifen im Interesse der Welt: Eine Studie zur Politischen Urteilskraft im Denken Hannah Arendts*. Bielefeld: Transcript.
Mellema G (2016) *Complicity and Moral Accountability*. Notre Dame, IN: University of Notre Dame Press.
Mihai M (2014) Theorizing agonistic emotions. *Parallax* 20(2): 31–48.
Mihai M (2016a) *Negative Emotions and Transitional Justice*. New York: Columbia University Press.
Mihai M (2016b) Theorizing change: between reflective judgment and the inertia of political *habitus*. *European Journal of Political Theory* 15(1): 22–42.
Mihai M (2019) Understanding complicity: memory, hope and the imagination. *Critical Review of International Social and Political Philosophy* 22(5): 504–522.
Mihai M (2022) *Political Memory and the Aesthetics of Care: The Art of Complicity and Resistance*. Stanford, CA: Stanford University Press.
Mills C (2007) White ignorance. In: Sullivan S and Tuana N (eds) *Race and Epistemologies of Ignorance*. Albany: State University of New York Press, pp. 13–38.
Morton S (2003) *Gayatri Chakravorty Spivak*. Abingdon: Routledge.
Mouzelis NP (2008) *Modern and Postmodern Social Theorizing: Bridging the Divide*. Cambridge: Cambridge University Press.
Mrovlje M (2018) *Rethinking Political Judgement: Arendt and Existentialism*. Edinburgh: Edinburgh University Press.
Müller H (1991) *Der Teufel sitzt im Spiegel: wie Wahrnehmung sich erfindet*. Berlin: Rotbuch.
Müller H (2001) *The Appointment*. New York: Metropolitan.
Müller H (2007) *Herztier*. Frankfurt am Main: Fischer Taschenbuch.
Müller H (2008) *Der König verneigt sich und tötet*. Frankfurt am Main: Fischer Taschenbuch.
Müller H (2009a) *Atemschaukel: Roman*. Munich: Carl Hanser.
Müller H (2009b) *Der Mensch ist ein Großer Fasan auf der Welt*. Berlin: Fischer Taschenbuch Verlag.
Müller H (2011) *Niederungen*. Frankfurt am Main: Fischer Taschenbuch.
Müller H (2015) *The Passport*. London: Serpent's Tail.
Müller H (2016) *Hunger und Seide*. Frankfurt am Main: Fischer Taschenbuch.
Müller H and Klammer A (2014) *Mein Vaterland war ein Apfelkern: ein Gespräch mit Angelika Klammer*. Munich: Carl Hanser.
Müller H and Lentz M (2010) *Lebensangst und Worthunger: im Gespräch mit Michael Lentz*. Berlin: Suhrkamp.
Müller H and Liiceanu G (2011) When personal integrity is not enough. *Eurozine*, 26 May. Available at: https://www.eurozine.com/when-personal-integrity-is-not-enough/ (accessed 20 July 2023).

Mutch A (2004) Constraints on the internal conversation: Margaret Archer and the structural shaping of thought. *Journal for the Theory of Social Behaviour* 34(4): 429–445.
Myers E (2008) Resisting Foucauldian ethics: associative politics and the limits of the care of the self. *Contemporary Political Theory* 7(2): 125–146.
Myers E (2013) *Worldly Ethics: Democratic Politics and Care for the World*. Durham, NC: Duke University Press.
Nelson D (2006) The virtues of heartlessness: Mary McCarthy, Hannah Arendt, and the anesthetics of empathy. *American Literary History* 18(1): 86–101.
Nixon R (2011). *Slow Violence and the Environmentalism of the Poor*. Cambridge, MA: Harvard University Press.
Nussbaum MC (2013) *Political Emotions: Why Love Matters for Justice*. Cambridge, MA: Belknap Press.
Oliver K (2004) Witnessing and testimony. *Parallax* 10(1): 78–87.
Oliver K (2010) Animal ethics: toward an ethics of responsiveness. *Research in Phenomenology* 40(2): 267–280.
Osiel MJ (2005) Modes of participation in mass atrocity. *Cornell International Law Journal* 38(3): article 7.
Osiel MJ (2009) *Making Sense of Mass Atrocity*. Cambridge: Cambridge University Press.
Owens P (2008) The ethic of reality in Hannah Arendt. In: Bell D (ed.) *Political Thought and International Relations: Variations on a Realist Theme*. Oxford: Oxford University Press, pp. 105–121.
Owens P (2017) Racism in the theory canon: Hannah Arendt and 'the one great crime in which America was never involved'. *Millennium: Journal of International Studies* 45(3): 403–424.
Peeters R (2009a) Truth, meaning and the common world: the significance and meaning of common sense in Hannah Arendt's thought, part 1. *Ethical Perspectives* 16(3): 337–359.
Peeters R (2009b) Truth, meaning and the common world: the significance and meaning of common sense in Hannah Arendt's thought, part 2. *Ethical Perspectives* 16(4): 411–434.
Pitkin HF (1981) Justice: on relating private and public. *Political Theory* 9(3): 327–352.
Porpora DV (1989) Four concepts of social structure. *Journal for the Theory of Social Behaviour* 19(2): 195–211.
Porpora DV (2015) *Reconstructing Sociology: The Critical Realist Approach*. Cambridge: Cambridge University Press.
Probyn-Rapsey F (2010) Complicity, critique and methodology: Australian con/texts. In: Guanglin W and Carter DJ (eds.) *Modern Australian Criticism and Theory*. Qingdao: China Ocean University Press, pp. 218–228.

Protevi J (2009) *Political Affect: Connecting the Social and the Somatic*. Minneapolis: University of Minnesota Press.
Rabinbach A (2004) Eichmann in New York: the New York intellectuals and the Hannah Arendt controversy. *October* 108: 97–111.
Rawls J (1993) *Political Liberalism*. New York: Columbia University Press.
Rosa H (2013) *Social Acceleration: A New Theory of Modernity*. New York: Columbia University Press.
Rosa H (2017) Das Tempo des sozialen Wandels und die Formen der Reflexivität: ein Drei-Stadien-Modell (Replik auf Margaret S. Archer). In: Lindner U and Mader D (eds) *Critical Realism Meets kritische Sozialtheorie: Ontologie, Erklärung und Kritik in den Sozialwissenschaften*. Bielefeld: Transcript, pp. 147–166.
Rosa H (2019) *Resonance: A Sociology of Our Relationship to the World*. Cambridge: Polity Press.
Sanders M (2002) *Complicities: The Intellectual and Apartheid*. Durham, NC: Duke University Press.
Sanyal D (2015) *Memory and Complicity: Migrations of Holocaust Remembrance*. New York: Fordham University Press.
Sayer A (1992) *Method in Social Science: A Realist Approach*. London: Routledge.
Sayer A (2009) Reflexivity and the habitus. In: Archer MS (ed.) *Conversations about Reflexivity*. Abingdon: Routledge, pp. 120–134.
Schaap A (2001) Guilty subjects and political responsibility: Arendt, Jaspers and the resonance of the 'German question' in politics of reconciliation. *Political Studies* 49(4): 749–766.
Schaap A (2020) Do you not see the reason for yourself? Political withdrawal and the experience of epistemic friction. *Political Studies* 68(3): 565–581.
Schabas WA (2000) *Genocide in International Law: The Crimes of Crimes*. Cambridge: Cambridge University Press.
Schabas WA (2001) Enforcing international humanitarian law: catching the accomplices. *International Review of the Red Cross* 83(842): 439–460.
Schiff J (2013) The varieties of thoughtlessness and the limits of thinking. *European Journal of Political Theory* 12(2): 99–115.
Schiff JL (2014) *Burdens of Political Responsibility: Narrative and the Cultivation of Responsiveness*. New York: Cambridge University Press.
Schwartz JP (2016) *Arendt's Judgment: Freedom, Responsibility, Citizenship*. Philadelphia: University of Pennsylvania Press.
Seigworth GJ and Gregg M (2009) An inventory of shimmers. In: Gregg M and Seigworth GJ (eds) *The Affect Theory Reader*. Durham, NC: Duke University Press, pp. 1–25.
Shklar JN (1990) *The Faces of Injustice*. New Haven, CT: Yale University Press.

Shouse E (2005) Feeling, emotion, affect. *M/C Journal* 8(6). DOI: 10.5204/mcj.2443.
Sindic D (2013) Arendt and the politics of theory and practice: beyond ivory towers and philosopher-kings. *Theory and Psychology* 23(4): 499–517.
Smith O and Brisman A (2021) Plastic waste and the environmental crisis industry. *Critical Criminology* 29(2): 289–309.
Spivak GC (1999) *A Critique of Postcolonial Reason: Toward a History of the Vanishing Present*. Cambridge, MA: Harvard University Press.
Steinberger PJ (1990) Hannah Arendt on judgment. *American Journal of Political Science* 34(3): 803–821.
Steinberger PJ (2018) *Political Judgment: An Introduction*. Cambridge: Polity Press.
Sterenborg J, Grasso N, Schouten R et al. (2019) The Ocean Cleanup System 001 performance during towing and seakeeping tests. *Proceedings of the ASME 2019 38th International Conference on Ocean, Offshore and Arctic Engineering, Volume 1: Offshore Technology; Offshore Geotechnics*. DOI: 10.1115/OMAE2019-96207.
Stone-Mediatore S (2016) Storytelling/narrative. In: Disch L and Hawkesworth M (eds) *The Oxford Handbook of Feminist Theory*. New York: Oxford University Press, pp. 934–955.
Sweetman P (2003) Twenty-first century dis-ease? Habitual reflexivity or the reflexive habitus. *Sociological Review* 51(4): 528–549.
tenBroek J (1966) The right to live in the world: the disabled in the law of torts. *California Law Review* (54)2: 841–919.
Terada R (2003) *Feeling in Theory: Emotion after the 'Death of the Subject'*. Cambridge, MA: Harvard University Press.
Terada R (2008) Thinking for oneself: realism and defiance in Arendt. *Textual Practice* 22(1): 85–111.
Thaler M (2011) Political judgment beyond paralysis and heroism. *European Journal of Political Theory* 10(2): 225–253.
Thaler M (2018) Reconciliation through estrangement. *Review of Politics* 80(4): 649–673.
Thiele LP (2006) *The Heart of Judgment: Practical Wisdom, Neuroscience, and Narrative*. Cambridge: Cambridge University Press.
Van Buren HJ III and Schrempf-Stirling J (2022) Beyond structural injustice: pursuing justice for workers in post-pandemic global value chains. *Business Ethics, the Environment and Responsibility* 31(4): 969–980.
Villa DR (1999) *Politics, Philosophy, Terror: Essays on the Thought of Hannah Arendt*. Princeton, NJ: Princeton University Press.
Vogelmann F (2017) *The Spell of Responsibility: Labor, Criminality, Philosophy*. London: Rowman & Littlefield International.
Vogler G (2016) Power between habitus and reflexivity – introducing Margaret Archer to the power debate. *Journal of Political Power* 9(1): 65–82.

Vogler G (2020) Enriching responsiveness to complicity through a disposition towards world-in-formation. *Arendt Studies* 4: 83–105.

Vogler G (2021) Bridging the gap between affect and reason: on thinking-feeling in politics. *Distinktion: Journal of Social Theory* 22(3): 259–276.

Vogler G and Tillyris D (2021) Arendt and political realism: towards a realist account of political judgement. *Critical Review of International Social and Political Philosophy* 24(6): 821–844.

Wacquant L (2016) A concise genealogy and anatomy of habitus. *Sociological Review* 64(1): 64–72.

Waller BN (2011) *Against Moral Responsibility*. Cambridge, MA: MIT Press.

Walsh P (2015) *Arendt Contra Sociology: Theory, Society and Its Science*. Farnham: Ashgate.

Walsh P (2017) Hannah Arendt on thinking, personhood and meaning. In: Baehr P and Walsh P (eds) *The Anthem Companion to Hannah Arendt*. London: Anthem Press, pp. 155–174.

Walzer M (1994) *Thick and Thin: Moral Argument at Home and Abroad*. Notre Dame, IN: University of Notre Dame Press.

Weidenfeld MC (2011) Comportment, not cognition: contributions to a phenomenology of judgment. *Contemporary Political Theory* 10(2): 232–254.

Weidenfeld MC (2013) Visions of judgment: Arendt, Kant, and the misreading of judgment. *Political Research Quarterly* 66(2): 254–266.

Wimalasena L (2017) Reflexivity and women's agency: a critical realist morphogenetic exploration of the life experience of Sri Lankan women. *Journal of Critical Realism* 16(4): 383–401.

Wimalasena L (2022) Critical realism, reflexivity and the missing voice of the subaltern: the case of postcolonial Sri Lanka. In: Jammulamadaka N and Ul-Haq S (eds) *Managing the Post-Colony South Asia Focus: Ways of Organising, Managing and Living*. Singapore: Springer, pp. 101–120.

Wimalasena L & Marks A (2019) Habitus and reflexivity in tandem? Insights from postcolonial Sri Lanka. *Sociological Review* 67(3): 518–535.

Yar M (2000) From actor to spectator: Hannah Arendt's 'two theories' of political judgment. *Philosophy and Social Criticism* 26(2): 1–27.

Young IM (2001) Equality of whom? Social groups and judgments of injustice. *Journal of Political Philosophy* 9(1): 1–18.

Young IM (2011) *Responsibility for Justice*. New York: Oxford University Press.

Zerilli LMG (2005a) *Feminism and the Abyss of Freedom*. Chicago: University of Chicago Press.

Zerilli LMG (2005b) 'We feel our freedom': imagination and judgment in the thought of Hannah Arendt. *Political Theory* 33(2): 158–188.

Zerilli LMG (2012) Value pluralism and the problem of judgment: farewell to public reason. *Political Theory* 40(1): 6–31.
Zerilli LMG (2013) Embodied knowing, judgment, and the limits of neurobiology. *Perspectives on Politics* 11(2): 512–515.
Zerilli LMG (2015) The turn to affect and the problem of judgment. *New Literary History* 46(2): 261–286.
Zerilli LMG (2016a) *A Democratic Theory of Judgment*. Chicago: University of Chicago Press.
Zerilli LMG (2016b) 'The machine as symbol': Wittgenstein's contribution to the politics of judgement and freedom in contemporary democratic theory. In: Bevir M and Gališanka A (eds) *Wittgenstein and Normative Inquiry*. Leiden: Brill, pp. 127–151.

Index

Note: The index is organised in alphabetical order using the word-by-word method.

alienation, 39–40, 43, 142–3, 151, 153, 168
Applebaum, Barbara, 28, 90
Archer, Margaret
  and duality, 87–92, 109, 117
  and analytical dualism, 93–102, 117, 124–6
  and reflexivity 102–7, 124–6, 145
Arendt, Hannah
  and crisis of modernity, 36–40
  and judgement, 4, 34–6, 42, 47–58
  and responsibility, 21
  and pluralist politics, 5, 40–6
Azmanova, Albena, 6, 81–2

being-in-the-world, 100, 117, 142
Beausoleil, Emily, 1, 4, 25
blame, 2, 3, 8, 18, 20–2, 24, 28, 31–2, 60, 64, 87–8, 114
Bourdieu, Pierre, 7, 25, 67, 87–9, 103

common and community sense, 55–8, 80–3

common world, 39–42, 48, 55–7, 70, 92, 114–19, 121–3, 127–8, 130, 132–3, 135, 139, 153–8
  flourishing or hospitable, 5–6, 47, 61, 119, 130–1, 155–6, 164–8
complicity, 2–6, 16–32, 34–5, 87–92, 114, 120–33, 136, 139
complicity-as-being, 3–4, 11, 16, 22–4, 32, 120

emotion, 77–80, 101, 103, 117–18, 144
ethics of responsiveness, 4, 25–31, 87–92, 119, 121, 132, 165

Ferrara, Alessandro, 80–1, 83

guilt, 18–19, 21, 28, 88

Habermas, Jürgen, 5, 65–6, 77
Hayward, Clarissa, 29–30, 91–2, 119
human condition or nature, 38–9, 41, 43, 86, 117–18

being human, 23, 29, 31, 38, 100, 127, 139, 141, 147, 151
human agency, 7, 8, 10, 86, 89–92, 97, 100–2, 106, 117–19, 125–8, 144, 147–8
human plurality, 35–43, 118–19, 123–4, 128–31, 151–8

ignorance, 25–6, 28, 29, 90–2, 119, 141
imagination, 48–9, 52, 68–71, 119
impartiality or impartial, 52–5, 71–4, 80
intersubjective, 6, 12, 36, 30, 65–6, 76, 80–3, 99, 115, 126

judgement
  aesthetic, 35, 51, 65–8
  determinant, 68–9
  moral, 2, 6, 11, 18, 34, 64, 77, 87
  reflective, 34, 36, 41, 47, 53, 56, 60, 64, 67–9, 74, 81–3

Kant, Immanuel, 35–6, 38, 51–2, 56–7, 66–7

love of the world, 30, 44–6, 92, 123

methodological individualism, 2, 11, 17–19, 25, 28, 34, 87, 98, 105, 108, 117, 119, 124–5, 132, 144, 146, 165, 167
Müller, Herta, 13, 135–59
Myers, Ella, 30–1, 92, 122–4

public realm or sphere, 36, 40–5, 54, 56, 59, 60, 70, 76, 81, 133, 151

Rawls, John, 5–6, 77
realism, realist, 44, 79, 96–101, 115, 154, 156
  engagement with reality, 4, 7–10, 36–7, 47, 96, 110, 115–21, 132
reason, 2, 6–7, 11, 17–18, 20, 34, 36, 40, 42, 50, 52, 64, 69–70, 73, 75, 77–9, 81, 115, 133
representative thinking, 52, 56–60
responsibility
  collective, shared or political, 4, 9, 13, 21–2, 24–5, 30, 32, 124, 133, 165
  personal or moral, 20, 24, 126

Schiff, Jade, 24, 26–8, 74, 83, 89–91, 129
situated or social embedded agency, 12, 25, 91, 164
  embodied, 71, 76, 78, 100–2, 110, 117–18, 131, 135, 144
social transformation or change, 8–9, 17, 25, 27, 30, 91, 93–8, 102, 108–9, 125–6, 132–3
  social conditioning, 7 9, 31, 65, 71, 74, 80, 86, 92, 94–6, 102–3, 119
storytelling, 27, 32, 53–4, 71–4
structure and agency, 7–10, 86–9, 92–5, 102–3, 110, 117, 119

validity, 6–7, 56, 58, 64–71, 80–1

worldliness, 118
world-disclosure, 35, 42, 71

Young, Iris Marion, 3, 20–2, 24–5, 88, 119, 122, 165

Zerilli, Linda, 10, 68–71, 76, 78

EU representative:
Easy Access System Europe
Mustamäe tee 50, 10621 Tallinn, Estonia
Gpsr.requests@easproject.com